STUDENT GUIDE

Dudley W. Curry
Ph.D., C.P.A.
Professor of Accounting
Southern Methodist University

Cost Accounting

A Managerial Emphasis

FOURTH EDITION

CHARLES T. HORNGREN

PRENTICE-HALL, INC., *Englewood Cliffs, New Jersey 07632*

10 9 8 7 6 5 4 3 2 1

0-13-179705-0

Printed in the United States of America

Prentice-Hall International, Inc., *London*
Prentice-Hall of Australia Pty. Limited, *Sydney*
Prentice-Hall of Canada, Ltd., *Toronto*
Prentice-Hall of India Private Limited, *New Delhi*
Prentice-Hall of Japan, Inc., *Tokyo*
Prentice-Hall of Southeast Asia Pte. Ltd., *Singapore*
Whitehall Books Limited, *Wellington, New Zealand*

Contents

Preface

This student guide has been designed to supplement the fourth edition of Charles T. Horngren's *Cost Accounting: A Managerial Emphasis.* Its purpose is to help you master the concepts, techniques, and analytical approaches presented in the textbook.

The student guide is not intended as a substitute for the textbook; rather, it is to serve as an aid in using the textbook to learn cost accounting. The student guide will help you to understand the main ideas and their interrelationships and to reinforce your understanding through immediate application in the self-test and practice exercises.

Each student guide chapter begins with a brief introduction aimed at helping you gain a clear perspective of the corresponding textbook chapter. This is followed by a chapter review summary that organizes and restates important points to increase your understanding and retention before going on to the self-test and practice exercises. These consist of multiple-choice and true-false questions, completion statements, drills, and short problems designed to measure and reinforce your learning. In solving these, you will think through important ideas and relationships and improve your working knowledge of them.

Solutions to all the self-test and practice exercises are presented at the back of the student guide. The solutions facilitate the self-teaching process by providing immediate feedback—somewhat in the manner of a programmed-learning textbook. By comparing your own answers with the solutions, you can determine whether you are actually receiving, absorbing, and retaining the intended meaning of the textbook. If you did not arrive at the correct answer and fail to understand the reason, consult the appropriate sections of the textbook.

It is important to emphasize that all parts of the self-test and practice exercises cannot be answered solely on the basis of the student guide. This will undoubtedly hold true also for quizzes and examinations given by your instructor. Therefore, do not rely upon the student guide to the exclusion of the textbook.

Here are two suggested sequences for using this student guide in conjunction with the textbook:

PLAN A

1. Study the textbook chapter.
2. Solve the self-study problem(s) in the textbook chapter.
3. Compare your work with the textbook solution(s).
4. If you made any errors, review the appropriate parts of the textbook.
5. Read the corresponding chapter of the student guide.
6. Answer all the self-test and practice exercises in the student guide chapter.
7. Check your answers with the solutions at the back of the student guide.
8. If you made any errors, review the appropriate parts of the textbook.
9. Solve homework problems assigned from the textbook by your instructor.

PLAN B

1. Study the textbook chapter.
2. Read the corresponding chapter of the student guide.
3. Answer all the self-test and practice exercises in the student guide chapter.
4. Check your answers with the solutions at the back of the student guide.
5. If you made any errors, review the appropriate parts of the textbook.
6. Solve the self-study problem(s) in the textbook chapter.
7. Compare your work with the textbook solution(s).
8. If you made any errors, review the appropriate parts of the textbook.
9. Solve homework problems assigned from the textbook by your instructor.

For valuable ideas and assistance, I am indebted to Professor Charles T. Horngren of Stanford University, numerous students in my classes at SMU and the University of Arizona, and Ken Cashman of Prentice-Hall.

Suggestions and comments from users are welcome.

Dudley W. Curry

Southern Methodist University

The Accountant's Role in the Organization

1

This first chapter is designed to give us a useful perspective concerning modern systems of cost accounting (*management accounting systems*). This is done by describing the basic elements of the management decision process, by explaining the main purposes of managment accounting systems, and by delineating the management accountant's role in large business organizations. Chapter 1 introduces one of the major themes of the entire book: the *cost-benefit approach* to obtaining information for management decisions.

REVIEW SUMMARY

A. In almost every organization, the accounting system is the major quantitative information system.

1. A cost accounting system should be designed primarily to assist management in making decisions.

2. Decision making involves both routine and nonroutine choices of actions to reach certain objectives.

3. A method for systematically aiding management to make choices is often called a *decision model.*

4. A decision model helps a manager by providing him with the means for measuring the effects of different actions that might be chosen to obtain a particular objective.

B. You should study very carefully the important textbook Exhibit 1-1, which illustrates the sequence of the main steps in the decision process.

1. *Information:* Obtaining information pertaining to a management decision.

2. *Prediction Method:* Using the information to predict helpful future costs (and other data).

3. *Decision Model:* Using the predicted data to reach a decision.

4. *Implementation:* Taking action to carry out the decision.

5. *Results and Feedback:* Evaluating performance for the purpose of improving subsequent information, predictions, decisions, and implementation methods.

C. Exhibit 1-1 also serves as a useful framework for identifying some important aspects of the management process.

1. *Planning* is the selection of objectives and appropriate decision models (prediction and decision making).

2. *Control* is the process of achieving organizational objectives in an optimal manner (implementation and feedback).

3. Planning and control are not separable functions, but are *interactive.*

D. It is important to use the cost-benefit approach to obtain information for management decisions.

1. Like other economic goods, accounting information is a commodity with a price.

2. Therefore, the cost of obtaining information should be compared with the expected benefits to be obtained.

3. The optimal accounting measure or system is one that produces the most net benefit after the costs of obtaining the information are deducted.

4. Thus, for decision purposes, the optimal accounting measure or system is not necessarily the one that produces the most accurate or the most economically realistic information.

E. A distinction should be observed between two types of decisions.

1. A choice of the appropriate management *action* must, of course, be made.

2. Linked with such a choice is the selection of the appropriate *information* or accounting measurement.

3. The information decision is often delegated to the accountant by management.

4. Be sure to notice that the cost-benefit approach is fundamental to both the action decision and the information decision.

F. The chief accounting executive, or chief management accountant, is often called the *controller.*

1. The principal functions of the controller are:

a. Planning for control,

b. Reporting and interpreting, and

c. Evaluating and consulting.

2. In contrast, the principal functions of the corporate treasurer are:

a. Provision of capital,

b. Investor relations, and

c. Short-term financing, banking, etc.

3. Note that the controller deals more directly with the operating problems of a company than does the treasurer, who is concerned more with financial matters.

4. The controller has duties somewhat analogous to those of a ship's navigator.

G. A general distinction should be observed between *line* authority and the *staff* function.

1. Line managers, such as sales and production executives, are directly responsible for the principal operations of a business.

2. As shown in textbook Exhibit 1-2, the controller's authority is basically of the *staff* type—that is, giving advice and service to other departments:

a. Service departments, such as the storekeeper and purchasing agent, which aid the work of producing departments, and

b. Producing and operating departments, such as the production superintendent and the assembly foreman.

3. As shown in Exhibit 1-3, the controller has direct or *line* authority only over the members of his own department, such as those employees who conduct internal audits, keep cost records, or prepare payrolls.

H. Two principal roles must be performed simultaneously by the chief accountant of an organization:

1. The watchdog role for top managers:

a. This is the scorekeeping task of accumulating and reporting data, a regular day-to-day routine involving large volumes of work and many completion deadlines.

b. Examples are indicated in Exhibit 1-3: general accounting procedures and maintenance of cost records.

2. The helper role for all managers:

a. This role includes the attention-directing and problem-solving tasks of experienced accountants who work directly with management decision makers on nonroutine problems.

b. Examples indicated in Exhibit 1-3 are, respectively, performance analysis and special reports.

3. The controller's responsibility for playing both these roles often requires large organizations to divide accountants' duties into the specialties shown by Exhibit 1-3.

SELF-TEST AND PRACTICE EXERCISES*

(A) For each of the following multiple-choice and true-false statements, select the single most appropriate answer, and enter its identification letter in the space provided:

C 1. A modern management accounting system should be designed for the main purpose of: (a) developing historical costs for inventory valuations; (b) providing data for income tax returns; (c) aiding decision makers.

b 2. The essence of the management process is: (a) raising capital; (b) decision making; (c) training employees; (d) evaluating performance.

b 3. The function of a decision model is to: (a) make the choice of a course of action; (b) furnish measurements of the effects of different possible actions; (c) specify a certain method for predicting future costs; (d) eliminate the need for managers to make decisions.

D 4. Management accounting is intended primarily to service the needs of: (a) stockholders; (b) creditors; (c) external decision makers; (d) internal decision makers.

b 5. Control is the process of setting upper limits on expenditures: (a) true; (b) false.

A 6. In the practice of management, the planning and control processes are: (a) interactive; (b) independent; (c) separable; (d) identical.

b 7. The implementation and feedback phases of the management decision process should be viewed as separable subparts: (a) true; (b) false.

E 8. Feedback provided by the decision process may suggest changes in: (a) the information system; (b) the prediction method; (c) the decision model; (d) the implementation method; (e) all of these.

b 9. Since an accounting system must be maintained to meet the requirements of income taxation and external reporting, the cost of accounting information may be safely ignored in making management decisions: (a) true; (b) false.

C 10. From a management viewpoint, the selection of a method of computing or reporting cost should be based mainly on: (a) accuracy of measurement; (b) reflection of economic reality; (c) the cost of the method compared with its benefits.

C 11. Basically, the management decision maker must make: (a) an action choice; (b) an information choice; (c) both of the above; (d) neither of the above.

* Answers and solutions to all self-test and practice exercises are given in the back of the *Student Guide*.

A 12. The controller's authority is basically of the: (a) staff type; (b) line type.

B 13. The controller has direct authority over: (a) line departments; (b) members of the accounting department; (c) both of the above; (d) neither of the above.

D 14. The controller is most aptly compared to the ship's: (a) captain; (b) engineer; (c) cook; (d) navigator; (e) executive officer.

D 15. The principal functions of the controller include: (a) providing capital; (b) arranging short-term financing; (c) both of the above; (d) neither of the above.

C 16. The controller's office furnishes advice and service to: (a) producing departments; (b) service departments; (c) both of the above; (d) neither of the above.

A 17. The watchdog function of the chief accountant includes the task(s) of: (a) scorekeeping; (b) attention directing; (c) problem solving; (d) all of the above.

(B) Complete each of the following statements:

1. Modern systems of cost accounting may be called Manangement or Managerial accounting systems.
2. Decision making deals with choices of Alternative Actions to attain specific objectives or goals.
3. A method for helping management to arrive at the most appropriate decision is frequently called a decision model.
4. The information that is produced by a decision model for the possible improvement of the decision process is called Feed back.
5. The management planning process is the selection of objectives or goals and appropriate decision models.
6. The optimal accounting measure or system for management decision purposes should be determined through the Cost-benefit approach.
7. The chief accounting executive, or chief management accountant, is often called the controller.
8. The two principal roles that must be performed simultaneously by the chief accountant of an organization are the watchdog role for top managers and the helper role for all managers.

(C) For each of the following pairs, use the code shown below to indicate the usual type of authority of the first-named party over the second-named party:

L: line authority
S: staff authority
N: no authority

____ 1. controller
billing clerks

____ 2. production superintendent
payroll clerks

____ 3. financial vice-president
shipping foreman

____ 4. manufacturing vice-president
drill press foreman

____ 5. assistant controller
storekeeper

____ 6. chief inspector
controller

____ 7. president
chairman of the board

____ 8. manufacturing vice-president
plant maintenance foreman

____ 9. controller
production superintendent

____ 10. assistant controller
internal auditor

(D) Classify each of the following departments of a manufacturing company either as a service department (S) or as a producing department(P):

____ 1. chief inspector

____ 2. power plant

____ 3. product grinding

____ 4. curing process

____ 5. plant personnel

____ 6. toolroom

____ 7 parts assembly

____ 8. machinery maintenance

____ 9. plant air conditioning

____ 10. material cutting

An Introduction to Cost Terms and Purposes

2

In this chapter we continue our preliminary exploration of management accounting systems by studying some basic cost concepts used throughout the book. No single kind of cost is exclusively useful in all situations, since there are many different costs for many different purposes.

This chapter explains the fundamental relationships among decision alternatives, cost objectives, and the design of a management accounting system. Also included is a description of the contrasting behavior of fixed and variable costs and an important survey of the basic cost terminology for manufacturing operations.

REVIEW SUMMARY

A. Costs are generally defined as resources sacrificed or foregone to achieve a specific objective.

1. A cost objective is any activity for which a separate measurement of costs is desired.

2. The particular decision alternatives that managers expect to consider have a direct influence on the determination of cost objectives against which costs will be accumulated by the accounting system.

3. Modern cost accounting systems are built around probable cost objectives that can be anticipated (such as products and departments) to serve routine uses:

a. For inventory valuation and income determination.

b. For management planning and control decisions.

B. Among the most useful concepts in the entire field of management accounting are those concerning the behavior of different kinds of costs when there are changes in the level or volume of activity of a chosen cost objective, such as units of products sold, tons shipped, or hours worked.

1. *Variable costs* are those costs that change *in total* in proportion to changes in the volume of activity.

a. Variable costs are the same *per unit* of activity at different levels of activity.

b. Examples of variable costs are direct materials used, direct labor, and sales commissions.

c. Notice how variable costs can be graphed against cost objectives in textbook Exhibits 2-1 and 2-2.

2. *Fixed costs* are those costs that are the same *in total* over a wide range of activity volume within a given time period.

a. Fixed costs are not the same *per unit* of activity at different levels of activity; instead, fixed costs on a per-unit basis would vary inversely with changes in activity volume.

b. Examples of fixed costs are executive salaries, fire insurance, and straight-line depreciation.

c. The wide range of activity volume over which total fixed costs would not change is called *the relevant range.*

d. Exhibits 2-3 and 2-4 illustrate some of these ideas graphically.

3. An identification of *cost-behavior patterns* (*cost functions*) helps describe the relationships between total costs and cost objects.

a. For simplicity, we assume at this stage that all costs can be classified as fixed or variable.

b. In addition, cost functions are usually assumed to be linear rather than curvilinear.

c. Further, in practice, activity is assumed to be measurable in only one specified dimension, such as product units, labor hours, sales dollars, etc.

4. Unit cost figures often represent averages based on a total cost that includes both fixed and variable elements. For this reason, unit cost data should be used with great caution for predictive and decision purposes—as pointed out in the textbook example of the $1,000 party fee for a musical group.

C. As a useful background for the later study of planning and control concepts—which are equally applicable to both manufacturing and nonmanufacturing activities—we review some basic cost terminology for manufacturing operations.

1. The cost to manufacture a tangible product has three basic elements.

a. *Direct-material costs* are the costs of all materials that are physically observable as being identified with the finished good and that may be traced to the finished good in an economically feasible way. Examples are lumber and hardware for a furniture manufacturer.

b. *Direct-labor costs* are the costs of all labor that is physically traceable to the finished good in an economically feasible manner. Examples are the labor of lathe operators and product assemblers.

c. *Indirect manufacturing costs* are all costs other than direct materials and direct labor that are associated with the manufacture of the finished good. Examples are supplies, supervisory labor, and depreciation.

d. Indirect manufacturing costs are also called factory overhead, factory burden, manufacturing overhead, manufacturing expenses, and so forth.

e. Some indirect manufacturing costs are variable and some are fixed.

f. Direct material plus direct labor is called *prime cost;* direct labor plus factory overhead is called *conversion cost.*

2. Note in Exhibit 2-5 how the three elements of cost are typically shown in a company's schedule of cost of goods manufactured.

D. A fundamental distinction must be made between two general types of costs, as summarized in Exhibit 2-6.

1. *Product costs* are *inventoriable costs;* that is, they are measures of assets (unexpired costs) until they are sold and become cost of goods sold, which is an expense (expired cost).

a. Instead of the single merchandise inventory of a nonmanufacturing company, a manufacturing company could show three inventory items in its balance sheet: *finished goods, work in process,* and *materials and supplies.*

b. Two basic ways of accounting for inventories are the *perpetual-inventory method,* which requires a continuous record of inventory transactions, and the *periodic-inventory method,* which relies on physical inventory counts.

2. Period costs are *expired costs* (expenses); they include, in addition to cost of goods sold, the *non-inventoriable costs* usually listed as selling and administrative expenses.

E. There is some additional cost terminology you should become familiar with:

1. *Cost of sales* is often used as a synonym for cost of goods sold, which, of course, is an expense.

2. *Indirect-labor costs,* a major part of factory overhead, include the wages and salaries of various factory service employees, idle time of direct labor, and even overtime premium of direct labor—despite the association of the overtime with specific jobs, provided such association is due to the random scheduling of such jobs instead of the special characteristics of the jobs themselves.

3. *Payroll fringe costs,* such as payroll taxes and the costs of employee benefits, are generally classified as factory overhead.

SELF-TEST AND PRACTICE EXERCISES

(A) For each of the following multiple-choice and true-false statements, select the single most appropriate answer and enter its identification letter in the space provided:

A 1. Accountants usually define costs as resources sacrificed or foregone to obtain a specific objective: (a) true; (b) false.

c 2. The purposes for which modern accounting systems accumulate costs include : (a) inventory valuation and income determination; (b) management planning and control decisions; (c) all of the above; (d) none of the above.

d 3. Costs that vary inversely with changes in the volume of activity include: (a) total variable costs; (b) total variable costs divided by activity volume; (c) total fixed costs; (d) total fixed costs divided by activity volume; (e) none of the above.

B 4. The relevant-range concept pertains to the range of activity volume over which unit variable costs would tend to remain stable: (a) true; (b) false.

A 5. In practice, cost-behavior patterns are usually assumed to be: (a) linear; (b) curvilinear; (c) both of the above; (d) neither of the above.

c 6. Unit costs often represent averages that include: (a) fixed costs; (b) variable costs; (c) both of the above.

b 7. In general, if unit costs are multiplied by the number of product units at a certain level of activity, the result would be a total cost that is also appropriate for a different level of activity: (a) true; (b) false.

E 8. The three basic elements of manufacturing cost are direct materials, direct labor, and: (a) indirect materials and labor; (b) selling and general expenses; (c) fixed factory overhead; (d) cost of goods sold; (e) none of the above.

b 9. In general, factory-overhead costs are: (a) direct manufacturing costs; (b) indirect manufacturing costs; (c) both of the above; (d) neither of the above.

b 10. Examples of direct labor include wages of: (a) material handlers; (b) product assemblers; (c) both of the above; (d) neither of the above.

D 11. Cost of goods sold is: (a) an expense; (b) an expired cost; (c) a period cost; (d) all of the above; (e) none of the above.

b 12. In general, the idle time of direct labor should be included as direct-labor cost: (a) true; (b) false.

A 13. The overtime premium earnings of direct-labor employees are usually included as part of factory-overhead cost: (a) true; (b) false.

A 14. When inventories are accounted for by keeping a continuous record of changes in them, the method is called: (a) perpetual-inventory method; (b) periodic-inventory method; (c) both of the above; (d) neither of the above.

C 15. For a manufacturing company, the cost of goods available for sale during a given period is: (a) the beginning inventory of finished goods; (b) the cost of goods manufactured during that period; (c) the sum of the above; (d) none of the above.

A 16. Total manufacturing costs incurred plus the decrease in work-in-process inventory is equal to cost of goods manufactured: (a) true; (b) false.

(B) Complete each of the following statements:

1. Any activity for which a separate measurement of costs is desired is called Cost Objective.

2. The collection of costs in an organized way by an accounting system is called Cost Accumulation.

3. Cost-behavior patterns may be called Cost functions.

4. Prime cost is the total of Direct material cost and Direct Labor cost.

5. Direct-labor cost plus factory-overhead cost is called Conversion cost.

6. Minor materials that become part of a manufactured product but that cannot feasibly be traced to specific physical units are called Indirect materials or supplies.

7. Sales less cost of goods sold is equal to Gross Profit.

8. Product costs are synonymous with Inventoriable costs.

9. The three major inventory classifications that might appear among the assets shown on the balance sheet of a manufacturing company are Finished goods inventory, Work in Process inventory, and Material & Supplies inventory.

10. Such items as payroll taxes and the costs of employee benefits are usually included as part of factory-overhead cost and are called Payroll fringe benefit costs.

11. The cost of goods available for sale less the ending inventory of finished goods is equal to Cost of Goods Sold.

12. In a merchandising company, merchandise purchases plus the beginning inventory of merchandise is equal to Cost of Goods Available For Sale.

(C) Classify each of the following costs in two ways: (a) as variable costs (V), or fixed costs (F); (b) as inventoriable costs (I), or non-inventoriable costs (N):

	(a) V or F	(b) I or N
0. Example: Direct labor	V	I
1. Salary of company controller	F	N
2. Fire insurance on direct materials	F	I
3. Property taxes on finished goods held for sale	F	N
4. Direct materials	V	I
5. Rent paid for store building	F	N
6. Commissions paid to salesmen	V	N
7. Overtime premium of lathe operators	V	I
8. Straight-line depreciation of factory equipment	F	I
9. Straight-line depreciation of trucks used for delivery of sales to customers	V	I
10. Idle time of assembly labor	V	I

(D) You are given the following data of Perfect Square Domino Manufacturing Company for 19_2.

Sales		$350,000
Depreciation machinery		4,000
Direct factory labor		70,000
Factory heat, light, and power		3,000
Factory supplies used		2,000
Indirect factory labor		28,000
Miscellaneous manufacturing expenses		1,000
Purchase of direct materials		88,000
Rent, factory building		12,000
Selling and administrative expenses		120,000
Inventories:	Dec. 31, 19_1	Dec. 31, 19_2
Direct materials	$22,000	$ 20,000
Finished goods	39,000	45,000
Work in process	18,000	12,000

1. Prepare in good form a schedule of cost of goods manufactured for 19_2.

2. Prepare in good form the 19_2 income statement.

Cost-Volume-Profit Relationships

3

In this chapter we examine several basic concepts that are widely used in management decision making for planning and control. The principal technique used here is often called *breakeven analysis,* but it is actually more broadly applicable than this name would suggest. Breakeven analysis is a useful approach for studying the relationships among activity volume, variable expenses, fixed expenses, and net income. Such a study may more aptly be called *cost-volume-profit analysis.*

The idea that is most helpful in understanding this subject is *contribution margin,* which is the excess of sales over variable expenses. This excess can be expressed in various terms: total dollars, dollars per product unit, percentage of sales, or ratio to sales.

The chapter also introduces *sensitivity analysis* and the *contribution approach* to income statements, and it includes a useful appendix showing how cost-volume-profit analysis is affected by income taxes.

A. The *breakeven point* is that point of activity (level of sales volume) where total revenues equal total expenses. At this point there is neither profit nor loss.

1. The *equation method* of determining the breakeven point is based on the fundamental relationships among the principal elements of the income statement:

$$\text{Sales} = \text{Variable Expenses} + \text{Fixed Expenses} + \text{Net Income}$$

a. The breakeven point in terms of *product units* is computed by solving the equation for X, where sales is X times the selling price per unit, net income is zero, fixed expenses are expressed in total dollars, and variable expenses are expressed as X times the *variable expense per product unit.* See the textbook equation example.

b. The breakeven point in terms of *total dollar sales* is computed by solving the equation as above, except that sales is X and variable expenses are expressed as X times the *ratio or percentage of variable expenses to sales.*

2. Instead of using the equation method, one can often find the breakeven point more quickly and more easily by using an equivalent but streamlined approach called the *contribution-margin method.* This merely utilizes a special form of the basic equation:

$$\text{Sales} = \frac{\text{Fixed Expenses} + \text{Net Income}}{\text{Contribution Margin}}$$

a. The breakeven point in terms of *product units* is computed simply by dividing total fixed expenses by the *contribution margin per product unit.*

b. The breakeven point in terms of *total dollar sales* is determined simply by dividing total fixed expenses by the *contribution-margin ratio* or *percentage of sales.*

3. The *graphic approach* (textbook Exhibit 3-1), which is useful in visualizing the concept of breakeven analysis, can utilize either of two methods for plotting expenses:

a. Placing fixed expenses below variable expenses, or

b. Placing fixed expenses above variable expenses (preferred by many because it depicts more clearly the key concept of contribution margin).

4. The sales in terms of product units or total sales dollars that must be made to attain a certain *target net income* can be computed either by the equation method or by the contribution-margin method.

a. The equation method would be the same as described above except that the target net income is used instead of zero net income.

b. The contribution-margin method is the same as described above except that the target net income is combined with total fixed expenses before dividing by the contribution margin per unit, ratio, or percentage.

B. Certain important cost-volume-profit assumptions are customarily made when breakeven charts are prepared.

1. The relationships between total sales and total expenses are usually assumed by accountants to be those that would apply only to the *relevant range:* the rather wide band of activity volume over which total fixed expenses would not change.

2. In contrast to the somewhat simplified relationships implied by accountants' breakeven charts, the economists' breakeven charts usually reflect the more realistic *curvilinear relationships* between sales and variable expenses over a more complete range of activity volume.

3. Essentially, accountants assume *linear relationships* between costs and activity volume:

a. All costs are divisible into the strictly fixed and variable elements defined in Chapter 2.

b. Unit selling prices and unit variable costs are constant at different activity levels.

c. No changes in efficiency and productivity occur at different volume levels.

d. Activity volume is the only relevant factor affecting costs.

C. Because costs, volume, and profits are interrelated, a change in any predicted factor could affect the breakeven point and net income.

1. In order to cope with such uncertainty, a manager can apply a *sensitivity analysis* to a cost-volume-profit model.

a. Different assumptions can be made for certain critical factors in a given case in order that their effects on the breakeven point and net income can be determined.

b. Thus, sensitivity analysis can provide an immediate financial measure of the consequences of possible *prediction errors,* and this can help managers focus on the most sensitive aspects of a particular plan of action before making potentially costly commitments. See the textbook section on cost of prediction error.

2. Changes (or prediction errors) in unit variable costs will affect the breakeven point, contribution margin, and net income.

3. Basic changes (or prediction errors) in production or distribution may alter both fixed and variable costs and affect the contribution margin, breakeven point, activity volume, and net income.

4. A *profit-volume graph,* or *P/V chart* (Exhibit 3-2), is often helpful in understanding the impact of volume changes on net income.

a. The horizontal scale or axis of the P/V chart shows units of volume; the vertical scale shows net income in dollars.

b. A net-income line is plotted so that it indicates the breakeven point where it crosses the horizontal scale.

D. The activity volume of an organization can be measured in different ways.

1. If the entire physical volume is measurable in *uniform terms,* such as product units, patient-days, or student credit hours, the breakeven volume in total sales dollars can be determined by first computing the number of breakeven units and then simply multiplying by the uniform selling price per unit.

2. Alternatively (when the entire physical volume is measurable in uniform terms), the breakeven volume in *total sales dollars* could be computed as described above in A.1.b. and A.2.b.: Divide total fixed expenses by the *contribution-margin percentage or ratio,* which is the total contribution margin divided by total sales.

3. However, for *multi-product companies,* only the second method could be used.

E. The contribution approach to income statements differs basically from the traditional pattern of the income statement.

1. The two approaches differ in their primary classification of costs.

a. The *traditional approach* makes a primary classification of costs according to manufacturing and nonmanufacturing functions, emphasizing the *gross profit margin* available to cover selling and administrative expenses.

b. The *contribution approach* makes a primary classification of costs into variable and fixed categories, emphasizing the *contribution margin* available to cover fixed costs.

2. In contrast to the traditional structure of the income statement, the measurement and reporting of contribution margins can provide important advantages to management.

a. Contribution margins and ratios can help management identify the products to emphasize or redesign and those to de-emphasize or drop.

b. Contribution margins may aid management in making decisions concerning selling-price changes and special sales promotions.

c. Contribution-margin data can be useful in deciding how to utilize most profitably machines, materials, and other resources.

d. In general, the contribution approach enables management to understand more clearly the cost-volume-profit relationships and therefore to determine more realistically the combination of products, selling prices, and sales volume necessary to attain target profits.

SELF-TEST AND PRACTICE EXERCISES

(A) For each of the following multiple-choice and true-false statements, select the single most appropriate answer and enter its identification letter in the space provided:

____ 1. Breakeven analysis is useful primarily for: (a) minimizing income taxes; (b) reporting to stockholders and creditors; (c) complying with requirements of government contracts; (d) making management decisions for planning and controlling operations.

____ 2. Contribution margin is sales minus total fixed expenses: (a) true; (b) false.

____ 3. The breakeven point can be expressed in terms of: (a) product units; (b) total sales dollars; (c) either of the above; (d) neither of the above.

____ 4. The breakeven point can be calculated by dividing total fixed expenses by: (a) the contribution-margin ratio; (b) variable costs per product unit; (c) the margin-of-safety percentage; (d) any of the above; (e) none of the above.

____ 5. The contribution-margin idea is reflected in a breakeven graph more clearly by placing fixed expenses: (a) below variable expenses; (b) above variable expenses.

____ 6. The number of product units that must be sold to earn a specified amount of net income can be calculated by dividing the contribution margin per product unit into: (a) total fixed expenses; (b) the specified amount of net income; (c) the sum of the above; (d) none of the above.

____ 7. The accountant's breakeven charts are usually: (a) linear; (b) nonlinear; (c) curvilinear.

____ 8. The economists' breakeven charts usually depict: (a) constant unit selling prices at different activity levels; (b) constant unit variable costs at different activity levels; (c) both of the above; (d) neither of the above.

____ 9. One of of the several assumptions upon which accountants' breakeven charts are usually based is that no changes in efficiency and productivity take place at different activity levels: (a) true; (b) false.

____ 10. The principal purpose of breakeven charts is to serve as proof of the validity of the breakeven points determined by the equation approach: (a) true; (b) false.

____ 11. Sensitivity analysis is designed to measure: (a) the effects of proposed plans on human behavior; (b) the financial consequences of possible prediction errors; (c) the defects on decision models.

____ 12. As sales exceed the breakeven point, a low contribution-margin percentage would result in lower profits than would a high contribution-margin percentage: (a) true; (b) false.

____ 13. The breakeven point for a given case would be decreased by an increase in: (a) total fixed costs; (b) the contribution-margin percentage; (c) either of the above; (d) neither of the above.

E 14. The vertical axis of the P/V chart shows: (a) units of volume; (b) costs in dollars; (c) contribution margin in dollars; (d) margin of safety in dollars; (e) none of the above.

A 15. The contribution approach to the income statement makes a primary classification of expenses according to: (a) cost behavior; (b) operating functions of the business; (c) relative sizes of the expenses.

b 16. In multi-product firms, a shift in sales mix from products with high contribution-margin ratios to products with low contribution-margin ratios would cause the breakeven point to be: (a) lower; (b) higher; (c) unchanged.

(B) Complete each of the following statements:

1. A key concept that is useful in understanding breakeven analysis is contribution margin.

2. In the usual breakeven graph, the horizontal scale or axis represents Activity Volume.

3. The linearity assumption for breakeven charts is likely to be most accurate within the Relevant Range of activity volume.

4. Breakeven analysis by accountants usually assumes that the only relevant variable affecting costs is Activity Volume.

5. The expected values of a decision model will be affected by changes or errors in critical data inputs. A technique that measures this effect is called Sensitivity Analysis.

6. An increase in total fixed costs in a given case would cause the breakeven point to Increase.

7. In multi-product companies, the relative combinations of products sold is called the Sales mix.

(C) Given for Adjustable Products, Inc.:

Sales price per product unit	$	40
Variable expenses per product unit		30
Total fixed expenses		600

Find:

1. Contribution margin per product unit Unit Selling price − Unit Variable Expenses .... $ 10

2. Breakeven sales in units Total fixed expenses ÷ unit contribution margin .... 60 units

3. Sales in units that will produce a net income of \$250 600 + 250 ÷ 10 = 850 ÷ 10 .... 85 units
The sum of Total Fixed expenses + the target net Income ÷ the unit contribution margin

40 − 6 − 30 = \$4 per unit

4. Sales in units that will produce a net income of 15% of sales 40 × 15% = \$6.00 600 ÷ 4 = ... 150 units
Unit sales price less the unit net income less the unit variable cost; Dividing this into the total fixed expenses gives us the required sales in units

5. Net income, if 80 product units are sold .... $
Each unit would contribute \$10 toward total fixed expenses, therefore net Inc =
$(10)\cdot(80) = 800 - 600 = 200$

6. The breakeven sales in units, if variable expenses were increased by $3 per unit and if total fixed expenses were decreased by $110 .... 20 units

CTM = 40 - (30+3) 7 per unit

T.F. Exp = 600 - 110 = 490

BE in Sales = 490 ÷ 7 = 70 units

7. If the company desires a net income of $200 on a sales volume of 100 units, what must the unit selling price be, assuming no changes in the $30 variable expenses per unit or the $600 total fixed expenses? .... $ 38

CTM = 200 + 600 = 800 ÷ 100 = 8 per unit

Selling Price = Variable cost per unit + the unit CT. margin 30 + 8 = 38

(D) Given for Aggregate Sales Company:

Sales	$60,000
Total fixed expenses	12,000
Total variable expenses	42,000

Find:

1. Net income when sales are $60,000 (as above) .... $ 6000

60,000 - 12000 - 42000 = 6000

2. Contribution-margin ratio or percentage .... 30 %

(60,000 - 42,000) ÷ 60000 = 18000 ÷ 60000 = 30%

3. Breakeven sales .... 12000 ÷ 30% = 40000 .... $ 40,000

4. Sales that would produce a net income of $9,000, assuming no changes in the contribution-margin ratio or in total fixed expenses .... $ ~~120000~~ 70,000

~~(12000 + 9000) ÷ 30% = 21000 ÷ 30% = 70,000~~

~~OR~~

~~S = 12000 + 70% S + 20% S = 12000 + 90% S~~

~~10% S = 12000~~

~~S = 12000 ÷ 10% = 120,000~~

12000 + 9000 ÷ 30% = 21000 - 30% = 70,000

5. Sales that would produce a net income of 20% of sales, assuming no changes in the contribution-margin ratio or in total fixed expenses .... $ 120000

12000 ÷ 30% - 20% = 12000 ÷ 10% = 120,000

OR

S = 12000 + 70% + 20% = 12000 + 90% S

10% S = 12000

S = 12000 ÷ 10% = 120,000

6. Breakeven sales if total fixed expenses are reduced by $2,000 and if selling prices are reduced by 10% per product unit, assuming no changes in variable expenses per product unit .... $ 45000

T Fix Exp = 12000 - 2000 = 10,000

Dollar Sales - 42000 ÷ 60000 - 10% of 60,000 = 42000 ÷ 54000 = 7/9 ctm = 2/9

The new breakeven sales would be the new total fixed expenses divided by the new contribution margin ratio

10,000 ÷ 2/9 = 10,000 × 9/2 = 45000

(E) Given for Dual-View Lens Corporation for 19_8:

	Fixed	Variable	Total
Manufacturing cost of goods sold	$80,000	$120,000	$200,000
Selling expenses	20,000	80,000	100,000
Administrative expenses	30,000	10,000	40,000
Sales			365,000

1. Prepare an income statement in the traditional form:

2. Prepare an income statement using the contribution approach:

3. Compute the operating income if sales volume increased 10% without any change in unit selling prices:

Job-Order Accounting: An Illustration of Systems Design

4

This chapter presents the framework of the job-order system of product costing for a manufacturing company. Described are the basic records and procedures involved in management planning and control and in accumulation of costs for inventory valuation and income determination. Also explained are the principal transactions and their entries in the controlling accounts and subsidiary ledgers.

The simple diagram in Exhibit 4-5 of the textbook is an excellent focal point for our study of the job-order cost system, because it includes the principal general-ledger accounts used in manufacturing accounting and it clearly shows the flow of costs from the originating accounts, through the inventories, and to the cost of sales. Using this diagram for a background, we can more easily comprehend the various technical procedures and relationships covered in the chapter. This material can serve as a valuable part of our foundation for understanding and using many of the ideas contained in the remainder of the book, especially in the next eight chapters.

REVIEW SUMMARY

A. In management accounting systems, costs are usually accumulated to meet both internal management needs and external reporting requirements.

1. A major aim of such systems is the accumulation of costs *by departments or cost centers* to assist planning and control by pinpointing responsibility.

2. Another major objective is the accumulation of costs *by products* for purposes of inventory valuation and income determination.

3. *Job-order costing* is suitable for use by companies that manufacture custom-made products or other products that are readily identified by individual units or batches, each of which receives varying degrees of attention and skill.

a. Such products would include furniture, machinery, highway bridges, drilling platforms for off-shore oil exploration, and space modules for voyages to the moon.

b. Nonmanufacturing situations for which the job-order system would be suitable include advertising agencies, auto repair, public accounting practice, social welfare cases, and research projects.

4. In contrast to job-order costing, *process costing* is appropriate when there is a mass production of uniform units, which usually flow continuously through a series of standard production steps called operations or processes.

a. Such products would include textiles, chemicals, petroleum products, cement, bricks, newsprint, ice cream, and breakfast foods.

b. Nonmanufacturing situations for which the process system would be appropriate include banks, insurance companies, schools, libraries, and many government services.

5. Some features are common to both job-order and process-costing methods:

a. Product costs per unit are determined by averaging (process-costing operations typically use larger denominators for this purpose than job-costing operations).

b. In addition to accumulating costs by products, each costing method also accumulates costs in cost centers or departments for planning and control purposes.

B. Several basic forms and documents are used in a typical job-order cost system.

1. The central document is the *job-order* or *job-cost sheet*, textbook Exhibit 4-1.

a. The job-order or job-cost sheet is used to accumulate product costs by identifiable lots of product.

b. The file or collection of job orders for uncompleted jobs serves as the subsidiary ledger for Work-in-Process Control, a general-ledger account.

c. In effect, the file of these cost sheets for uncompleted jobs is a perpetual book inventory of work in process.

2. Two other perpetual book inventories are also usually maintained in subsidiary ledgers:

a. The *stores cards* (Exhibit 4-6), which represent costs and quantities of materials on hand, are controlled by the Stores Control account in the general ledger.

b. The *finished-goods stock cards,* which measure costs and quantities of completed goods held for sale, are controlled by the Finished Goods Control, a general-ledger account.

3. The individual *factory department overhead cost sheets* (Exhibit 4-7), which contain the details of various kinds of manufacturing expenses actually incurred, make up a subsidiary ledger, which is controlled by the Factory Department Overhead Control account.

4. *Stores requisitons, labor work tickets,* and *labor clock cards* (Exhibits 4-2, 4-3, and 4-4) serve two basic purposes:

a. They are used as bookkeeping media for charging direct costs to jobs and indirect costs to overhead departments.

b. They are used to aid in fixing responsibility for the control and usage of both direct and indirect materials and labor.

C. In practice, the general-ledger entries for transactions of job-order cost systems are typically oriented toward measuring inventory costs rather than serving the needs of management responsibility and cost control.

1. Usually the charges for *prime costs* (direct material and direct labor) are taken directly to the Work-in-Process Control and not through intermediate department accounts for responsibility and cost control (Exhibit 4-8).

2. However, costing for control is not overlooked in job-order cost systems, but is usually accomplished by the preparation of daily or weekly summaries of the source documents for material and labor costs (material requisitions, labor work tickets, and labor clock cards).

D. Most factory-overhead costs are indirect manufacturing costs and thus cannot easily be identified with specific jobs.

1. Therefore, the amount of factory-overhead cost applicable to specific jobs must be estimated by using rates based upon total direct-labor cost, total direct-labor hours, total machine-hours, or some other base for allocating indirect costs to jobs.

2. *Rather accurate* overhead cost rates for a given period could be calculated at the end of such period by using actual overhead costs and actual overhead allocation bases, but the resulting cost information would usually *not be available on a timely basis* for several important purposes:

a. Making interim measurements of product inventory costs and operating net income,

b. Currently relating factory-overhead costs to products for purposes of planning and control, and

c. Using manufacturing cost as one of the important factors in setting selling prices of products finished during the period.

3. Therefore, instead of using the more accurate *actual* or *historical* rates for applying overhead costs to production, most companies use the less accurate but more timely *predetermined* rates that are based upon forecasted or budgeted amounts of factory-overhead costs and the overhead rate base (such as budgeted total direct-labor costs or hours).

4. These predetermined factory-overhead cost rates are typically used on an *annualized basis* rather than a monthly basis for two important reasons:

a. To overcome the volatility in computed unit costs due to changes in the level of activity (the denominator reason), and

b. To avoid the volatility in computed unit costs due to seasonal variations in total factory-overhead costs (the numerator reason).

E. Accounting for total factory-overhead costs involves actual overhead, applied overhead, and the difference between these two amounts.

1. *Actual overhead cost* is the amount of overhead cost incurred on the accrual accounting basis.

a. Actual overhead cost is debited to Factory Department Overhead Control and its subsidiary ledger, the factory department overhead cost sheets.

b. The offsetting credit entries are made to such accounts as Stores Control, Accrued Payroll, Unexpired Insurance, Allowance for Depreciation, and Accounts Payable.

2. *Applied overhead cost* is found by multiplying the predetermined overhead rate by the actual (historical) amount of the overhead rate base (such as total direct-labor costs or hours).

a. Applied overhead cost is debited to Work-in-Process Control and its subsidiary ledger, the individual job-cost sheets.

b. The offsetting credit is made to Factory Overhead Applied, a contra or offset account to Factory Department Overhead Control.

3. The difference between applied and actual overhead is called either:

a. *Overapplied overhead* or *overabsorbed overhead* if the applied amount is greater than the actual amount, or

b. *Underapplied overhead* or *underabsorbed overhead* if the applied amount is less than the actual amount.

4. *At the end of the year,* there is typically only a small amount of under- or overapplied overhead cost, and it is usually closed out by a debit or credit, respectively, to Cost of Sales, in contrast to the more accurate method of prorating the amount over three accounts in proportion to the unadjusted overhead portions of their balances:

a. Cost of Sales,
b. Finished Goods, and
c. Work in Process.

5. *For interim financial statements,* there could be quite a large amount of under- or overapplied overhead cost, and this should usually not be carried through cost of sales for the interim period because significant deviations from the annual average could have been caused by seasonal influences on overhead costs and their application to production.

a. An underapplied overhead balance may be shown in an interim balance sheet as a current asset item.

b. An overapplied overhead balance may be shown in an interim balance sheet as a deferred credit or as an inventory offset.

SELF-TEST AND PRACTICE EXERCISES

(A) For each of the following multiple-choice and true-false statements, select the single most appropriate answer and enter its identification letter in the space provided:

___ 1. Companies that are engaged in the mass production of like product units, which flow continuously through a series of uniform production steps, would usually cost such products by: (a) the job-order costing method; (b) the process costing method.

___ 2. Accounting systems for manufacturers accumulate costs for the purposes of: (a) planning and control; (b) valuing inventories and measuring net income; (c) both of the above; (d) neither of the above.

___ 3. Examples of products for which a job-order costing system would probably be suitable include: (a) newsprint; (b) auto repairs; (c) both of the above; (d) neither of the above.

___ 4. Examples of products for which a process costing system would probably be suitable include: (a) printing; (b) mining; (c) both of the above; (d) neither of the above.

___ 5. Product costs per unit are determined by an averaging process in: (a) a job-order cost system; (b) a process cost system; (c) both of the above; (d) neither of the above.

___ 6. When a job-order cost system is used, costs are usually not accumulated in cost centers or departments: (a) true; (b) false.

___ 7. The file of cost sheets for uncompleted jobs serves as a perpetual book inventory of work in process: (a) true; (b) false.

___ 8. A perpetual book inventory is represented by: (a) the finished-goods stock cards; (b) the stores requisitions; (c) both of the above; (d) neither of the above.

B 9. Documents that are used as a basis for charging costs to jobs and overhead departments include: (a) stores cards; (b) labor work tickets; (c) both of the above; (d) neither of the above.

b 10. The subsidiary ledger for Factory Department Overhead Control contains entries for applied factory overhead: (a) true; (b) false.

A 11. A historical rate for applying factory-overhead cost to products would be preferred to a predetermined rate if the criteria used included: (a) accuracy; (b) timeliness; (c) both of the above; (d) neither of the above.

A 12. In a job-order cost system, costing for control purposes is usually accomplished by the frequent preparation of summaries of the source documents for labor and material costs: (a) true; (b) false.

b 13. When predetermined rates are used for applying factory overhead to production, they should usually be calculated to cover: (a) a month; (b) a year.

E 14. Overapplied factory overhead is the excess of applied factory overhead over the amount of: (a) budgeted factory overhead; (b) predicted factory overhead; (c) forecasted factory overhead; (d) all of the above; (e) none of the above.

A 15. The usual end-of-year treatment of underapplied factory overhead is to: (a) debit Cost of Sales; (b) credit Cost of Sales; (c) debit Cost of Sales and appropriate inventory accounts; (d) credit Cost of Sales and appropriate inventory accounts; (e) none of the above.

A 16. The preferred treatment of underapplied factory overhead in interim financial statements is to report it as a current asset item: (a) true; (b) false.

b 17. The amount of under- or overapplied factory overhead would, in general, tend to be larger at the end of the year than at any interim date: (a) true; (b) false.

(B) Complete each of the following statements:

1. Companies that manufacture products that are readily identified by individual units or batches, each of which receives different kinds of attention and skill, would usually find the Job order costing system more suitable than the Process costing system.

2. For planning and control purposes, costs can be accumulated in Cost centers or dept.

3. The subsidiary ledger for Work-in-Process Control consists of Cost sheets for uncompleted Jobs.

4. A document used to aid in fixing responsibility for the control and usage of materials is Stores Requisitions.

5. Applied factory overhead should be debited to Work in Process Control and to Job cost sheets.

6. The predetermined factory-overhead rate can be determined by dividing budgeted factory overhead cost by Budgeted Direct Labor or Mach. hours.

7. Applied factory-overhead cost is calculated by multiplying overhead rate by Actual amount of the Rate base.

8. At the end of the year, if the overapplied factory-overhead cost is to be handled in a theoretically accurate manner, it should be prorated by credit ~~Cost of Sale~~ Credit entries to three accounts: Cost of Sales, Finish Goods, and Work in Process

(C) Given for Forward Calendar Company:

Budgeted factory-overhead cost	$220,000
Budgeted direct-labor hours	200,000 hr
Actual factory-overhead cost	$226,000
Actual direct-labor hours	210,000 hr

Find:

1. Predetermined overhead rate 220,000 ÷ 200,000 = 1.10 per hr . . . . . $\_\_\_\_\_\_$
2. Applied factory-overhead cost 210,000 × 1.10 = 231,000 . . . . . $\_\_\_\_\_\_$
3. Amount of underapplied factory-overhead cost 231,000 − 226,000 = 5000 . . . . . $\_\_\_\_\_\_$

or

Amount of overapplied factory-overhead cost . . . . . $\_\_\_\_\_\_$

(D) The Great Works Producing Corporation presents the following selected general-ledger accounts showing balances at April 1 of the current calendar year:

Cash	
10,000	

Accrued Payroll	
	-0-

Work-in-Process Control	
41,000	

Unexpired Insurance	
1,000	

Stores Control	
32,000	

Finished Goods Control	
148,000	

Allowance for Depreciation	
	70,000

Factory Dept. Overhead Control	
62,000	

Cost of Sales	
200,000	

Accounts Payable	
	27,000

Factory Overhead Applied	
	63,000

Sales	
	310,000

Correct balances at April 30 of the current year include:

Accrued Payroll	$ 3,000(Cr.)
Stores	$ 30,000(Dr.)
Work in Process	$ 47,000(Dr.)
Finished Goods	$152,000(Dr.)

The April transactions of Great Works Producing Corporation are summarized as follows:

(a)	Cash sales	$105,000
(b)	Materials purchased on account	42,000
(c)	Direct materials used	39,000
(d)	Direct factory labor incurred	16,000
(e)	Indirect materials used	______
(f)	Indirect factory labor incurred	______
(g)	Factory insurance expired	300
(h)	Factory depreciation	1,700
(i)	Factory utility services purchased on account	3,000
(j)	Factory overhead applied: 125% of direct-labor cost	______
(k)	Accounts payable paid	49,000
(l)	Factory payroll paid	22,000
(m)	Cost of goods manufactured	______
(n)	Cost of goods sold	______

Required:

1. Calculate the dollar amounts to fill the five blanks in the above list of transactions (e f, j, m, n).

2. Post the amounts for all April transactions to the general-ledger accounts on the preceding page, using each transaction letter to cross-reference your posted debits and credits.

Budgeting in General: Profit Planning

5

In this chapter we study a useful planning and control device called the *budget.* This is a comprehensive plan that quantifies an organization's goals in terms of specific financial and operating objectives. The master budget is a coordinated set of detailed forecasts adopted by management as guidelines for future operations. The principal budget schedules and statements contain measurements in dollar amounts, but in many cases these figures are based on predictions of such nonmonetary data as material quantities, product units, and labor hours.

Mainly, we examine here the general framework of the master budget and some techniques for assembling data into budget schedules and statements. Particularly helpful is the comprehensive textbook illustration, which you should follow through, step by step. In addition, the chapter briefly surveys sales forecasting techniques and the use of budgets in computer-based simulation models. This chapter provides useful background and perspective for the next few chapters.

REVIEW SUMMARY

A. A *budget* is a quantitative expression of an organization's plan of action and an aid to the coordination and implementation of the plan.

1. The budget is helpful to management in making two broad types of decisions:

a. *Financing decisions* deal with the obtaining of funds for acquisition of resources.

b. *Operating decisions* are concerned with the acquisition and utilization of scarce resources.

2. The budget is valuable to very small units as well as to large organizations.

3. Budgets have several significant advantages when properly used:

a. They compel management to face the task of planning.

b. Budgets aid in translating plans into explicit terms that can be useful as a basis for evaluating actual performance in the future.

c. Budgets also serve to communicate management plans, to coordinate these plans, and to carry them out.

B. Budgets can be classified in at least two ways:

1. They may be classified as to the length of time covered.

a. The usual period for planning and control budgets is one year, which can be divided into months or quarters and which can also be kept continuously extended for one year in advance.

b. Long-term budgets of ten or more years can be used for basic changes in products and manufacturing facilities.

2. The budgeted financial statements, sometimes called *pro forma statements,* may be classified also as to general type of budget.

a. *Operating budgets,* such as the sales, production, and expense budgets, are elements of the budgeted income statement.

b. *Financial budgets* include the budgeted balance sheet, the budgeted statement of sources and applications of funds, and the budgets for cash receipts and disbursements.

C. The final master budget is the product of several preliminary drafts, each of which may lead to decisions that require an additional draft.

1. Two principal levels of exhibits are included.

a. *Schedules* show details for such areas as sales, production, and expenses.

b. *Main statements* include the income statement, the balance sheet, and summaries of cash receipts and disbursements.

2. Several basic steps are typically followed in preparing the final budget exhibits:

a. Make the forecast of sales by products in both units and dollars.

b. Prepare the budget for the number of units to produce that, with beginning inventories, will meet the needs of sales and also bring ending inventories up to the target levels.

c. Construct schedules for material, labor, and overhead costs to support the production activity determined in the preceding step.

d. Make the cost-of-goods-sold budget.

e. Prepare the various expense budgets.

f. Construct the budgeted income statement.

g. Make cash budgets that show, in addition to expected cash receipts and disbursements, financing plans involving loans and temporary investments.

h. Prepare a balance sheet that is projected to the end of the budget period.

D. The forecast of sales volume is usually the keystone of the entire budget structure, but it is often difficult to predict reliable sales figures.

1. Many factors should be considered, such as:

a. Past sales volume,

b. General economic and industry conditions,

c. Market research studies,

d. Pricing policies, and

e. Advertising, competition, and other factors.

2. Usually, in forecasting sales, it would be wise not to rely entirely upon a single producedure, but to use some suitable combinations of three particular procedures:

a. Individual salesmen and sales managers of the organization combine their predictions after considering such factors as previous sales volumes, economic indicators, and competitive conditions.

b. Predict sales by using a statistical approach such as trend measurements, cycle projections, and correlation analysis.

c. The top executives and administrators of the organization hold a meeting, express their opinions, and arrive at a group judgment as to predicted sales.

E. Master budgets are helpful foundations for the construction of computer-based simulation models that are often called *financial planning models* or *total models.*

1. Such models are mathematical statements or relationships among a company's activities and selected related factors, both internal and external.

2. The models are used not only for preparing and revising budgets, but also for comparing the effects of various decision alternatives (*sensitivity analysis*).

3. The degree of sophistication of such models range from the standard general-purpose simulators, available on a rental basis, to the more comprehensive models that must be designed to meet the complex requirements of specific organizations.

4. As in all information decisions, the selection of computer-based simulation models should be determined by a *cost-benefit approach.*

SELF-TEST AND PRACTICE EXERCISES

(A) For each of the following multiple-choice and true-false statements, select the single most appropriate answer and enter its identification letter in the space provided:

B 1. In general, a budget for a given year's operations would consist of the actual operating data for the immediately preceding year: (a) true; (b) false.

C 2. A budget aids management in: (a) making operating decisions; (b) making financing decisions; (c) both of the above; (d) neither of the above.

B 3. Budgets are usually of significant value only to large organizations: (a) true; (b) false.

B 4. A budgeted balance sheet would be classified as: (a) an operating budget; (b) a financial budget; (c) both of the above; (d) neither of the above.

C 5. Operating budgets would include: (a) the production budget; (b) the expense budgets; (c) both of the above; (d) neither of the above.

B 6. The usual starting point in preparing a master budget is making forecasts of cash receipts and disbursements: (a) true; (b) false.

C 7. In making a production budget for a given period, consideration should normally be given to: (a) predicted beginning inventories of the period; (b) desired ending inventories of the period; (c) both of the above; (d) neither of the above.

A 8. As a basis for judging operating results, it is usually better to use expected performance than to use past performance: (a) true; (b) false.

E 9. In preparing a master budget, the last step is usually the preparation of the forecasted: (a) income statement; (b) cash receipts; (c) sales; (d) production; (e) balance sheet.

D 10. It is usually feasible to forecast sales without considering; (a) general economic conditions; (b) competition; (c) both of the above; (d) neither of the above.

A 11. Arriving at a sales forecast by forming a group judgment composed of the opinions of top company officers is usually: (a) a fast method; (b) an excellent method; (c) both of the above; (d) neither of the above.

B 12. A usually effective way of forecasting sales is to rely entirely on the predictions of the individual salesmen and sales managers of the organization: (a) true; (b) false.

C 13. Ordinarily, a budget would include: (a) predicted income tax expenses; (b) predicted income tax liability; (c) both of the above; (d) neither of the above.

E 14. Potential cash deficiencies would usually be determined by: (a) the sales budget; (b) the pro forma balance sheet; (c) the expense budgets; (d) the projected income statement; (e) the cash budgets.

A 15. Units of materials to purchase would be equal to budgeted materials usage: (a) plus the desired ending inventory of materials and minus the beginning inventory of materials; (b) plus the beginning inventory of materials and minus the desired ending inventory of materials; (c) both of the above; (d) neither of the above.

C 16. A financial planning model can be used: (a) in the preparation and revision of budgets; (b) for sensitivity analysis; (c) both of the above; (d) neither of the above.

(B) Complete each of the following statements:

1. Budgets may be called projections, forecasted statements, predicted statements, or Pro forma statements.

2. Budgets should help to communicate management Plans, to coordinate these Plans, and to implement them.

3. A budget that always shows a 12-month forecast by adding a month or quarter in the future as the month or quarter just ended is dropped is called a continuous budget.

4. In preparing a master budget, it is usually best to start with a forecast of Sales.

5. Budgeted units of product to manufacture may be determined by adding The Desired Inventory of Finished Goods to budgeted sales and subtracting The beginning Inventory of Finished Goods from this total.

6. Cash budgets can be helpful to managers in avoiding unnecessary cash deficiencies and idle cash balances.

7. Computer-based simulation models constructed on the foundation of master budgets are often called Financial Planning Models.

8. The selection of computer-based simulation models should be determined by a Cost benefit approach.

(C) Given for the Four-C Company:

	Case 1	Case 2
Beginning inventory	1,300 units	2,850 units
Expected sales	10,000 units	9,500 units
Desired ending inventory	1,800 units	1,200 units
Find budgeted purchases	10500 units	7850 units

(D) Given for Credit Claim Corporation:

	Case 1	Case 2
Beginning balance of accounts receivable	$ 75,000	$ 42,100
Expected sales on account	243,000	349,500
Expected collections from customers	285,000	324,400
Find expected ending balance of accounts receivable	$33000	$ 67200

(E) Given for Cash-Plan, Inc.:

	Case 1	Case 2
Beginning cash balance	$ 4,200	$ 2,700
Expected cash receipts	98,000	73,600
Expected cash disbursements	87,000	80,800
Minimum ending cash balance desired	8,000	8,500
Find estimated amount (1. or 2.):		
1. Necessary to borrow	$	$ 13000
2. Available for repayment of loans and interest	$ 7200	$

(F) Given for Summ-Totall Material Company:

	Finished Product X	Finished Product Y
Number of units to be produced	2,000 units	3,000 units
Number of pounds of Material A needed for each finished product unit	10 lb	15 lb
Number of square feet of Material B needed for each finished product unit	20 ft	6 ft

	Material A	Material B
Beginning inventories of materials	6,000 lb	15,000 ft
Desired ending inventories of materials	10,000 lb	8,000 ft
Purchase price of materials per pound, per square foot	$4.00	$6.00

Find:

	Material A	Material B
1. Number of material units (pounds or square feet) needed for production of both finished products	65000 lb	58000 ft
2. Cost of materials needed for production	$260,000	$348 000
3. Number of material units to be purchased	69000 lb	51000 ft
4. Cost of materials to be purchased	$276000	$306000

Systems Design, Responsibility Accounting, and Motivation

6

Management accounting systems are also called management control systems or, simply, control systems. Their purpose is to assist management in making decisions to achieve the general and specific objectives of an organization.

Because the human behavioral aspects of a management accounting system are crucial to its success, they should be given paramount consideration in the design, operation, and evaluation of the system. This chapter focuses on some related ideas: motivation of people, potential behavioral advantages of budgets, responsibility accounting, the controllability of costs, and other important aspects of control systems relating to human behavior.

REVIEW SUMMARY

A. Control-system design has a basic relationship to the *motivation* of people.

1. Of prime important is *goal congruence,* the harmony of individual and group objectives with those of the organization for the encouragement of effective behavior toward organizational goals.

2. Interdependent with goal congruence is the problem of developing effective *incentive* to induce efforts toward goals—often provided by the appropriate use of performance-evaluation reports.

3. Because accounting data and control systems are economic goods, we must always use the *cost-benefit approach* to choosing information devices for management decisions.

a. Thus, at the inception of an organization, when it may be small and fairly simple, physical observation alone may be quite adequate as an informal information system.

b. However, as an organization grows and becomes more complex, it may be desirable to develop more elaborate systems, such as budgets and responsibility-accounting frameworks for profit centers and investment centers.

B. Most control systems rely heavily on budgets, which can have three important advantages:

1. Budgets can strongly influence management to anticipate changing conditions and to formulate strategies for dealing with expected changes.

2. Budgets show what should be accomplished under expected conditions and thus can provide a better basis than past performance for judging current performance.

3. Budgets are comprehensive action plans for the entire organization and therefore can be extremely helpful in communicating top-management plans, coordinating the plans among the segments of the organization, and implementing the plans.

4. However, the ability of a budget to achieve these advantages depends more on its understanding and acceptance by members of the organization than on the excellence of the accounting techniques for gathering and assembling the budget data.

C. When decision making within a given organization is subdivided into certain areas of management responsibility (cost centers, profit centers, and investment centers), some form of *responsibility-accounting system* should usually accompany this subdivision.

1. Because the design of a system and the design of an organizational structure are actually interdependent, they should not be designed separately.

2. Responsibility-accounting systems (also called profitability-accounting systems or activity-accounting systems) recognize various decision centers throughout an organization and trace costs (and revenues, assets, and liabilities, where appropriate) to the individual manager who is primarily responsible for making decisions about the costs in question.

3. Responsibility reports (performance reports) should be prepared periodically to provide the manager of each decision center with figures on those items subject to his control, as illustrated in textbook Exhibit 6-2.

4. Such reports may show only the budgeted amounts and the variances of actual amounts from budgeted amounts.

a. This focus on the variances illustrates *management by exception.*

b. Managers thus need not waste their time and effort on those parts of the reports that reflect the smoothly running phases of operations.

D. It is important but difficult to distinguish between controllable and uncontrollable costs.

1. *Controllable costs* are costs directly influenced by a given manager within a given time span.

2. In practice it is often not easy to fix responsibility or controllability for a given cost.

a. Two or more persons may have a direct influence on the cost.

b. Some persons may indirectly influence costs that appear to be under the direct control of another.

3. In reporting *uncontrollable costs,* there are conflicting views.

a. Most advocates of responsibility accounting favor excluding the uncontrollable items from a performance report.

b. However, another view is that uncontrollable items that are indirectly caused by the existence of a department should be included in the department manager's report so that he can become more aware of their impact on total organization costs and benefits.

4. In general, the length of the time period involved must also be considered in determining whether a cost is controllable.

5. Variances arising from a responsibility-accounting system should not be used to "fix the blame," but rather to help suggest possible causes of variances or to identify persons who should be asked to explain the variances.

6. In evaluating performance, we should distinguish between evaluating the *manager* as an individual and the *subunit* as an investment, because some costs of a subunit are not controllable by the manager (rents, property taxes, etc.).

E. We must understand some of the typical effects of control systems on human behavior.

1. The *formal organization controls,* such as budgets, may impose quantitative standards of performance that motivate employees toward organizational goals.

2. However, in addition, there are two important types of *informal* controls that can significantly influence employee behavior (Exhibit 6-3):

a. *Group controls* tend to confine employee behavior close to accepted behavior norms.

b. *Individual controls* imposed by personal aspirations and expectations tend to keep employee behavior directed toward personal goals.

3. Effective *goal congruence* means that, in addition to the harmony of subgoals with top-management goals, individual managers must accept the subgoals as their own personal goals.

a. However, the influence of accounting measurements on acceptance of subgoals as personal goals may be outweighed by other influences, such as family, religion, and opinions of colleagues.

b. Significantly helpful in inducing management acceptance of subgoals as personal goals are strong endorsement of system goals by top management and meaningful participation by managers in setting goals.

F. Several additional matters illustrate the overriding importance of a behavioral orientation for a successful management control system.

1. Goal congruence can be complicated by the use of *multiple goals* for the organization; these may be interdependent and even somewhat conflicting—for example, profitability and public responsibility.

2. Another danger to guard against is the emphasis on a short-run goal, such as sales or net income, at the risk of poor long-run results.

3. A *human resources accounting system* has been advocated by psychologist Rensis Likert to remedy the motivational errors caused by the conventional accounting system's emphasis on the measurement of short-run performance.

a. Likert would integrate his system with conventional accounting procedures, thus explicitly recognizing the importance of these procedures for measuring performance.

b. He would debit assets (not expenses) for the costs of recruiting and training managers.

c. He would then use an amortization procedure to charge these costs to expense over the expected useful lives of the managers.

4. A universal problem is *slack* or *padding* in the budget of an organization, intentionally created by managers as a protective device and therefore difficult to eliminate through motivation.

5. Although management accounting systems should clearly delineate responsibility, they should also avoid a too-rigid separation of responsibility that might cause costly competition among managers and lack of cooperation toward the overall benefit of the organization.

6. It is important in decision making to motivate employees toward the preparation of accurate source documents for reliable scorekeeping.

7. In general, cost information for management-decision purposes would be more useful if developed and analyzed through the *contribution approach* rather than traditional accounting methods.

SELF-TEST AND PRACTICE EXERCISES

(A) For each of the following multiple-choice and true-false statements, select the single most appropriate answer and enter its identification letter in the space provided:

____ 1. The human behavioral aspects of a management accounting system are usually not essential to its success: (a) true; (b) false.

____ 2. In the design of effective control systems, goal congruence and incentive should be viewed as: (a) important characteristics; (b) independent of each other; (c) both of the above; (d) neither of the above.

____ 3. In selecting such technical devices as budgets for generating goal congruence and incentive in a control system, one should base his choice solely upon: (a) the cost of the devices; (b) their ability to generate goal congruence and incentive; (c) their degree of sophistication; (d) none of the above.

____ 4. For evaluating performance and planning it is best to compare current results with: (a) historical records of the organization: (b) average performance of similar organizations; (c) budget data.

____ 5. The effect of budgets on the formulation of overall strategies of an organization is: (a) significant; (b) insignificant.

____ 6. If a budget is carefully developed, it should be: (a) rigidly adhered to; (b) deviated from or adjusted if there are some definite changes in conditions.

____ 7. Of greater importance in budgeting are: (a) human aspects; (b) accounting techniques.

____ 8. The design of a management accounting system and the design of an organizational structure are: (a) interdependent; (b) inseparable; (c) both of the above; (d) neither of the above.

____ 9. Most advocates of responsibility accounting feel that the manager of each decision center should be provided periodically with performance reports showing: (a) total costs of his decision center; (b) costs of only those items subject to his control.

____10. As the time period lengthens in a given case, the number of costs that are controllable becomes: (a) larger; (b) smaller.

____11. In practice, the fixing of responsibility or controllability for a given cost is usually: (a) easy; (b) difficult.

____12. Controllable costs are equivalent to variable costs: (a) true; (b) false.

____13. The variances developed in a responsibility-accounting system should be used primarily to help identify: (a) persons who can explain the variances; (b) persons who can be blamed for the variances; (c) persons who made or approved the budget forecasts.

____14. In general, it is appropriate to use the same subunit costs for evaluating the subunit as an investment and for evaluating the subunit manager as an individual: (a) true; (b) false.

____15. Effective goal congruence implies: (a) harmony of subgoals with top-management goals; (b) acceptance by individual managers of subgoals as their personal goals; (c) both of the above; (d) neither of the above.

____16. The use of multiple goals for an organization can make goal congruence more difficult: (a) true; (b) false.

____17. Psychologist Rensis Likert advocated an accounting procedure aimed at curing some motivational errors caused by the conventional accounting system's emphasis on: (a) the going-concern concept; (b) historical costs; (c) objectivity; (d) short-run performance.

____18. Goal congruence means the acceptance of certain goals by managers as their personal goals. The goals to be accepted by managers are the goals of: (a) the organization; (b) stockholders; (c) accountants; (d) customers; (e) none of the above.

____19. Helpful influences on managers' acceptance of the organization's subgoals as their personal goals include: (a) meaningful participation by managers in setting goals; (b) endorsement of subgoals by top management; (c) both of the above; (d) neither of the above.

____20. In general, cost accounting information for management-decision purposes would be more useful if developed and analyzed through: (a) traditional accounting methods; (b) the contribution approach.

____21. Weak management control systems are due almost invariably to: (a) the technical aspects of the system; (b) the human behavioral aspects of the system.

(B) Complete each of the following statements:

1. The first target of a good management accounting system should be ____________ .

2. In selecting such technical devices as budgets for use in a control system, one should use the____________ approach.

3. In ____________ accounting systems (also called profitability-accounting systems or activity-accounting systems), costs are traced to various decision centers of the organization.

4. In performance reports to managers of decision centers, the focus on ____________ of actual amounts from budgeted figures illustrates a form of "management by ____________ ____________."

5. Costs that are directly influenced by a manager during a given time span are called ____________ costs.

6. In the ____________ accounting system advocated by psychologist Rensis Likert, the costs of recruiting and training managers would be charged initially to ____________accounts.

7. Informal group controls within an organization tend to keep employee behavior close to ________ .

(C) Part of the organization chart of Adam Taylor Company appears below:

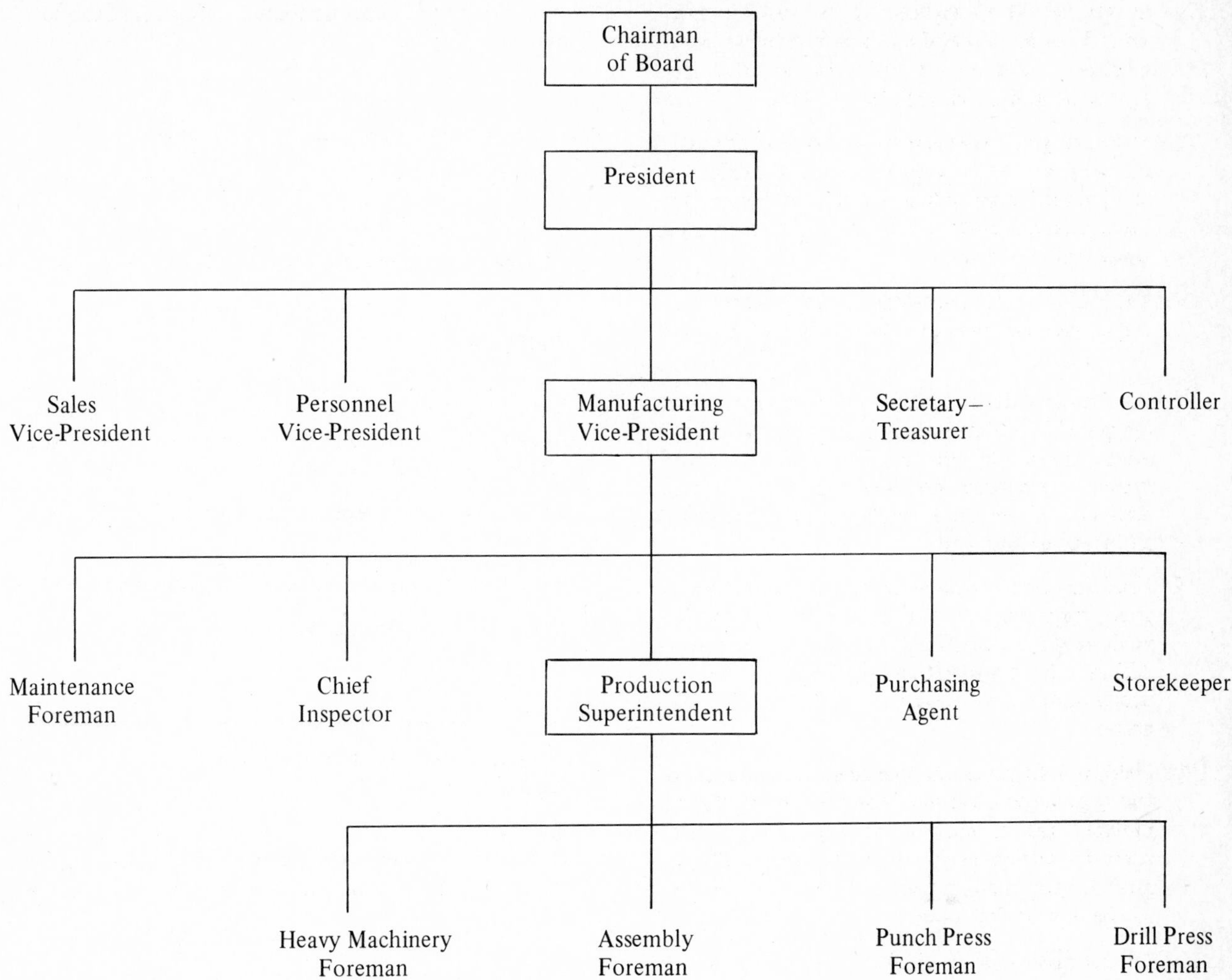

For each item listed below, indicate by "Yes" or "No" whether it should be classified in Adam Taylor Company as a variable cost and as a controllable cost:

	Variable Cost	Controllable Cost: By Controller	Controllable Cost: By Punch Press Foreman	Controllable Cost: By Production Superintendent	Controllable Cost: By Manufacturing Vice-President
1. Direct material used in drill press department					
2. Salary of personnel vice-president					
3. Supplies used by purchasing agent					
4. Straight-line depreciation in punch press department					
5. Secretary's salary in controller's department					
6. Direct labor used in punch press department					

Standard Costs: Direct Material and Direct Labor

7

Standard costs are production and operating costs that are carefully set in advance to measure what these costs should be under certain conditions. Such predetermined costs are used primarily to help managers judge and improve performance. The principal technique employed for this purpose is the analysis of variances of actual costs from standard costs. In addition to the main purpose, standard costs are used also to help construct budgets, obtain product costs, and streamline bookkeeping.

In this chapter, we learn how to compute, account for, and use price and efficiency variances for direct-material costs and direct-labor costs. Included also is a brief section on the use of learning curves in setting standards. Standard costs for factory overhead are explained in Chapters 8 and 9.

REVIEW SUMMARY

A. Standard costs are *predetermined* costs representing target costs that should be attained; they are part of carefully prepared sets of criteria for accomplishing specific tasks.

1. Standard costs assist management in improving performance.

a. Variances are determined by comparing actual costs incurred with standard costs.

b. Such feedback helps management plan and control operations.

2. If standards are currently attainable, as we assume in this book, they are conceptually the same as budgets, except that we will view *standards* in terms of *unit* costs and *budgets* in terms of *total* costs.

3. The general approach to *cost variance analysis* is first to compute the total cost variance and then to subdivide this into two elements.

a. *The total cost variance* is the difference between inputs at actual prices and outputs at standard costs allowed, an unfavorable variance occurring when the former amount is larger.

b. *Price* or *rate variance* is generally the difference between inputs at actual prices and inputs at standard prices, or the difference in unit price or rate times the actual inputs used, an unfavorable variance occurring when actual price exceeds standard price.

c. *Efficiency, usage,* or *quantity variance* is generally the difference between actual inputs at standard prices and inputs that should have been used at standard prices, or the difference between actual inputs and inputs that should have been used times the standard unit price, an unfavorable variance occurring when actual usage exceeds standard usage.

4. Textbook Exhibit 7-1 shows a graphical analysis of direct-labor cost variances; note that the relationships are linear and that the total variance (flexible-budget variance) is equal to the algebraic sum of the price and efficiency variances.

5. A *key concept* in standard costs is the expression of outputs, not as the actual number of product units produced, but as the *standard number of input units allowed,* such as pounds of materials or hours of labor. This is the number of input units that should have been utilized to produce the actual output of good product units.

B. Some general aspects of standard-cost systems deserve special mention:

1. The step-by-step evolution of a control system within most organizations probably occurs as follows:

a. Physical observations.

b. Historical records.

c. Static budgets.

d. Standard costs and flexible budgets.

e. Each more sophisticated system includes the principal features of the preceding systems.

2. Standard costs can be classified into three main types:

a. *Basic cost standards* are used without change over several years for the purpose of revealing trends. However, such standards are seldom used, because changes in standards would be required by frequent improvements in the design and manufacture of products.

b. *Perfection, ideal, maximum-efficiency,* or *theoretical standard costs* are absolute minimum costs under the best possible operating conditions with existing product specifications and manufacturing facilities. Although rarely attainable, such standards might be productive because of their motivational effects.

c. *Currently attainable standards* are the costs that should be incurred under near-term efficient operating conditions. These standards make allowance for normal spoilage, lost time, and ordinary breakdowns in machinery.

d. Because currently attainable standards are difficult to reach but possible to achieve, variances are more likely to be slightly unfavorable than favorable. Such standards may be used simultaneously for product costing, master budgets, and motivation.

3. Basically, line personnel have the responsibility for setting standards and budgets, but the accounting department performs the functions of translating physical standards into monetary terms and reporting operating performance in comparison with standards.

4. In practice, the theoretical *combined* or *joint variance* for price and quantity is usually not separately recognized, but is included in the price variance, which, in the case of materials, is typically the responsibility of the purchasing officer (Exhibit 7-2).

5. Because interdependencies among manufacturing materials and methods may permit desirable tradeoffs between price and efficiency variances, one should interpret individual variances with caution.

6. The foundation of a standard-cost system is usually composed of engineering or physical estimates–made in varying degrees of rigor–of material and product quantities, labor time, and operation methods.

7. Standard costs are determined by multiplying the physical standards by price factors, thus placing all standards in the company on a dollar basis and making it easier to single out the more costly items for managerial attention.

C. Standard material prices are used to help evaluate the performance of the purchasing officer in acquiring appropriate materials at the right price.

1. The standard material prices are usually forecasted prices and are often set jointly by the purchasing officer and the accounting department.

2. The variance of actual material prices from standard prices should usually be recorded, not at the time materials are *issued* to production, but at the time they are *purchased,* thus permitting faster corrective action and making the reported price variations more useful for control purposes.

D. Standard material quantities are used to aid in judging the efficiency with which direct materials are used in manufacturing finished products.

1. The standard material quantities may be determined from engineering studies, sample production runs, and historical records of material usage.

2. These standard quantities may be set jointly by the engineering, production, and cost accounting departments.

3. Although the specific procedures to be used for controlling the usage of materials would depend mainly on the circumstances of the particular case, it is always important that these procedures be carried out on a *timely* basis.

E. Because labor wage rates usually depend on union contracts, they are not generally subject to as much managerial control as are labor hours.

1. If labor-price standards are kept current, price variances are usually rather small.

2. Labor-price variances could result from such sources as using a man with a wrong wage rate for a certain task or using workers whose individual rates differ slightly from the average rate set as the standard.

F. Because of human elements, it is usually a complicated task to determine labor-efficiency standards, also called labor-time, labor-performance, or labor-quantity standards.

1. The most widely used method is time and motion study.

2. Allowances are usually made for such factors as fatigue, rest time, and faulty material.

3. For control purposes, setup or "make ready" costs should not be averaged with regular direct-labor costs but should be separately identified.

G. When entries are made in the general-ledger accounts for monthly summaries of standard-cost transactions, as is usually the case, these entries may be made for direct-material costs in different ways:

1. For management control purposes, variances should be isolated as early as feasible.

a. Price variances are recorded at the time of material *purchases* on the basis of price differences for the total material quantities actually purchased.

b. Efficiency variances are recorded at the time of material *issuances* on the basis of the quantities shown by the *excess material requisitions* at standard material prices.

c. Under this method, the uniform use of standard prices in the perpetual book inventories for materials would avoid many of the clerical difficulties that would follow from the need to make such cost-flow assumptions as first-in, first-out, or last-in, first-out.

2. Another general-ledger procedure for materials is less desirable for current control of purchasing activities, but it is often used in practice:

a. Price variances are recorded at the time of material *issuances* on the basis of price differences for the total material quantities actually issued.

b. Efficiency variances may be recorded at the time of material *issuances,* as in the method described above in 1b.

c. Under this method, the use of many different actual prices in the perpetual book inventories for materials would tend to increase the clerical work that would follow from the need to assume a particular cost-flow sequence.

3. Recordkeeping costs can be saved by adopting a standard-cost system.

a. Actual costs of materials, work in process, and finished goods need not be traced to batches of product on a daily basis; only records of physical counts would be kept.

b. Monthly consumption of material and labor can be totaled by operation or department without tracing the consumption to individual jobs.

H. Variances should be investigated without delay if it appears that they are significantly large and are not random in nature.

I. Learning curves aid in predicting costs and setting standards for new production processes.

1. During a learning phase, the time needed per product unit becomes progressively smaller at some constant rate.

2. Typical items for which standard costs should be adjusted during this phase are labor, power, and other related overhead.

SELF-TEST AND PRACTICE EXERCISES

(A) For each of the following multiple-choice and true-false statements, select the single most appropriate answer and enter its identification letter in the space provided:

____ 1. Standard costs are determined for a given period after a careful analysis of the actual production costs for that period: (a) true; (b) false.

____ 2. A standard-cost system can be used with: (a) a job-costing system; (b) a process-costing system; (c) either a job-costing or a process-costing system; (d) neither a job-costing nor a process-costing system.

____ 3. In general, a price variance is the difference between actual and standard unit prices multiplied by the actual inputs: (a) true; (b) false.

____ 4. The efficiency variance is often called: (a) usage variance; (b) quantity variance; (c) both of the above; (d) neither of the above.

____ 5. The total cost variance to be explained for a given item would be the difference between actual outputs at standard costs allowed and actual inputs at actual prices: (a) true; (b) false.

____ 6. Standard hours allowed are the standard hours allowed for: (a) actual output of good production; (b) budgeted or standard output of good production.

____ 7. When costs and variances are computed in a standard-cost system, outputs are usually expressed in terms of: (a) actual good product units; (b) budgeted or planned product units; (c) actual number of input units allowed for standard output of product units; (d) standard number of input units allowed for actual output of product units.

____ 8. Perfection or ideal standards are the most widely used standards: (a) true; (b) false.

____ 9. When currently attainable standards are used, variances are more likely to be: (a) favorable rather than unfavorable; (b) unfavorable rather than favorable.

____ 10. The simultaneous use of standard costs for control, product costing, master budgets, and motivation is a major benefit to be derived from the use of: (a) basic standards; (b) maximum-efficiency standards; (c) currently attainable standards.

____ 11. The accounting department of an organization has the basic responsibility for setting performance standards: (a) true; (b) false.

____ 12. In practice, the theoretical combined or joint variance for price and quantity is usually: (a) recognized separately; (b) excluded from variance calculations; (c) included as part of the efficiency variance; (d) included as part of the price variance.

____ 13. Engineering or physical estimates usually form the basis for setting standard costs: (a) true; (b) false.

____ 14. An unfavorable material-efficiency variance would be calculated by multiplying the quantity of excess materials used by: (a) standard material unit prices; (b) actual material unit prices; (c) neither of the above.

____ 15. Labor-time standards usually make allowances for human fatigue, rest time, and faulty material: (a) true; (b) false.

____ 16. Variance accounts with debit balances generally reflect cost variances that are: (a) favorable; (b) unfavorable.

____ 17. If material-price variances are recorded in the general ledger at the time of material purchases, the book inventory of materials would be maintained on the basis of: (a) actual costs; (b) standard costs.

____ 18. No corrective action to an existing process need be made for a random variance: (a) true; (b) false.

____ 19. During the learning phase of a new production process, productivity in units per hour tends to: (a) stay about the same; (b) decrease; (c) increase.

(B) Complete each of the following statements:

1. ____________________ are carefully predetermined costs to be used by managers as ________ aids in controlling operations.

2. Managers are assisted in evaluating performance by comparisons of ______________ costs of operations with ______________ costs of operations.

3. The two main causes of differences between actual and standard costs are ____________________ variances and ____________ variances.

4. When currently attainable standards are used, it is helpful to view standards in terms of ______________ costs and budgets in terms of ______________ costs.

5. Unchanging cost standards that are used over several years to spotlight trends are called ______________ cost standards.

6. When a a variance account has a debit balance, this usually means that there is an excess of a certain ____________________ cost over its related ____________________ cost.

7. It is usually more feasible to recognize material-price variations at the time materials are ______________, and material-quantity variations when materials are ______________.

8. Standard material prices are useful in judging the performance of the ______________ officer.

9. If book inventories of materials are maintained on the basis of ______________ costs, it would not be necessary to assume a cost-flow sequence such as ______________ or ______________.

10. Labor ________________ are usually more subject to managerial control than are labor ________________.

11. ________________ curves are useful for predicting costs and setting ________________ for new production processes.

(C) The Mustang Saddle Corporation, which uses a standard cost accounting system, provides the following data concerning its operations during last week:

Finished units produced	200 units
Standard labor-hours allowed per product unit	5 hours
Standard wage rate per hour	\$6.00
Actual wage rate per hour	\$5.50
Total direct-labor hours actually used	1,100 hr

1. Show calculations of costs and variances in the spaces provided in the Analysis Framework given below. Ignore payroll taxes and all other payroll deductions and fringe labor costs. Use F for favorable variances and U for unfavorable variances.

2. Using the Journal provided, prepare one compound journal entry to record direct-labor costs and variances for the week.

1. Analysis Framework

(1) Actual Inputs at Actual Prices	(2) Actual Inputs at Standard Prices	(3) Actual Outputs at Standard Prices
1,100 @ 5.50 per hr	1100 @ \$6.00 per hR	1000 @ \$6.00
\$6050 F	6600u	6000 F

Price Variance	Efficiency Variance
.50 X 1100	100 X \$6
550F	600u

Flexible-Budget Variance

6050 - 6000

50u

2. Journal

Work in Process	6000	
Efficiency Variance	600	
Price Variance		550
Accrued Payroll		6050

(D) Peruna Medicinal Products, Inc., which uses a standard-cost accounting system, provides the following data concerning its operations during last week:

Finished units produced	300 units
Standard material pounds allowed per product unit	10 lb
Standard material price per pound	\$2.00
Actual material purchase price per pound	\$1.80
Actual quantity of materials purchased	4,000 lb
Actual quantity of materials used in production	3,500 lb

1. Show calculations of costs and variances in the spaces provided in the Analysis Framework shown below. Assume that the stores account is to be carried on a *standard* price basis. Use F for favorable variances and U for unfavorable variances.

2. Using the journal provided, prepare journal entries for direct-material costs and variances:

   (a) Purchase of direct materials.

   (b) Usage of direct materials.

1. Analysis Framework

(1) Actual Inputs at Actual Prices	(2) Actual Inputs at Standard Prices (Purchases)	(2) Actual Inputs at Standard Prices (Usage)	(3) Actual Outputs at Standard Prices
4000 @ 1.80	4000 @ 2.00	3500 @ 2	3000 lbs @ 2.00
\$ 7200	8000	7000	6000

Price Variance	Efficiency Variance
.20 x 4000 = 800 F	500 @ 2 = 1000 U

2. Journal

		Debit	Credit
(a)	Stores	8000	
	D.M. Price Varians		800
	Accouts Pay.		7200
(b)	WIP.	6000	
	Eff V. U	1000	
	Stores		7000

Flexible Budgets and Overhead Control

8

We have studied some basic relationships between the volume of activity and expenses or costs. However, it is not sufficient to say simply that all costs may be neatly divided into only two groups: costs that are unaffected by changes in the volume of activity (fixed costs), and costs that change proportionately to changes in the volume of activity (variable costs). Other cost-behavior patterns make it necessary to understand some additional types of costs: mixed, committed fixed, discretionary fixed, and engineered variable costs.

In this chapter, we explore these costs and their implications for management planning and control. More specifically, we focus on two main tools for decisions and feedback: the *flexible budget* for controlling variable overhead costs, and the *work-measurement approach* for controlling certain types of nonmanufacturing costs.

REVIEW SUMMARY

A. In contrast to a *static budget,* which is a single plan tailored to a certain target volume level, a *flexible budget* is prepared for a range of activity.

1. Although standard costs are of particular importance in the control of direct material and labor, and departmental budgets are helpful in the control of factory overhead, flexible budgets can properly include all manufacturing costs, and selling and administrative expenses as well.

2. The variable-cost items in a flexible budget can be used as bases for actual cost comparisons because they are automatically geared to changes in volume.

3. The key idea in a flexible budget is the *budget formula,* which, in the case of proportionately variable costs, is simply the cost rate per unit of product or activity, as illustrated by textbook Exhibit 8-1.

a. By using the budget formula, one can construct a budget that can be easily tailored later as a comparison basis for the particular activity level actually attained, as shown in Exhibit 8-2.

b. However, because the flexible-budget performance report ordinarily does not show a foreman's deviation from his scheduled production volume, it would be helpful to report also the data for actual and scheduled production volume.

4. In many cases, the selection of a proper measure of production volume or activity would not be easy, and several helpful selection criteria should be used.

a. The activity measure should have a causal relationship to the variable cost.

b. The activity unit should not be significantly affected by variable factors other than volume.

c. Measurement units should be easily understandable and inexpensively obtainable.

d. The measure of budgeted activity must be under adequate control and not be subject to the influence of inefficient operations. Therefore, a better measure for this purpose would be the *standard* labor or machine-hours allowed for units produced, rather than the *actual* labor or machine-hours used.

5. In understanding and using a flexible-budget approach for the variance analysis of *variable* factory overhead, we find it quite helpful to follow the direct-labor analysis approach described in the preceding chapter.

a. The *budget variance* for variable factory-overhead cost is similar to the total variance for direct-labor cost. It is the difference between the actual costs incurred and the budget based on the standard hours of work allowed for units produced (column 4 of Exhibit 8-3).

b. The subdivision of the budget variance for variable overhead into *spending variance* and *efficiency variance* is similar to the split of the total direct-labor variance into *price variance* and *efficiency variance* (last two columns of Exhibit 8-3).

c. The *spending variance* is the difference between the actual costs incurred and the budget based on the actual hours of work.

d. The *efficiency variance* is the difference between the budget based on the actual hours of work and the budget based on the standard hours of work allowed for units produced.

6. Flexible budgets include both fixed and variable costs, as shown in Exhibit 8-4.

a. The portion of the budget representing fixed costs will remain constant despite fluctuations in production volume.

b. Each variable-budget item may be determined by an appropriate formula.

B. In addition to simple fixed and variable costs, there are other cost-behavior patterns (*cost functions*).

1. Accountants and managers generally make two simplifying assumptions in determining cost functions:

a. Cost behavior can be sufficiently explained by only a *single* measure of activity volume, such as labor hours.

b. *Linear* (straight-line) approximations to cost behavior are sufficiently accurate even though nonlinear behavior is widespread.

2. Relying mainly on historical data, the accountant thus typically uses a formula to represent the appropriate cost function:

$$y' = a + bx$$

where y' is the total predicted cost (the dependent variable).
a is a constant (the fixed-cost element).
b is a coefficient (the variable-cost rate).
x is the independent variable (the measure of activity volume).

3. Some costs are called *mixed costs* because they contain both a fixed element and a variable element; for example: repairs, power, and the rental of a delivery truck for a fixed cost per month plus a variable cost based on mileage.

a. Although fixed and variable cost elements should theoretically not be included in one account, mixed costs are generally not separated in accounting practice.

b. However, mixed costs can be budgeted by using the formula given above. Helpful in implementing this formula are *scatter charts* and the *high-low method* (Exhibits 8-6 and 8-7).

C. *Fixed costs* are costs that are not affected in total by changes in activity volume during a given year.

1. Fixed costs come into existence as a result of far-reaching decisions.

2. Fixed costs may be subdivided for planning and control purposes into committed costs and discretionary costs.

3. *Committed fixed costs* are incurred because of a company's basic organization or the ownership of such long-term assets as land, buildings, machinery, and equipment.

a. Examples of committed fixed costs are certain administrative salaries, insurance, property taxes, rent, and depreciation of fixed assets.

b. Committed fixed costs, the least responsive of fixed costs to short-term decisions, cannot be decreased without jeopardizing a company's ability to meet its long-range goals.

4. *Discretionary fixed costs,* also called *managed* or *programmed costs,* originate from periodic appropriation decisions to implement top-management policies.

a. Examples of discretionary fixed costs are the costs of advertising, sales promotion, employee training programs, and research and development.

b. In contrast to committed fixed costs, discretionary fixed costs are more difficult to measure and evaluate in terms of their outputs.

c. In some cases, discretionary fixed costs, which are more easily influenced by management on a short-term basis than are committed fixed costs, may seem to have the behavior pattern of a variable cost.

d. You should especially note that discretionary fixed costs, unlike most other costs, are not subject to ordinary engineering input-output analysis.

e. Thus, managers rarely know if they are spending proper amounts for such functions as public relations, industrial relations, legal advice, accounting services, and management training.

D. *Engineered variable costs* exist when an optimum relationship between inputs and outputs is closely specified.

1. For example, a chair may have one back, four legs, two armrests, etc.

2. Most types of variable costs have such an explicit physical relationship with volume.

E. Measurement is needed for management control of costs.

1. *Work measurement* is a formal analysis of a task, its size, the methods used in its performance, and its efficiency. This can also be called an engineered variable-cost approach.

a. By using such techniques as time and motion study, one can set standard unit costs that can indicate in advance the number of resource units needed for a given quantity of some specified work.

b. These standards also permit analyses of the efficiency and effectiveness with which the resources are being used to do the work.

c. Advocates of work measurement contend that this is the only satisfactory way to control the costs of some nonmanufacturing types of activities, the most prominent being such high-volume, repetitive tasks as billing, mailing, and payroll operations.

2. However, most organizations do not use work-measurement techniques for controlling their nonmanufacturing costs.

a. Instead, they treat such costs in their budgets as discretionary fixed costs.

b. The actual expenditures are then periodically evaluated in the light of the desired objectives.

SELF-TEST AND PRACTICE EXERCISES

(A) For each of the following multiple-choice and true-false statements, select the single most appropriate answer and enter its identification letter in the space provided:

____ 1. A flexible budget is constructed for: (a) a range of activity; (b) a certain target volume level.

____ 2. Flexible budgets may be used for: (a) variable-overhead costs only; (b) variable- and fixed-overhead costs only; (c) direct-material, direct-labor, and variable-overhead costs only; (d) manufacturing costs only; (e) manufacturing costs and nonmanufacturing costs.

____ 3. Ordinarily, flexible-budget performance reports would show a departmental foreman's deviation from his scheduled production volume: (a) true; (b) false.

____ 4. After a flexible budget is prepared, it can ordinarily be used, without further adjustment, for comparisons of actual variable costs: (a) true; (b) false.

____ 5. The key idea in flexible budgets is: (a) the forecasting of a specific volume of activity; (b) the exclusion of fixed costs from the budget: (c) the use of a budget formula; (d) the tentative or contingent nature of forecasts of fixed costs.

____ 6. The activity unit (measure of production activity) to be used in flexible budgets should not be greatly affected by variable factors other than volume of activity: (a) true; (b) false.

____ 7. For the measurement of activity incorporated in flexible budgets, it would usually be better to use: (a) standard labor- or machine-hours allowed for units produced; (b) actual labor- or machine-hours used.

____ 8. It is helpful to use similar cost-analysis approaches for: (a) direct-labor cost and fixed factory-overhead cost; (b) direct-material cost and fixed factory-overhead cost; (c) variable factory-overhead cost and direct-labor cost.

____ 9. The efficiency variance for variable factory overhead is the difference between the budget based on the standard hours of work allowed for units produced and: (a) the budget based on the actual hours of work; (b) the actual costs incurred.

____10. Cost behavior is generally assumed by accountants and managers to be: (a) approximately linear rather than nonlinear; (b) dependent on a single variable rather than several; (c) both of the above; (d) none of these.

___11. Mixed costs are defined as those costs that contain both manufacturing and nonmanufacturing elements: (a) true; (b) false.

___12. The inclusion of fixed- and variable-cost elements in one account is: (a) theoretically proper; (b) generally done in practice; (c) both of the above; (d) neither of the above.

___13. Fixed costs that arise from periodic appropriation decisions that directly reflect top-management policies are called: (a) fixed asset-ownership costs; (b) fluctuating fixed costs; (c) committed fixed costs; (d) discretionary fixed costs.

___14. It is likely that the committed-fixed-cost classification would include: (a) sales promotion costs; (b) the cost of employee training programs; (c) both of the above; (d) neither of the above.

___15. In contrast to committed fixed costs, discretionary fixed costs are: (a) more easily influenced by management on a short-term basis; (b) more difficult to measure and evaluate in terms of their outputs; (c) both of the above; (d) neither of the above.

___16. Work measurement is an engineered variable-cost approach to cost control: (a) true; (b) false.

___17. Most organizations use the work-measurement approach in controlling their nonmanufacturing costs: (a) true; (b) false.

___18. In general, the application of work-measurement techniques to certain types of nonmanufacturing costs assumes that such costs are discretionary fixed costs: (a) true; (b) false.

(B) Complete each of the following statements:

1. In contrast to a __________ budget, a __________ budget is prepared for a range of activity.

2. For strictly variable costs, the budget formula used in flexible budgets is ____________________.

3. The budget variance for variable factory-overhead cost is the difference between __________ and the budget based upon ____________________.

4. The spending variance for variable factory-overhead cost is similar to the __________ variance for direct-labor cost.

5. The spending variance for variable factory-overhead cost is the difference between __________ and the budget based on ____________________.

6. Cost-behavior patterns may also be called ____________________.

7. Costs that include both fixed and variable elements are called __________.

8. Discretionary fixed costs may also be called __________ costs or __________ costs.

9. Fixed costs that arise from the possession of plant and equipment or from the existence of a certain basic organization are known as __________ fixed costs.

10. In controlling nonmanufacturing costs, most organizations treat such costs as __________ costs.

11. The high-low method can be useful in analyzing the behavior of __________ costs.

(C) Given for a certain factory-overhead cost of Mixed Products Company:

	Jan.	Feb.
Volume of activity in direct-labor hours for the month	30,000	40,000
Total cost for the month	$ 9,500	$12,000

Find:

1. The variable cost rate per direct-labor hour . . . . $_____

2. The fixed cost per month . . . . $_____

(D) The following data pertain to the Longhorn Boot Corporation, which uses a standard cost accounting system:

Product units manufactured: 200
Direct labor:
    Standard hours allowed: 7 hours per product unit
    Standard wage rate: $6 per hour
    Actual direct labor: 1,500 hours, total cost $8,800
Variable factory overhead:
    Standard cost allowed: $4 per direct-labor hour
    Actual variable-overhead cost incurred: $5,100.

Compute the following variances, using F to indicate favorable variances and U to indicate unfavorable variances:

1. Direct-labor flexible-budget variance . . . . $_____

2. Direct-labor price variance . . . . $_____

3. Direct-labor efficiency variance . . . . $_____

4. Variable factory-overhead flexible-budget variance .... $______

5. Variable factory-overhead spending variance.......................... $______

6. Variable factory-overhead efficiency variance .... $______

Standard Absorption Costing: Overhead Variances

9

The preceding chapter explained the differences in the behavior and controllability of various types of costs. This chapter stresses the usefulness of distinguishing between variable and fixed costs in the analysis of factory-overhead variances. Also emphasized is the need to recognize and understand the two purposes of factory-overhead accounting: management control and product costing.

We study here, for both the fixed and variable elements of factory overhead, the setting of predetermined rates, the analysis of overhead variances, and the general-ledger treatment of overhead costs. This chapter, by providing a helpful combination of standard costs and flexible budgets, can enhance our understanding and grasp of the ideas presented in the two preceding chapters.

The two key textbook illustrations for understanding the analysis of overhead variances are Exhibits 9-2 and 9-4.

REVIEW SUMMARY

A. For *variable* factory-overhead costs, the determination of application rates, the general-ledger accounting for costs, and the analysis of variances should be done separately from the *fixed* factory-overhead rate setting, cost accounting, and variance analysis.

1. The predetermined variable-overhead rate can be calculated from data included in the flexible budget for variable factory overhead.

2. This variable-overhead rate is computed by dividing the total variable factory overhead at a given level of activity by the standard activity at that level (often expressed in terms of direct-labor hours allowed). See textbook Exhibit 9-1.

3. A separate set of general-ledger accounts is maintained for variable factory-overhead cost: Variable Factory Overhead Control (debit) and Variable Factory Overhead Applied (credit).

a. The difference between the balances of these two accounts is the under- or overapplied overhead, which is equal to the *flexible-budget variance for variable overhead*. See Exhibit 9-2.

b. The flexible-budget variance can be broken down into the *spending and efficiency variances* which are computed as explained in the preceding chapter. See Exhibit 9-2.

c. Although the variable-overhead variances may be computed and reported on a monthly basis, they need not be isolated formally in individual ledger accounts.

B. Because *fixed* factory-overhead costs do not change *in total* over wide ranges of activity, the *unit costs* do change, and this causes a difficulty in determining standard costs per product unit at different levels of production volume, a difficulty that does not arise with *variable* overhead.

1. In order to obtain a single standard product cost per unit for pricing and inventory uses, it is necessary to select in advance an appropriate annual activity or volume level for division into the budgeted fixed factory overhead for the year.

a. The activity level preselected for this purpose, which is called the *denominator level* (often expressed in terms of direct-labor hours allowed), can have a significant effect on the fixed-overhead rates and standard unit costs. See Exhibit 9-3.

b. The preferred denominator level is one that best expresses the production capability of the plant and thus helps to measure the utilization of plant capacity.

c. Nevertheless, fixed-overhead rates based upon a single denominator level would have only limited significance for management control purposes, and would be used primarily for product costing and long-run pricing.

2. As in the case of variable-overhead costs, a separate set of general-ledger accounts is also maintained for fixed factory-overhead cost: Fixed Factory Overhead Control (debit), and Fixed Factory Overhead Applied (credit).

a. The difference between the balances of these two accounts is the under- or overapplied overhead, which can be divided into two parts:

b. The *budget variance for fixed overhead* is the difference between the actual fixed-overhead cost incurred and the budgeted fixed-overhead cost. See Exhibit 9-4, which clearly shows why this budget variance is *always equal* to the *spending variance* for fixed overhead.

c. The *denominator variance for fixed overhead* is the difference between budgeted fixed-overhead cost and applied fixed-overhead cost (the actual production on the basis of the standard hours allowed at the standard fixed-overhead rate per hour). See Exhibit 9-4.

d. Again, as in the case of variable overhead, the fixed-overhead variances may also be calculated and reported each month, but they need not be carried in individual ledger accounts.

C. Because fixed-overhead rates are used mainly for product costing and pricing, variance analysis has limited usefulness for planning and control purposes.

1. The fixed-overhead budget variances serve to direct managerial attention to changes in price factors, but these variances are often beyond immediate managerial control.

a. An unfavorable budget variance for fixed overhead would be the excess of the actual fixed-overhead cost incurred over the budgeted fixed-overhead cost. A favorable variance would be the reverse of this relationship.

b. A comparison of the actual and budget amounts for the *individual items* of fixed overhead might yield information of some value in the management control of total fixed-overhead costs.

2. The fixed-overhead denominator variance is unfavorable if the standard hours allowed for actual production are less than the denominator level of activity.

a. Most companies consider such variances to be beyond immediate management control, because the failure to achieve denominator volume is often due to noncontrollable causes such as storms, strikes, unusual accidents, shortages of skilled production workers, or general economic conditions.

b. However, subnormal volume could result from such controllable causes as idleness due to faulty production scheduling, or machinery breakdowns due to poor maintenance.

3. The fixed-overhead denominator variance is favorable if the standard hours allowed for actual production are more than the denominator level of activity. This would indicate better-than-expected utilization of available facilities.

4. Although overhead-cost analysis varies from company to company, it is always important to distinguish between fixed and variable overhead as being separate management problems.

D. An excellent review of the basic analysis and journal entries for a standard-cost system is quite efficiently provided by the comprehensive self-study problem at the end of textbook Chapter 9. Note particularly the helpful analytical framework shown in Exhibit 9-8.

SELF-TEST AND PRACTICE EXERCISES

(A) For each of the following multiple-choice and true-false statements, select the single most appropriate answer and enter its identification letter in the space provided:

C 1. In the management accounting for factory-overhead costs, it is desirable to treat variable and fixed overhead separately in: (a) the predetermination of application rates; (b) the analysis of cost variances; (c) both of the above; (d) neither of the above.

C 2. It is desirable to maintain separate general-ledger accounts for: (a) actual and applied factory overhead; (b) fixed and variable factory overhead; (c) both of the above; (d) neither of the above.

A 3. The predetermined rate for variable factory-overhead cost can be readily computed from the information ordinarily included in the flexible budget for variable overhead: (a) true; (b) false.

B 4. The variable factory-overhead rate may be computed by dividing the total variable factory overhead at a given level of activity by: (a) the actual activity at that level; (b) the standard activity at that level.

E 5. The applied amount of fixed factory-overhead cost should be: (a) debited to Fixed Factory Overhead Applied; (b) credited to Fixed Factory Overhead Control; (c) debited to Fixed Factory Overhead Control; (d) credited to Work-in-Process Control; (e) none of the above.

D 6. The actual amount of variable factory-overhead cost incurred should be: (a) debited to Work-in-Process Control; (b) credited to Variable Factory Overhead Applied; (c) credited to Variable Factory Overhead Control; (d) debited to Variable Factory Overhead Control; (e) none of the above.

B 7. The variable factory-overhead variances that are computed and reported at regular intervals must be entered regularly in individual general-ledger accounts: (a) true; (b) false.

A 8. The standard-cost sheets for manufactured products should include fixed factory-overhead cost: (a) true; (b) false.

C 9. For variable factory-overhead costs, the flexible-budget variance is the difference between the standard hours allowed at the standard variable-overhead rate for products produced and: (a) actual outputs times the actual variable-overhead rate; (b) actual inputs times the standard variable-overhead rate; (c) actual inputs times the actual prices; (d) none of the above.

B 10. An unfavorable spending variance for variable factory-overhead cost would be the excess of actual variable overhead incurred over: (a) variable overhead applied; (b) actual inputs at the standard variable-overhead rate; (c) standard hours allowed at the standard variable-overhead rate; (d) actual inputs at the actual prices; (e) none of the above.

C 11. An unfavorable efficiency variance for variable factory-overhead cost would be: (a) the excess of variable overhead applied over actual inputs at standard rates; (b) the excess of actual inputs at standard rates over actual inputs at actual rates; (c) the excess of actual inputs at standard rates over flexible budget based on actual outputs; (d) the excess of actual inputs at actual rates over actual inputs at standard rates; (e) none of the above.

B 12. The predetermined rates for fixed factory overhead are useful primarily for: (a) management control purposes; (b) product costing and pricing purposes.

A 13. When the standard hours allowed are greater than the denominator level of activity used for setting the fixed-overhead rate, there is: (a) a favorable denominator variance; (b) a favorable budget variance; (c) an unfavorable denominator variance; (d) an unfavorable budget variance; (e) none of the above.

A 14. For fixed factory-overhead costs, the budget variance is the difference between the budgeted costs and: (a) actual fixed overhead; (b) applied fixed overhead; (c) neither of the above.

A 15. The predetermined rate for applying fixed factory-overhead costs is usually based on some activity or volume level predicted for a period of one year: (a) true; (b) false.

A 16. The fixed factory-overhead variances should be: (a) computed and reported at regular intervals; (b) entered regularly in individual general-ledger accounts; (c) both of the above; (d) neither of the above.

B 17. The fixed-overhead budget variances are usually within immediate managerial control: (a) true; (b) false.

A 18. Most companies consider fixed-overhead denominator variances to be: (a) beyond immediate management control; (b) within immediate management control.

A 19. If the standard hours allowed for actual production are less than the denominator level of activity, this would indicate: (a) below-expected utilization of available facilities; (b) better-than-expected utilization of facilities.

(B) Complete each of the following statements:

1. In the management control of factory-overhead costs, it is useful to divide such costs into Variable factory overhead and FIXED factory overhead.

2. The two principal purposes of factory-overhead cost accounting are MANAGEMENT PLANNING and CONTROL Product costing + PRICING

3. The actual amount of variable-overhead cost incurred should be recorded by a Debit entry to the Variable Factory Overhead control account.

4. The applied amount of variable factory-overhead cost should be debited to the WORK in Process Control account and credited to the Variable Factory overhead Applied account.

5. The actual amount of fixed factory-overhead cost should be debited to the Fixed Factory OH account and credited to the Accrued payroll, Allowance for Depreciation accounts.

6. The flexible-budget variance for variable factory-overhead costs can be broken down into the spending variance and the efficiency variance.

7. The difference between variable overhead applied and actual variable overhead incurred is always equal to the Flexible budget variance for variable factory overhead. If the applied amount is larger than the actual amount, the variance is favorable.

8. The activity or volume level used for the calculation of the predetermined rate for fixed factory overhead is called the denominator level.

9. The under- or overapplied amount for fixed factory-overhead cost is composed of the budget variance and the denominator variance.

10. Underapplied fixed factory overhead would be the excess of the balance of the Fixed FOH control account over the balance of the Fixed Factory OH Applied account.

(C) You are given the following data for the Razorback Coverall Company:

Products manufactured	400 units
Standard variable-overhead cost per unit, 1.5 direct-labor hours at $2.00	$3.00
Actual direct-labor hours used	700 hr
Actual variable-overhead cost incurred	$1,350

1. Compute the following amounts:
   (a) Actual labor-hours used at the standard variable-overhead rate 1400

   (b) Actual product units made at standard variable-overhead cost 1200

   (c) Flexible-budget variance for overhead .... $ 150

(d) Spending variance . . . . $ 50

(e) Efficiency variance . . . . $ 200

For each variance, indicate whether it is favorable (F) or unfavorable (U).

2. Make the journal entries to summarize the above facts for the general ledger:

(D) The following information pertains to the operations of the Red Raider Exterminator Corporation:

Budgeted fixed-overhead cost	$1,800
Actual fixed-overhead cost	$1,750
Denominator level of activity	300 hr
Standard hours allowed for work done on product units manufactured	280 hr

1. Compute the following amounts:
   (a) Standard rate for fixed overhead . . . . $____per hr

   (b) Applied fixed overhead . . . . $______

(c) Under- or overapplied fixed overhead .... $________

(d) Budget variance .... $________

(e) Denominator variance .... $________

For each variance, indicate whether it is favorable (F) or unfavorable (U).

2. Make the journal entries to summarize the above facts in the general ledger:

Income Effects of Alternative Product-Costing Methods

10

In designing and operating modern planning and control systems, management must choose from some costing alternatives that can produce significantly different results. This chapter examines some of these alternatives, their effects on the measurements of product costs and income, and their impacts on some operating decisions.

The chapter contains four major subjects: (I) an analytical comparison of the absorption-costing approach and the contribution approach to income measurement; (II) an examination of the inventory and income effects of choosing various activity levels for absorption costing; (III) a study of the inventory and income effects of using different treatments for standard-cost variances; and (IV) an overview of budgetary control. Although these matters are by no means unrelated, they may be considered independently. For the convenience of separate study and review, each self-study problem in the textbook and each section of the review summary and exercises in this study guide has been identified with one of the four major sections of the textbook chapter.

REVIEW SUMMARY

I. CONTRIBUTION APPROACH TO INCOME MEASUREMENT

A. The contribution approach to income measurement differs basically from the absorption-costing approach demonstrated in Chapter 9.

1. *Absorption costing* is the traditional approach to income measurement.

a. *Fixed* factory-overhead costs are treated as *product costs* and are therefore *included in product inventories* and cost of goods manufactured and sold, along with direct-material, direct-labor, and *variable* factory-overhead costs.

b. This approach is more widely used than the contribution approach, must be used for income tax purposes, and is generally accepted for making financial reports to external parties.

2. The *contribution approach* to income measurement involves *direct costing* or *variable costing.*

a. *Fixed* factory-overhead costs are treated as *period costs* (charged directly to expense) and are therefore *excluded from product inventories,* which include only direct-material, direct-labor, and *variable* factory-overhead costs.

b. Direct costing is growing in use for internal performance reports to management, but it is not acceptable for income tax purposes or external reporting.

3. As you can easily see in textbook Exhibit 10-1, the two approaches differ in their primary classification of costs.

a. Absorption costing makes a primary classification of costs according to manufacturing and nonmanufacturing functions, emphasizing the *gross profit margin* available to cover selling and administrative expenses.

b. Direct costing makes a primary classification of costs into variable and fixed categories, emphasizing the *contribution margin* available to cover fixed costs.

4. The difference between the two income-measurement approaches is essentially the difference in the *timing* of the charge to expense for fixed factory-overhead cost.

a. In the absorption-costing method, fixed factory overhead is first charged to inventory and is therefore not charged to expense until the period in which the inventory is sold and included in cost of goods sold (an expense).

b. However, in the direct-costing method, fixed factory overhead is charged to expense immediately, and only variable manufacturing costs are included in product inventories.

c. Therefore, if inventories increase during a period (production exceeds sales), the direct-costing method will generally report less net income than will the absorption-costing method; when inventories decrease, the opposite effect will occur.

II. ROLE OF VARIOUS ACTIVITY LEVELS IN ABSORPTION COSTING

B. When absorption costing is used, reported profits can be significantly affected by the choice of an activity level for use as a denominator in computing fixed-overhead rates.

1. The activity level that is chosen should be related to the capacity of available plant, equipment, and other resources, such as people and materials.

a. Such a capacity, called *practical capacity* or *practical attainable capacity,* is the maximum level at which the plant (or department or other subdivision thereof) can operate efficiently, allowing for unavoidable operating interruptions.

b. This capacity is an upper limit specified by management for current planning and control purposes, after considering engineering factors and the economic tradeoffs that must be made in providing for upward trends in customer demand and for the seasonal and cyclical fluctuations in customer demand.

2. Two levels of capacity utilization are commonly used:

a. *Normal activity* is the level of capacity utilization that will meet average customer demand over a period (often five years) that includes seasonal, cyclical, and trend factors.

b. *Expected annual activity*, also called *master-budgeted activity,* is the expected level of capacity utilization for the coming year.

3. The choice of the level of capacity utilization to be used would affect the *predetermined rate* for applying fixed-overhead cost to production, as demonstrated by Exhibit 10-2.

a. If *normal activity* were used to compute a normal rate, unit costs of fixed overhead would not be influenced by annual fluctuations in volume, and there would tend to be overapplications of overhead in some years that are offset by underapplications in other years. Thus, the use of a normal rate would provide a yearly and monthly measure of the cost of idle capacity.

b. If *expected annual activity* were used to compute the predetermined rate for fixed overhead, product and inventory costs would tend to fluctuate merely because of annual differences in utilization of facilities.

4. For various nontheoretical reasons, expected annual activity is generally used as the activity base for computing the predetermined fixed-overhead rate.

a. There is a widespread conviction that the year is the key time period and that overhead costs for the year should be assigned to the year's production.

b. Using the normal rate would require long-run forecasting, and this cannot be done accurately.

c. The accounting profession and the Internal Revenue Service do not approve of carrying forward on the balance sheet the annual amounts of under- or overapplied factory-overhead cost.

5. Reasons are given by some managements for using practical capacity as an activity base for the predetermined fixed-overhead rate.

a. Lower unit costs and higher profits can be obtained on such a larger-volume basis.

b. Selling prices based on such lower unit costs would be more competitive and thus would induce higher volume and profits.

6. However, expected annual activity is usually regarded as an appropriate overhead-rate base for the purposes of current planning and control. This is because expected annual activity is the basis for the year's master budget, which is the principal short-run planning and control tool.

7. Exhibit 10-3, accompanying the solution to the textbook self-study problem, shows that the use of different activity bases for developing product-costing overhead rates results in different inventory valuations and different net incomes.

a. There is a striking difference in the measure of utilization of facilities, the denominator variance.

b. Note carefully the basic reasons for the substantial differences in the reported inventories and net incomes.

III. STANDARD-COST VARIANCES AND THE INCOME STATEMENT

C. When accounting entries for the transactions of a standard-cost system are made in the general-ledger accounts, different methods are available for disposing of the account balances for the variances of actual costs from standard costs, as illustrated by the Bridget example in the textbook, page 306.

1. If *currently attainable standards* are used for product costing, the variances can be viewed as measures of efficiency (credit) or inefficiency (debit).

a. No parts of these variances would be viewed as positive or negative product costs, and therefore the variances would not be prorated among inventories and cost of sales.

b. The entire amounts of such variances may be treated in the income statement either as direct charges or credits to cost of goods sold or as separate charges or credits after the gross margin (or gross profit) on sales.

2. On the other hand, if the standards are *not currently attainable* because they are perfection standards or not up to date, and if the variances are large enough to materially distort net income and inventory figures, the variances should be prorated.

a. The proration would be in proportion to the related standard-cost charges included in the affected accounts.

b. Material-price variances should be prorated over five accounts: Direct Material Efficiency Variance, Stores, Work-in-Process, Finished Goods, and Cost of Goods Sold.

c. The adjusted material-efficiency variance, the labor variances, and the overhead variances should be prorated over three accounts: Work-in-Process, Finished Goods, and Cost of Goods Sold.

IV. OVERVIEW OF BUDGETARY CONTROL

D. This section of the textbook can help you improve your perspective concerning the budgets, variances, and product-costing methods described in Chapters 5 through 10.

1. For control purposes, all variances can be assigned to three major types: price, efficiency, and volume.

2. As shown in textbook Exhibit 10-4, the *volume variance* (column 5) is used to account for the difference between the master (static) budget and the flexible budget.

3. Such a volume variance reflects the changes in budgeted costs and revenues due *solely* to the difference between the actual activity volume and the planned activity volume.

4. This volume variance should not be confused with the *denominator variance* of Chapter 9, which is a specialized variance pertaining only to the analysis of *fixed factory overhead* when absorption costing is used.

SELF-TEST AND PRACTICE EXERCISES

(A) For each of the following multiple-choice and true-false statements, select the single most appropriate answer and enter its identification letter in the space provided:

I. CONTRIBUTION APPROACH TO INCOME MEASUREMENT

____ 1. The traditional approach to income measurement makes a primary classification of costs according to their behavior patterns: (a) true; (b) false.

____ 2. The contribution approach to income measurement emphasizes: (a) the gross profit margin; (b) the contribution margin; (c) both of the above; (d) neither of the above.

____ 3. The traditional costing approach uses: (a) variable costing: (b) direct costing; (c) absorption costing; (d) all of the above; (e) none of the above.

____ 4. Treated as period costs by the absorption-costing method are: (a) variable factory-overhead costs; (b) fixed factory-overhead costs; (c) both of the above; (d) neither of the above.

____ 5. Fixed factory-overhead costs may be included in product inventories by: (a) the traditional approach to income measurement; (b) the contribution approach to income measurement; (c) both of the above; (d) neither of the above.

____ 6. The contribution approach is not acceptable for income tax purposes: (a) true; (b) false.

____ 7. The differences between the two income approaches is basically the difference in: (a) the *total amount of fixed* overhead costs charged to expense; (b) the *total amount of variable* overhead costs charged to expense; (c) the *timing of fixed* overhead costs charged to expense; (d) the *timing of variable* overhead costs charged to expense.

____ 8. When sales exceed production for a given period, the traditional costing method tends to produce: (a) more profit than the contribution approach; (b) less profit than the contribution approach; (c) the same profit as the contribution approach.

II. ROLE OF VARIOUS ACTIVITY LEVELS IN ABSORPTION COSTING

____ 9. The practical capacity of a given plant is: (a) determined by calculating the maximum physical output that can possibly be obtained from existing machinery and equipment; (b) specified by management after considering the related engineering and economic factors; (c) measured by expected customer demand for our products.

____ 10. Practical plant capacity reflects an allowance for unavoidable operating interruptions: (a) true; (b) false.

____ 11. Reported profits would not ordinarily be greatly affected by the choice of an activity level for computing fixed-overhead rates: (a) true; (b) false.

____ 12. Normal activity is a level of capacity utilization that will meet average customer demand over a period that includes: (a) cyclical factors; (b) seasonal factors; (c) both of the above; (d) neither of the above.

____ 13. A monthly and yearly measure of the cost of idle capacity would be provided by a predetermined fixed-overhead rate based upon: (a) expected annual activity; (b) normal activity.

____ 14. In general, operating budgets that are used to judge current performance should be based upon a normal activity level: (a) true; (b) false.

____ 15. The activity level that can usually be predicted with greater accuracy is: (a) expected annual activity; (b) full capacity; (c) normal activity.

____ 16. In practice, under- or overapplied fixed-overhead costs are carried forward from year to year: (a) for income tax purposes; (b) for external reporting purposes; (c) both of the above; (d) neither of the above.

III. STANDARD-COST VARIANCES AND THE INCOME STATEMENT

B 17. If currently available standards are used for product costing, it would be consistent to view variances as: (a) positive or negative product costs; (b) measures of efficiency or inefficiency.

C 18. Standard-cost variances should be prorated to cost of sales and inventory accounts when the variances are due to the use of standards that are: (a) perfection standards; (b) out-of-date standards; (c) either of the above; (d) neither of the above.

B 19. When standard-cost variances are to be prorated among several accounts, the prorations should be based upon the related: (a) actual costs in the accounts; (b) standard costs in the accounts.

A 20. If all standard-cost variances are prorated among inventories and cost of goods sold, the reported net income would be the same as under an actual historical costing procedure: (a) true; (b) false.

B 21. Favorable standard-cost variance accounts have: (a) debit balances; (b) credit balances.

IV. OVERVIEW OF BUDGETARY CONTROL

D 22. For control purposes, all variances can be divided into three principal categories: price, efficiency, and: (a) spending; (b) rate; (c) quantity; (d) volume.

B 23. The volume variance, as used in the textbook, is the difference between the flexible budget and: (a) the actual results; (b) the static budget; (c) neither of the above.

B 24. The volume variance, as used in the textbook, means virtually the same as the denominator variance: (a) true; (b) false.

A 25. The volume variance, as used in the textbook, measures changes in budgeted costs and revenues due to the difference between budgeted and actual activity volume: (a) true; (b) false.

(B) Complete each of the following statements:

I. CONTRIBUTION APPROACH TO INCOME MEASUREMENT

1. The contribution approach to income measurement classifies costs into FIXED and VARIABLE categories.
2. The direct-costing approach produces Contribution margins.
3. Treated as product costs by the variable-costing method are direct material costs, Direct labor costs, and variable overhead costs.
4. The contribution approach to income measurement is acceptable for Internal or Management reporting purposes.
5. The direct-costing method would tend to report lower profits than would the absorption-costing method when Production is greater than Sales for a given period.

II. ROLE OF VARIOUS ACTIVITY LEVELS IN ABSORPTION COSTING

6. The maximum level at which the plant can operate most efficiently, allowing for unavoidable operating interruptions, is called Practical Capacity.
7. Expected annual activity is a level of Capacity utilization that is also called Master Budgeted activity.
8. The activity level generally used as the base for calculating the predetermined rate for fixed factory-overhead cost is Expected Annual Activity.
9. Conceptually, when Normal Activity is the base, the yearly over- or underapplied fixed-overhead cost should be carried forward on the balance sheet.

10. When currently available standards are used for product costing, the entire amounts of variances may be shown in the income statement as direct charges or credits to Cost of Goods Sold or as separate charges or credits appearing after the gross profit on sales.

11. If a direct-labor price variance were allocated fully to other accounts, the titles of the accounts normally used would be Work in Process, Finished Goods, and Cost of Goods Sold.

12. If an unfavorable standard-cost variance were allocated to Cost of Goods Sold, the reported amount of Cost of Goods Sold would thus be Increased.

(C) Contribution Approach to Income Measurement

The Bear Cupboard Manufacturing Company provided the following data pertaining to its operations for the current calendar year:

Standard costs per product unit:		
Direct material	$ 3.00	
Direct labor	4.00	
Variable overhead	1.00	$ 8.00
Fixed overhead		2.00
Total		$10.00
Product units:		
In beginning inventory		10,000 units
Produced		90,000
Sold		80,000
In ending inventory		20,000
Selling and administrative expenses:		
Variable		$200,000
Fixed		100,000
Selling price per product unit		$ 15.00

1. Construct two income statements, using standard production costs for inventories and cost of goods manufactured, and ignoring income taxes:
   (a) Follow the absorption-costing method.
   (b) Follow the direct-costing method.
2. Reconcile the difference in net incomes shown by these two methods.

(C) 1. (a)

Bear Cupboard Manufacturing Company
Income Statement
For the Year Ending December 31, 197_
(Absorption-Costing Method)

(C) 1. (b)

Bear Cupboard Manufacturing Company
Income Statement
For the Year Ending December 31, 197_
(Direct-Costing Method)

(C) 2. **Reconciliation of Difference in Net Income:**

Absorption-costing method (a) .... $______

Direct-costing method (b) .... $______

Difference to be accounted for .... $______

Difference accounted for as follows:

(D) Role of Various Activity Levels in Absorption Costing

The Aggie Farm Equipment Company furnished the following data:

Fixed factory overhead for the year:	
Budgeted	$72,000
Actual	$74,000
Practical capacity per year	20,000 hr
Normal activity per year	16,000 hr
Expected annual activity	12,000 hr
Standard hours allowed for the work done in the year	13,000 hr

Compute the following amounts:

1. Using an expected annual activity basis:

(a) Fixed overhead rate per hour .... $______

(b) Total fixed overhead applied .... $______

(c) Under- or overapplied fixed overhead .... $________

2. Using a normal activity basis:

(a) Fixed overhead rate per hour .... $________

(b) Total fixed overhead applied .... $________

(c) Under- or overapplied fixed overhead .... $________

(E) Standard-Cost Variances and the Income Statement

The following data are supplied by the Owl Bookend Company, which uses a standard-cost accounting system:

Sales	$25,000
Standard cost of goods manufactured	$20,000
Selling and administrative expenses	$ 6,000
Favorable labor-rate variance	$ 400
Unfavorable labor-efficiency variance	$ 1,200
Product units manufactured	2,000 units
Product units sold	1,600 units
Beginning inventory of finished goods	none
Ending inventory of finished goods	400 units
Work-in-process inventories	none
Income taxes	ignore

1. Compute net income before giving effect to variances .... $________

2. Compute the net unfavorable variance . . . . $________

3. Assuming the net variance is treated as an expense, compute:

(a) Net income . . . . $________

(b) Cost of ending inventory of finished goods . . . . $________

4. Assuming the net variance is prorated between inventory and cost of goods sold, compute:

(a) Net income . . . . $________

(b) Cost of ending inventory of finished goods . . . . $________

5. Which net income figure would seem to be more consistent with the concept of *standard* costs: (3a) or (4a)? . . . . ________

6. Which ending inventory cost would seem to be more consistent with the concept of *historical* costs: (3b) or (4b)? . . . . ________

Relevant Costs and the Contribution Approach to Decisions

11

In this chapter we examine some concepts and techniques that are useful to management in making special decisions. In previous chapters, our studies dealt primarily with product costing and the routine control of operations. The *contribution approach*, which was one of the main concepts used in these studies, is also one of the two keys to understanding and analyzing the costs involved in nonroutine decisions. The other key is the idea of *relevant costs,* which are defined as the expected future costs that will differ for alternative actions under consideration by management. This is the major conceptual lesson of this chapter.

The basic function of the management accountant in decision making for special purposes is to select, measure, and analyze the costs that pertain to the available courses of action. Some of these important types of decisions that can benefit from a discriminating cost analysis are dealt with in this chapter. They include the acceptance or rejection of special orders, the manufacture or purchase of direct materials (make or buy), and the replacement of equipment.

REVIEW SUMMARY

A. Cost accountants process and report information for use by management in making decisions.

1. Such information should be *relevant* to the decisions.

2. Although *qualitative* factors may be decisive in many cases, accountants usually try to express as many decision factors as possible in *quantitative* terms, in order to reduce the number of qualitative factors to be judged.

B. It is essential that we clearly understand the meaning of *relevance* as it pertains to costs used in management decision processes.

1. Because the function of management decision making is to choose objectives and select appropriate courses of action for the future, decisions always involve *prediction.*

2. For this reason, the costs that are relevant to managerial decision making are the predicted costs that must be compared under available alternatives.

a. *These costs include only the expected future costs that will differ under alternatives.*

b. Although *historical costs* are often helpful in predicting future costs, *they are not relevant to the management decision itself.*

C. The *relevant-cost approach* is well suited to the choosing of appropriate activity levels for evaluating special orders.

1. When idle capacity permits the filling of special reduced-price sales orders that would not affect regular sales, average overall unit costs do not necessarily serve as the proper basis for evaluating these orders.

a. The only costs that would usually be relevant to such situations are the variable costs that would be affected by accepting the special sales orders, not the variable costs that are unaffected. See textbook Exhibit 11-2.

b. Because fixed costs would usually not be affected by the decision, they would usually be irrelevant. However, if the decision would affect certain fixed costs immediately or in the future, they should of course be given appropriate consideration.

c. On the basis of a relevant-cost approach, it is possible that some special orders should be accepted at selling prices below the average unit costs that include all fixed and variable costs—as in the textbook example.

2. The important point is that such decisions should depend primarily on the revenues and costs expected to be *different* among alternatives, whether or not accountants' reports to management also include any revenues and costs expected to be the same among alternatives.

D. For pricing decisions, the *contribution approach* can be quite useful to management.

1. Compared to the conventional or *absorption-costing approach*, the contribution approach has certain advantages.

a. The delineation of variable- and fixed-cost behavior patterns facilitates the development of pricing formulas for various activity levels in addition to the normal level.

b. The contribution approach provides insights that help in weighing the short-run benefits of cutting prices on special orders against the long-run benefits of not cutting such prices.

2. On the other hand, it has been claimed that the use of full manufacturing costs is better than the contribution approach to pricing decisions.

a. It has been argued that using the contribution approach in pricing decisions will result in underpricing and ultimate losses, whereas full manufacturing cost is a safer guide because it does not ignore fixed factory-overhead costs.

b. However, pricing decisions can be quite complex, and either method can lead to unprofitable pricing if used without understanding and judgment.

3. The contribution-margin approach reveals some factors more clearly than does the conventional approach and thus can help prevent decisions to sell products at less than out-of-pocket cost or to refuse contracts that could make contributions to fixed costs in an idle-capacity situation.

4. Another major influence sometimes affecting pricing decisions is the Robinson-Patman Act, which forbids price discrimination among competing customers except when justified by differences in costs.

a. However, contested cases have been decided on full-costing rather than direct-costing allocations.

b. Furthermore, price differentials that are justified are due mostly to distribution costs rather than to manufacturing costs.

5. Despite the strong theoretical attractions of the contribution approach, many managers coping with the "real world" tend to be more comfortable with full costs as approximations of the higher levels to which future costs seem inevitably to rise.

E. In addition to decisions involving special sales orders, there are several other important types of management decisions that can be assisted by the relevant-cost and contribution approaches, as illustrated in the series of helpful examples in the textbook.

1. When a multi-product plant is being operated at capacity, the orders that are accepted should maximize profits.

a. The criterion for maximum profits for a given capacity is the greatest possible contribution to profit per unit of the *constraining factor* or *resource.*

b. Constraining factors may include such resource measures as machine-hours, labor-hours, or cubic feet of space, but not necessarily the contribution-margin ratio per product unit. See Exhibit 11-3.

2. When manufacturers are confronted with the question of whether to make or buy a product, the decision may be based on qualitative factors, such as the quality of the products or long-run business relationships.

a. However, the decision may depend partly on the quantitative measurement of the difference in future costs among the alternatives, especially if idle productive facilities are involved.

b. Such relevant costs would not necessarily be restricted to variable costs, but could include fixed costs that may be avoided in the future.

3. The essence of the make-or-buy decision is how best to utilize available facilities after considering such alternatives as:

a. Leaving facilities idle

b. Buying products and renting out unused facilities

c. Buying products and using facilities for other products

4. In arriving at make-or-buy decisions, managers and accountants should be aware of several pitfalls:

a. Distorted unit costs could be produced by irrelevant allocations of a fixed cost that would not be affected by the decision.

b. Improper comparisons of *unit costs* not computed on the same basis could lead to the wrong decision. This error can be avoided by comparing *total costs* for alternatives.

F. Our definition of *relevant costs*—expected future costs that will differ among alternatives—excludes historical costs. Although past costs may be of aid in predicting future costs, they are irrelevant to the decision itself.

1. The historical cost of materials or finished inventories (whether obsolete or not) would be common to all future alternatives and therefore would not affect the differences in expected profits from such alternatives as:

a. Scrapping the inventory

b. Selling it at reduced prices

c. Remaking the inventory into other products and selling them at certain prices

2. For convenience in analyzing the alternatives under consideration, one can use as an *opportunity cost* the benefits promised by the best of the excluded alternatives (the copper example on text pages 349 and 350).

a. Opportunity cost is the maximum contribution or value that is sacrificed or given up by using limited resources for a certain purpose.

b. Because opportunity costs are derived from transactions that do not actually take place, they are not ordinarily entered in the accounting records.

3. The book value of old equipment is a past or historical cost and is therefore irrelevant to *making decisions*, although it might be relevant to *developing predictions* of future cash flows that are partly dependent on the income tax effects of the depreciation or sale of equipment.

a. Exhibits 11-4 and 11-5 are particularly helpful models for comparing costs in a machine-replacement situation.

b. As emphasized in the accompanying textbook example, note especially an important motivational aspect that should be recognized in such situations: the somewhat natural reluctance of a manager to replace a machine because of adverse effects on his perceived profit performance in the year of replacement.

SELF-TEST AND PRACTICE EXERCISES

(A) For each of the following multiple-choice and true-false statements, select the single most appropriate answer and enter its identification letter in the space provided.

___ 1. In managerial decision making, it is usually desirable to consider: (a) quantitative factors; (b) qualitative factors; (c) both of the above; (d) neither of the above.

___ 2. The function of management decision making always involves prediction: (a) true; (b) false.

___ 3. Historical costs may be: (a) relevant to decisions about the future; (b) helpful in predicting future costs; (c) both of the above; (d) neither of the above.

___ 4. Costs that are relevant to management decision making usually include all expected future costs: (a) true; (b) false.

___ 5. Costs that are relevant to decisions about the future might include: (a) an expected future fixed cost; (b) a past variable cost; (c) both of the above; (d) neither of the above.

___ 6. When there is idle plant capacity and reduced-price special orders are received, the relevant-cost approach: (a) would evaluate the orders on the basis of average overall unit costs; (b) might indicate acceptance of orders at prices below average overall unit costs; (c) both of the above; (d) neither of the above.

___ 7. The relevant-cost approach to evaluating reduced-price special orders implies that future fixed costs: (a) are irrelevant; (b) are usually relevant; (c) might be relevant.

___ 8. The approach that is more helpful in furnishing insights that help in weighing the short-run benefits of cutting prices on special orders against the long-run benefits of not cutting such prices is: (a) the absorption-costing approach; (b) the contribution approach.

___ 9. An approach to pricing decisions that can lead to unprofitable pricing if used without understanding and judgment is: (a) the contribution approach; (b) the full-costing approach; (c) either of the above; (d) neither of the above.

A 10. The pricing approach that is more helpful in preventing decisions to refuse contracts that could make contributions to fixed costs in an idle-capacity situation is: (a) the contribution-margin approach; (b) the conventional approach.

B 11. When a multi-product plant is being operated at capacity, orders that are accepted should maximize: (a) available machine-hours; (b) total profits; (c) contribution-margin ratio per product unit; (d) available labor hours; (e) cubic feet of factory space.

D 12. In deciding among alternatives for using inventories, their historical cost is irrelevant if the inventories are: (a) obsolete; (b) not obsolete; (c) either of the above; (d) neither of the above.

D 13. Amounts that are relevant to making predictions of future costs include: (a) disposal value of old equipment; (b) book value of old equipment; (c) both of the above; (d) neither of the above.

___ 14. Amounts that are relevant to choosing among alternative uses of certain materials on hand include: (a) their salvage value; (b) their book value; (c) both of the above; (d) neither of the above.

A 15. Opportunity costs: (a) are not ordinarily entered in the accounting records; (b) do not require dollar outlays; (c) both of the above; (d) neither of the above.

___ 16. The apportionment of joint costs to products appearing after the split-off point is often useful for cost-planning and control purposes: (a) true; (b) false.

(B) Complete each of the following statements:

1. Ideally, the information collected by accountants and reported to decision makers should be__________ .
2. Costs that are relevant to managerial decision making include only the __________ costs that __________ under alternative courses of action.
3. __________ costs may be relevant to the prediction of future costs but are not relevant to __________ .
4. It has been contended that the use of the __________ in pricing decisions will result in underpricing and ultimate company disaster.
5. The __________ Act forbids price discrimination among competing customers except when justified by differences in__________ .
6. It has been argued that, in comparison with the contribution approach, the __________ would be a safer guide in pricing decisions because it does not ignore __________ factory-overhead costs.
7. When a multi-product plant is being operated at capacity, the criterion for maximum profits is the largest contribution __________ .
8. The maximum contribution that is foregone by using limited resources for a particular purpose is called __________ .

(C) Bevo Enterprises, Inc., has an annual plant capacity of 2,500 product units. Its predicted operations for the year are:

Sales (2,000 units at $30 each)	$60,000
Manufacturing costs:	
Variable	$18 per unit
Fixed	$13,000
Selling and administrative expenses:	
Variable (sales commissions)	$ 2 per unit
Fixed	$ 2,000

Should the company accept a special order for 400 units at a selling price of $24 each and subject to half the usual sales commission rate per unit, assuming no effect on regular sales at regular prices? Show supporting computations.

(D) The Bruin Company has a used machine with a book value of $65,000, a present scrap value of $9,000, and an estimated remaining life of ten years. A new machine that is available at a cost of $84,000 has the same capacity, but it would reduce power costs by $6,000 per year. It has a predicted useful life of ten years. Neither machine will have a scrap value at the end of its useful life. Ignoring income taxes and the time value of money, which of the two alternatives should the company select: keep the old machine or replace it with the new machine? Show supporting computations.

(E) Stan's Cardinal Products Company has 2,400 hours of plant capacity available for manufacturing two products with the following characteristics:

	V	W
Selling price per unit	$10	$15
Variable expenses per unit	$ 7	$ 9
Units that can be manufactured in one hour (V or W)	10	4

Compute the number of its 2,400 available production hours that this company should devote to the manufacture of each product:

V____________________, W____________________.

(F) The Frog Novelty Manufacturing Corporation has three product lines: T, C, and U. The company furnished the following operating statement for its most recent year (in thousands of dollars):

	T	C	U	Total
Sales	120	150	180	450
Variable costs and expenses	80	90	100	270
Fixed costs and expenses:				
Annual salaries of product-line supervisors	17	20	23	60
Total company-wide fixed costs allocated equally to product lines	30	30	30	90
Total costs and expenses	127	140	153	420
Net operating income (loss)	(7)	10	27	30

1. Using a format similar to the above, prepare a projected operating statement on the assumption that Product T operations are discontinued with no effects on sales of the other product lines or on the total assets used by the company.

C	U	Total

2. On the basis of the statement you have prepared, would you advise the elimination of Product T operations? Why?

Cost Analysis and Capital Budgeting

12

In this chapter we shift our attention from the short-term, period-oriented aspects of management accounting for operations and turn toward the long-range, project-oriented features of planning and control for special decisions. Specifically, we study the problem of choosing among different proposals for large expenditures and their financing. Each occurrence of this problem is unique and typically involves a nonrecurring set of specific alternatives that may have different long-run effects on a company's profits and financial condition. Therefore, for each of the available alternatives, management should measure the expected results against the required investment. The planning, evaluation, and selection processes for special long-term projects are often referred to as *capital budgeting.*

This chapter describes and compares the principal capital-budgeting approaches (decision models) that are in general use. Of central importance is the concept of the time value of money and its use in measuring cash flows for decision purposes.

REVIEW SUMMARY

A. *Capital budgeting* means making long-term planning decisions for investments and their financing.

1. Such decisions typically involve special projects that require commitments over a period of several years.

2. For this reason, it is not necessarily appropriate to use the same planning and control models of traditional general-purpose accounting systems, which are designed primarily to meet the routine needs of current periods only.

3. This chapter concentrates on the conceptually superior approach to capital-budgeting decisions, the *discounted cash-flow (DCF) models*. The chapter also includes explanations of other models: urgency and persuasion, payback, and the accounting rate of return.

B. *Urgency and persuasion* do not provide a systematic approach that evaluates economic considerations on a timely and objective basis.

1. The urgency of critical situations caused by neglect and procrastination often limits management decisions to those that are not optimal.

2. Moreover, decisions based on the persuasive powers of managers who advocate different alternatives do not necessarily reflect appropriate consideration of valid evaluation data.

C. *DCF analysis* focuses on flows of cash instead of flows of revenues and expenses (net income).

1. This approach, which systematically weighs the time value of money, has two main variations:

a. The *internal rate of return*, or *time-adjusted rate of return*, is the rate of return (discount rate) that equates the amount invested at a given date with the present value of the expected cash inflows from the investment, as demonstrated in textbook Exhibits 12-2 and 12-3.

b. The *net-present-value model* uses a minimum desired rate of return (*hurdle rate* or *cutoff rate*) for discounting cash outflows and inflows to a given present date so that their net difference may be measured at that date, as illustrated in Exhibit 12-4.

2. Note especially that, because this approach is based upon flows of *cash* and not the *accrual* concepts of revenues and expenses, no adjustments should be made to cash flows for the periodic allocation of asset cost called *depreciation expense*. Instead, the *initial cost* of an asset is usually treated in DCF computations as a *lump-sum cash outflow* at time zero.

3. DCF models assume a world of certainty regarding interest rates and the amounts and timing of predicted cash flows.

D. Important differences should be recognized between the two variations of the discounted cash-flow approach. See helpful computations in textbook Example 2.

1. Different decision rules are used:

a. If the internal rate of return equals or exceeds the hurdle rate, accept the project; if not, reject the project.

b. If the net present value is zero or positive, accept the project; if negative, reject the project.

2. The internal rate of return usually requires more tedious manual calculations than are necessary for the net-present-value method, which can be more easily applied to situations with uneven periodic cash flows.

3. On the other hand, electronic computers can be programmed for calculations, and the internal rate of return is more widely used for two reasons:

a. The internal rates appear to be more easily interpreted than the net-present-value amounts.

b. The internal-rate-of-return method avoids the task of selecting a hurdle rate for discounting cash flows.

E. Whenever we make decisions involving future cash flows, we must recognize the risk and uncertainty that actual cash flows will not be the same as expected cash flows.

1. Therefore, *probability distributions* should be used in conjunction with expected cash flows, but these are described in later chapters.

2. *Sensitivity analysis* is a helpful way to cope with risk and uncertainty.

a. Sensitivity analysis is a technique that measures how the basic forecasted results in a decision model will be affected by changes in the critical data inputs that influence those results.

b. By providing an immediate financial measure of the possible errors in forecasting, sensitivity analysis helps managers to concentrate attention on the most sensitive decision factors in a given case, such as amounts of cash flows and useful lives of assets.

F. Two general aspects of DCF analysis deserve mention:

1. Such analysis is applicable to both profit-seeking and nonprofit-seeking organizations.

2. DCF models can be adjusted for general price inflation in either of two ways:

a. The discount rate is raised to include the effect of inflation, and cash flows are predicted on the basis of inflated expectations.

b. The discount rate excludes the effect of inflation, but predicted cash flows are reduced to the dollar basis before the expected inflation.

G. The relationships of several important items to discounted cash-flow analysis should be clearly understood:

1. Errors in forecasting future disposal values are usually not crucial, because the combination of relatively small disposal values and long time periods tends to produce small present values.

2. Current disposal values of old assets are most conveniently handled by offsetting them against the gross cash outlays for new assets.

3. Any additional investments that might be required for current assets (such as cash, receivables, and inventories) may be regarded as outflows at time zero, their terminal disposal values being regarded as inflows at the end of a project's useful life.

4. Depreciation and book values are ignored, because historical costs are irrelevant.

5. Income taxes, which do affect cash flows, are ignored in this chapter but are considered in the next chapter.

6. In the relevant-cost analysis of factory overhead, the only pertinent cost is the overhead that will differ among alternatives.

7. When cash-flow analysis is applied to two mutually exclusive projects, the one that shows the larger net present value should be undertaken.

8. Various complications in the use of capital budgeting are postponed to other chapters.

H. Another model used for capital-budgeting decisions is called *payback, payout*, or *payoff* (treated more fully in textbook chapter's Appendix B).

1. If there are uniform annual cash inflows, the initial cash investment is divided by the annual cash inflow to find the estimated number of years it will take to recoup the investment.

2. This may be useful in certain circumstances, *but it ignores the profitability of investments.*

I. Capital-budgeting decisions are sometimes based upon another model called *accounting rate of return, unadjusted rate of return, book value rate of return,* or *approximate rate of return* (treated more fully in textbook chapter's Appendix A).

1. The predicted amount of future average annual net income, or increase therein, is divided by the initial (sometimes average) amount of the required investment, or increase therein.

2. The accounting-rate-of-return method is widely used and aims at profit measurement by conventional accounting methods, *but it ignores the time value of money.*

J. In general, the best approach to long-range decisions is the discounted cash-flow method because, by explicitly and automatically weighing the time value of money, it aims at the overriding goal of maximizing long-run net cash inflows.

K. See the textbook problem for self-study and the accompanying Exhibit 12-6.

1. Note that the same net-present-value difference between two alternative projects can be obtained by either of two approaches for discounting cash flows to a common present date:

a. Calculate the net present value *of the cash flows* of each of the two projects and determine the difference between these two amounts (*the total-project approach*).

b. Calculate the net present value *of the cash flow differences* between the two projects (*the incremental approach*).

2. Note also the helpfulness of the "sketch of cash flows," a key step in solving problems of this type.

SELF-TEST AND PRACTICE EXERCISES

(A) For each of the following multiple-choice and true-false statements, select the single most appropriate answer and enter its identification letter in the space provided:

____ 1. Capital budgeting deals primarily with: (a) the current effects of routine decisions; (b) the long-run effects of special decisions.

____ 2. The planning and control methods used for general-purpose accounting systems are always well suited to both routine operating decisions and capital-budgeting decisions: (a) true; (b) false.

____ 3. The urgency-and-persuasion method is not recommended as a good model for capital-budgeting decisions: (a) true; (b) false.

____ 4. The time value of money is systematically weighed by: (a) the internal-rate-of-return model; (b) the net-present-value model; (c) both of the above; (d) neither of the above.

____ 5. DCF is usually feasible to use in situations where the predicted cash flows are: (a) even; (b) uneven; (c) both of the above; (d) neither of the above.

____ 6. The internal rate of return is the discount rate that equates the amount invested at a given date with the present value of the expected cash inflows from the investment: (a) true; (b) false.

____ 7. Depreciation is a periodic flow of: (a) cash; (b) expense; (c) both of the above; (d) neither of the above.

____ 8. If the minimum desired rate of return exceeds the internal rate of return expected from a certain project, the project should be rejected: (a) true; (b) false.

____ 9. When cash-flow analysis is applied to two mutually exclusive projects, the one that shows the smaller net present value should be: (a) accepted; (b) rejected.

____10. In DCF computations, depreciation is properly added to: (a) expected cash inflows; (b) expected cash outflows; (c) neither cash inflows nor cash outflows.

____11. The internal rate of return can usually be more easily applied to situations with uneven periodic cash flows than can the net-present-value method: (a) true; (b) false.

____12. DCF models: (a) are applicable to non-profit-seeking organizations; (b) cannot be adjusted for general price inflation; (c) both of the above; (d) neither of the above.

____13. Generally, in DCF analysis, we should ignore: (a) depreciation and book values; (b) income taxes; (c) both of the above; (d) neither of the above.

____14. In DCF analysis, the most convenient way to handle current disposal values of old assets is to: (a) treat them as cash inflows; (b) treat them as cash outflows; (c) offset them against gross cash outlays for new assets; (d) add them to the required investment in the project.

____15. The profitability of an investment is ignored by: (a) the net-present-value method; (b) the internal-rate-of-return method; (c) both of the above; (d) neither of the above.

____16. The payback model: (a) may be useful in certain circumstances; (b) ignores the profitability of investments; (c) both of the above; (d) neither of the above.

____17. The time value of money is ignored by: (a) the accounting-rate-of-return approach; (b) the internal-rate-of-return model; (c) both of the above; (d) neither of the above.

____18. Compared to the total-project approach for computing the net-present-value difference between two alternative projects, the incremental approach would usually produce: (a) a smaller present-value difference; (b) a larger present-value difference; (c) the same present-value difference.

(B) Complete each of the following statements:

1. Making long-term planning decisions for investments and their financing is called ______________________ ______________________.

2. The conceptually superior approach to capital-budgeting decisions is ______________________ ______________________.

3. The present value of a given amount due five years from now would be ______________ at a 10% discount rate than at an 8% discount rate.

4. The two main variations to the discounted cash-flow approach are ______________________ and ______________________ ______________________.

5. The internal rate of return is also called the ____________ ______________________.

6. A proposed project should be rejected if its net present value is ______________________ ______________________.

7. A technique that measures how the basic forecasted results in a decision model will be affected by changes in certain input data is called ______________________ ______________________.

8. In the relevant-cost analysis of factory overhead, the only pertinent cost is the overhead that ______________ ______________________.

9. If there are uniform annual cash inflows, the payback period can be computed by dividing the ______________ by the ______________ ______________________.

10. Essentially, the accounting rate of return is the predicted amount of ______________, or increase therein, divided by the initial (sometimes average) amount of the ______________, or increase therein.

11. When the incremental approach is used for determining the net-present-value difference between two alternative projects, one should calculate the present value of the ______________________ ______________________.

(C) Given for Optional Equipment Company:

Initial cost of a special purpose machine	$60,000
Predicted useful life	12 yr
Predicted residual value at end of useful life	$ 3,000
Predicted annual savings in cash operating expenses	$15,000
Minimum desired rate of return	16%
Present value of $1 due 12 years from now, using a 16% effective interest rate	$ 0.168
Present value of an annuity of $1 per year due at the end of each of 12 years from now, using a 16% effective interest rate	$ 5.197

Compute the following, ignoring income tax effects:

1. Present value of expected annual savings:

2. Present value of predicted residual value:

3. Total present value of expected cash inflows:

4. Net present value of expected cash inflows:

(D) Given for Auxiliary Products, Inc.:

Initial cost of a special purpose machine	$120,000
Predicted useful life (no terminal scrap value)	15 yr
Predicted annual savings in cash operating expenses	$ 20,000
Present value of an annuity of $1 for 15 years:	
Using a 14% effective interest rate	$ 6.142
Using a 16% effective interest rate	$ 5.575

Compute the internal rate of return to the nearest tenth of a percent, ignoring income tax effects . . . ______%

(E) Given for Apparatus Control Corporation:

Initial cost of proposed new equipment	$80,000
Predicted useful life	8 yr
Predicted residual value at end of useful life	none
Predicted savings per year in cash operating expenses	$16,000

Compute the following, ignoring income tax effects:

1. Payback period .... ____yr

2. Payback reciprocal (see textbook chapter, Appendix B) .... ____%

3. Depreciation expense per year by straight-line method .... $____

4. Predicted increase in future average annual net income .... $____

5. Accounting rate of return based on initial investment .... ____%

6. Accounting rate of return based on average investment .... ____%

A Closer Look at Capital Budgeting

13

Capital budgeting was introduced in the preceding chapter without the complications of income taxes. However, because they usually require relatively large cash outflows that depend for their amounts and timing upon the choices among alternative projects, income taxes almost always play a basic role in decision making. This chapter describes the treatment of income taxes and the function of depreciation in capital budgeting. In addition, several other important aspects of capital budgeting are examined: comparisons of projects having unequal lives, techniques for choosing from multiple alternatives within a total capital-budgeting constraint, and methods for determining the cost of capital.

REVIEW SUMMARY

A. Because the combined federal and state income tax rate may easily exceed 50% of corporate earnings, the income tax effects on cash and net income should not be ignored in capital budgeting.

1. Income taxes affect both the amount and the timing of cash flows.

2. Depreciation is a *noncash expense* used in computing periodic net income.

a. The basic relationships of depreciation to net income and cash flows are clearly shown in the textbook Exhibit 13-1, which should be studied very carefully.

b. Because depreciation expense is subtracted in arriving at the amount of periodic net income but is not a periodic cash disbursement, it may be *added back* to the net-income figure to arrive at current net cash inflow from all revenue-producing operations.

3. Although depreciation itself is not a cash inflow, the deductibility of depreciation from revenues in determining net income subject to taxes reduces income tax payments and thus serves as a *tax shield.*

a. The tax-savings effect of depreciation has a *present value* that is partially dependent upon the depreciation method chosen, as shown by the textbook Exhibit 13-2.

b. The double-declining-balance method and the sum-of-years'-digits method, which are two widely used accelerated-depreciation methods, produce higher present values for the tax savings than the straight-line method does.

4. Although consideration must be given to income tax effects in making capital-budgeting decisions, this does not require a change in the general approach described in the preceding chapter. See textbook Exhibits 13-3 and 13-4, and note carefully the following main points:

a. The same net-present-value difference between two alternative projects may be computed either by the total-project approach or by the incremental approach.

b. The *after-tax basis* is used to compute the present values of cash flows: cash operating costs, cash revenues, and the amounts expected to be received on disposals of assets.

c. The present value of the tax savings from depreciation is computed separately from other cash flows.

B. Occassionally, the net-present-value and internal-rate-of-return techniques produce *conflicting rankings* of mutually exclusive investment proposals, as indicated by Exhibit 13-5.

1. When alternative projects have unequal lives, differences in ranking by the two methods can occur because of different implicit assumptions as to the rate of return on the reinvestment of the cash proceeds at the end of the shorter project life.

2. The two approaches can be reconciled by using a common terminal date for alternative projects and by making explicit assumptions as to the appropriate rates for reinvestment of funds.

C. Theoretically, a general rule for evaluating capital projects would be to undertake any project with a *positive net present value* after discounting predicted cash flows at the minimum desired rate of return, but in practice, the rule is subject to some qualifications.

1. It may be necessary to practice *capital rationing* because of capital-spending budget limits influenced by such factors as management philosophy and the feasibility of obtaining funds from operations and security issues.

2. In the absence of capital rationing, the *excess-present-value index* would indicate the acceptance of the same projects indicated by the net-present-value approach.

3. However, in practice, capital-spending constraints are quite common, and the *net-present-value method* is the best general guide for choosing among investments of different sizes, as illustrated by Exhibit 13-6.

a. Optimal decisions would not always result from the use of the excess-present-value index.

b. If there are *investment indivisibilities* within a budget constraint, total returns in some instances would be maximized by accepting smaller, though less attractive, projects.

D. The minimum desired rate of return that we use as a discount rate in computing present values, or as a cutoff rate in selecting projects, is also called target rate, hurdle rate, financial standard, and—most frequently—*cost of capital*, or *k*.

1. Generally, the cost of capital is theoretically defined as the rate of return on a project that will leave unchanged the market price of the firm's stock, but in practice, the measurement of the cost of capital is complex and full of controversy.

2. The essentials of Van Horne's methods for computing the cost of typical sources of capital are summarized:

a. The cost of capital to be obtained by issuing mortgage bonds and other straight-debt securities is basically the after-tax interest rate.

b. For preferred stock, the cost of capital is the stated annual dividend rate.

c. For common stock, the cost of capital is the expected cash dividend yield on market price of the stock plus an expected constant rate of growth.

d. For retained earnings, the cost of capital is approximately the same as the cost of capital for common stock.

e. After the cost of each capital source has been estimated in a given case, a weighted-average cost of capital can be computed to give effect to the financing proportions from each capital source (capital structure proportions).

3. The rate of return to be used for evaluating investment proposals should also reflect the *degree of risk* involved.

a. The usual practice is to arbitrarily set higher rates as the perceived risk increases.

b. Appropriate diversification of investments can decrease risk (the essence of the *portfolio approach*).

SELF-TEST AND PRACTICE EXERCISES

(A) For each of the following multiple-choice and true-false statements, select the single most appropriate answer and enter its identification letter in the space provided:

____ 1. Because corporate income tax rates are often not large, the effects of income taxes on cash and net income may usually be safely ignored in capital budgeting: (a) true; (b) false.

____ 2. Income taxes may influence: (a) the amount of cash flows; (b) the timing of cash flows; (c) both of the above; (d) neither of the above.

____ 3. Depreciation is: (a) periodic cash inflow; (b) a periodic operating expense; (c) both of the above; (d) neither of the above.

____ 4. The current net cash inflow from all revenue-producing operations may be measured by adding net income and: (a) depreciation expense; (b) the income tax effect of depreciation expense; (c) depreciation expense less its income tax effect.

____ 5. Depreciation can affect cash flows by serving as an income tax shield: (a) true; (b) false.

____ 6. The after-tax effect of depreciation expense on the measurement of periodic net income is the periodic: (a) depreciation expense; (b) income tax effect of depreciation expense; (c) depreciation expense less its income tax effect.

____ 7. In contrast to the use of the double-declining-balance depreciation method, the use of the straight-line depreciation method would produce for the tax savings: (a) a larger present value; (b) a smaller present value; (c) about the same present value.

____ 8. Because it is appropriate to consider income tax effects in making capital-budgeting decisions: (a) the general approach of the preceding chapter must be changed; (b) the difference in the net present values of two alternatives computed by the incremental approach will not be the same as the difference computed by the total-project approach; (c) both of the above; (d) neither of the above.

____ 9. The use of the net-present-value and the internal-rate-of-return techniques to help determine the relative desirability of mutually exclusive investment proposals will produce conflicting rankings of projects: (a) always; (b) never; (c) occasionally.

____ 10. In the absence of capital rationing, all projects should be undertaken that have: (a) positive net present values using the minimum desired rate of return; (b) excess-present-value indexes above 100% using the minimum desired rate of return; (c) either of the above; (d) neither of the above.

____ 11. The best general guide for choosing among investments of different sizes is the excess-present-value index: (a) true; (b) false.

____ 12. In practice, the measurement of the cost of capital is: (a) fairly simple; (b) noncontroversial; (c) both of the above; (d) neither of the above.

____ 13. The overall cost of capital is the average of the short-term bank prime interest rate and the long-term borrowing rate of the strongest corporations: (a) true; (b) false.

____ 14. The cost of capital to be obtained from the issuance of bonds would ordinarily be computed on an after-tax basis: (a) true; (b) false.

____ 15. The cost of capital to be obtained from the issuance of preferred stock would often be approximately 50% of the pre-tax preferred dividend rate: (a) true; (b) false.

____ 16. For retained earnings, the cost of capital is approximately the same as the cost of capital for: (a) bonds; (b) preferred stock; (c) common stock.

____ 17. In dealing with risks, the generally prevailing practice today is: (a) to ignore the effect of risk on the rate of return to be used for evaluating investment proposals; (b) to use probability distributions; (c) neither of the above.

____ 18. An operating lease, in contrast to a financial lease, is one that: (a) is cancelable; (b) terminates before the rental payments have repaid the purchase price; (c) either of the above; (d) neither of the above.

(B) Complete each of the following statements:

1. A tax shield is provided by the deductibility of ____________ from ____________ in determining net income subject to taxes.

2. The ____________ method chosen will affect the ____________ of the related tax savings.

3. Two commonly used accelerated-depreciation methods are the ____________ method and the ____________ method.

4. When income taxes are involved, the present values of ____________ should be computed on the ____________ basis.

5. When differences in ranking of alternative projects with unequal lives are produced by the net-present-value and internal-rate-of-return techniques, this is caused by different implicit assumptions as to the rate of return on ______________________________

____

______________________________.

6. The selection of projects when there is an overall budget limit for capital expenditures is called ______

______________________________.

7. The minimum desired rate used in capital budgeting is most frequently called ______________________

______________________________.

8. The cost of capital to be obtained from the issuance of capital stock is ______________________

plus ______________________________

______________________________.

(C) Given for Old Guard Company's 197_ operations (000 omitted):

Sales	$500
Straight-line depreciation expense	$ 40
Other operating expenses, including cost of goods sold	$410
Income tax rate	(60%)

1. Prepare the income statement:

2. Compute the annual after-tax effect of depreciation expense on net income .... $______

3. Compute the annual tax savings from the depreciation deduction .... $______

4. Use three different approaches for computing the same after-tax net cash flow from all revenue-producing operations:

(a)

(b)

(c)

(D) The Instant Transit Company provides the following data:

Purchase price of special equipment	$100,000
Predicted useful life	10 yr
Predicted annual savings in cash operating costs	$ 30,000
Predicted residual value (terminal scrap value)	none
Depreciation method: straight line	
Minimum desired *after-tax* rate of return	10%
Income tax rate	60%
Present value of $1 at 10%:	
Due at the end of 5 years	$ 0.62
Due at the end of 10 years	$ 0.39
Present value of an annuity of $1 for 10 years:	
At 10%	$ 6.15
At 12%	$ 5.65
At 14%	$ 5.22

Compute the following on an *after-tax* basis:

1. The payback period .... ______yr

2. The internal rate of return to the nearest tenth of one percent .... ______%

3. The net present value of the investment .... $______

(E) The following projects of similar risk are available to Dilemma Unlimited:

Project	Total Cost	Present Value	Net Present Value	Excess-Present-Value Index
A	$15,000	$21,000	$______	______%
B	8,000	12,000	______	______
C	5,000	7,500	______	______
D	4,000	6,400	______	______
E	2,000	3,500	______	______
F	1,000	1,900	______	______

1. For each project, compute and make entries in the above schedule for the net present value and the excess-present-value index.

2. Assuming a total budget constraint of $25,000, which projects would you advise Dilemma to accept? List them below:

Project	Total Cost	Present Value	Net Present Value	Excess-Present-Value Index
______	$______	$______	$______	______%
______	______	______	______	______
______	______	______	______	______
______	______	______	______	______
______	______	______	______	______
Totals	$______	$______	$______	______%

3. Assuming a total budget constraint of $24,000, which projects would you advise Dilemma to accept? List them below:

Project	Total Cost	Present Value	Net Present Value	Excess-Present-Value Index
______	$______	$______	$______	______%
______	______	______	______	______
______	______	______	______	______
______	______	______	______	______
______	______	______	______	______
Totals	$______	$______	$______	______%

Inventory Planning, Control, and Valuation

14

Inventories include manufacturing materials held for use in production and finished products held for sale to customers. We seek to keep our inventories above the levels that would be insufficient for production or sales requirements and below the levels that would cause excessive inventory carrying costs or value deterioration. Holding inventories and other assets at appropriate levels helps to maximize long-run profits.

inventory control means the determination and maintenance of the optimum amount of investment in inventory. Explanations of various ways for accomplishing inventory control make up the principal content of this chapter, which also describes different methods of inventory valuation.

REVIEW SUMMARY

A. Inventories have some important managerial aspects.

1. Inventories permit prompt service to customers and a smooth flow of production operations.

2. If inventories are sufficient, they serve as cushions to absorb fluctuations in supply and demand.

3. Inventories also help minimize the interdependence of various parts of the organization.

4. Keeping inventories at levels that maximize profits (or minimize costs)—called *inventory control*—is not achieved merely by maintaining a high level of clerical accuracy in inventory records and documents.

B. Two main types of costs are relevant to inventory decisions:

1. *Ordering costs* are the clerical costs of preparing purchase or production orders and the special processing and receiving costs affected by the number of orders made.

2. *Carrying costs* include the desired rate of return on inventory investment and the costs of storage, breakage, obsolescence, deterioration, insurance, and personal property taxes.

3. These two types of costs are affected in opposite ways as the average size of the inventory increases because of larger orders at less frequent intervals: carrying costs increase, but ordering costs decrease.

C. One of the two key factors in applying inventory policy is the determination of the *economic order quanity* (EOQ), the optimum size of a normal purchase order for replenishing materials or a shop order for a production run.

1. The EOQ may be estimated by computing the annual carrying cost and the annual purchase-order cost (or setup cost) for each of several selected order sizes. The order size with the least total cost would be the approximate economic order quantity. This is illustrated by the key textbook Exhibit 14-1.

2. The EOQ may be computed more quickly and more accurately by a well-known formula:

$$E = \sqrt{\frac{2AP}{S}}$$

where E = Order size in units
A = Annual quantity used in units
P = Cost per purchase order
S = Annual cost of carrying one unit in stock one year

3. Total relevant costs may be easily computed by another widely used formula:

$$C = \sqrt{2APS}$$

D. The EOQ model for inventory decisions contains some important implications for accountants.

1. By studying the graph of relevant costs in Exhibit 14-2, you can easily see that the EOQ falls at the lowest point in a range where the total-cost curve tends to flatten.

a. In other words, the total costs are affected very little by errors in the approximations of unit costs; for example, the carrying cost per unit.

b. Thus, an important feature of inventory decisions is that they are usually not affected by small variations in cost estimates.

2. Inventory control for the benefit of the entire organization can often be complex and difficult because of the natural conflicts among the management objectives generally associated with the main functions of the business: sales, production, purchasing, and financing.

a. For example, a production manager would usually like to have longer (and less frequent) production runs, because they tend to produce lower annual costs chargeable to him, although larger inventories must be carried.

b. Thus, the performance-evaluation system must be designed so that the carrying costs are charged to the appropriate manager, even though not all such costs are recorded by the usual accounting system.

c. In general, the cost-benefit approach should be used in designing accounting and decision models, and accountants and managers must always be alert for important differences in motivations, results, and decisions arising from existing decision models and performance-evaluation models.

3. Some inventory costs are difficult to identify and to measure because they are *opportunity costs*, which ordinarily are not entered in conventional accounting records, for example:

a. Foregone quantity discounts,

b. Foregone contributions to profit from sales lost due to inventory shortages, and

c. Foregone fortuitous purchases because existing stock inhibits additional purchases.

4. Some inventory costs are not relevant to inventory planning and control decisions because they would be unchanged under different alternatives (for example, fixed rent or depreciation of warehouse).

E. The second key factor in applying inventory policy is the determination of the *reorder point*, the quantity level that automatically triggers a new order.

1. The inventory reorder point depends on several factors, which are graphed in Exhibit 14-3:

a. The *economic order quantity* was described above.

b. The *lead time* is the time interval between placing an order and receiving delivery.

c. The *demand during lead time* is the expected average usage during lead time.

d. The *safety stock* is the estimated minimum inventory quantity needed as a buffer or cushion against reasonable expected maximum usage.

2. The inventory reorder point is commonly computed as the safety stock plus expected average usage during lead time.

3. The optimum safety-stock level would minimize the total of two types of cost that are difficult to measure:

a. *Inventory carrying costs* include interest on investment, warehousing costs, and losses due to deterioration and obsolescence.

b. *Stockout costs* are costs of not carrying the inventory: expediting expenses and the costs of losing orders because of lack of inventory (loss of contribution margins and customer good will).

4. Exhibit 14-4 shows how the optimum safety stock can be estimated with the aid of probability measures of expected inventory usage.

F. When a huge number of different inventory items must be stocked, certain control techniques may be appropriate.

1. Physical methods for initiating a reorder of materials include the two-bin system, a red line to indicate the reorder level, and the special package method.

2. *The ABC approach* divides all inventory items into three classes based upon their *total consumption costs* (average usage for each item multiplied by the purchase price per unit).

a. Class A items have the highest consumption costs and therefore justify the closest control: frequent ordering, low safety stocks, and special attention in placing and following up orders.

b. Class C items have the lowest consumption costs and therefore justify less frequent ordering, higher safety stocks, and less paper work.

G. Inventory control is interdependent with production planning and requires systematic procedures for division of duties and handling of documents.

1. Although inventory control systems are being increasingly automated, human judgment is always needed when models must be revised to accommodate changing conditions.

2. The basic rules for internal control systems should always be observed; for example, the separation of recordkeeping duties from material-handling duties.

3. An example of systematic procedures for handling business documents is provided by Exhibit 14-6, which shows the paperwork routine for purchasing and receiving materials.

H. When identical material units are acquired at different times and prices, alternative methods are available for valuing inventories.

1. Essentially, these methods rest upon assumptions concerning the *sequence of cost flows*; that is, the method chosen directly affects the *timing* of the transfer of costs from inventory to expenses (costs of goods used or sold).

2. The *first-in, first-out method (FIFO)* assumes that the cost of the earliest-acquired stock is used first, whereas the *last-in, last-out method (LIFO)* makes the opposite assumption.

3. As a result, FIFO leaves the inventory valuation nearer current replacement costs, but LIFO tends to match current costs more closely with current sales.

4. By the same token, FIFO tends to match old costs with current sales, whereas LIFO values the inventory on an old-cost basis.

5. Therefore, compared to LIFO, the use of FIFO tends to show higher inventory and net-income measurements during periods of rising prices and lower figures for these when prices are falling.

a. If prices are rising, LIFO shows less income than FIFO, and thus it tends to postpone the payment of income taxes.

b. The use of LIFO also permits management to influence net-income measurement by deciding on the timing of purchases.

6. The average-inventory methods tend to produce figures for inventories and net income that fall between those for FIFO and LIFO.

7. The use of currently attainable standard costs produces variances that isolate the effects of price changes for managerial use (unlike FIFO, LIFO, and the average methods).

a. This prevents price fluctuations from distorting management appraisals of efficiency.

b. The use of standard costs also emphasizes and measures the impact of some price changes on overall company results.

SELF-TEST AND PRACTICE EXERCISES

(A) For each of the following multiple-choice and true-false statements, select the single most appropriate answer and enter its identification letter in the space provided:

____ 1. Inventory control means: (a) minimizing errors in inventory measurements; (b) maximizing clerical accuracy in inventory documents and records; (c) minimizing inventory losses from fire and theft; (d) decreasing the chances for improper use of inventory; (e) determining and maintaining inventory investment at the optimum level.

____ 2. Inventories are cushions: (a) to absorb planning errors and unforeseen fluctuations in supply and demand; (b) to facilitate smooth production and marketing operations; (c) both of the above; (d) neither of the above.

____ 3. Costs that are usually relevant to the inventory decision include: (a) carrying costs; (b) acquisition costs; (c) both of the above; (d) neither of these.

____ 4. EOQ is the optimum: (a) level of inventory; (b) time to order; (c) purchase quantity.

____ 5. EOQ is the quantity that would minimize the annual inventory carrying cost: (a) true; (b) false.

____ 6. The optimum size of a material-purchase order is the size that would minimize the annual purchase-order cost: (a) true; (b) false.

____ 7. Small variations in cost estimates usually have: (a) significant effects on inventory decisions; (b) no effects on inventory decisions.

____ 8. A production manager would usually prefer: (a) short production runs; (b) long production runs.

____ 9. A decrease in available quantity discounts would tend to have the following effect on the economic order quantity: (a) increase; (b) no effect; (c) decrease.

____10. Examples of inventory costs that would usually not be relevant to inventory decisions include: (a) imputed interest on investment in inventories; (b) salaries of storekeepers and clerks; (c) both of the above; (d) neither of these.

____11. The inventory reorder point would tend to be increased by: (a) a decrease in the expected usage of material during lead time; (b) an increase in the expected usage of material during lead time; (c) neither of the above.

____12. The quantity of the safety stock plus average usage during lead time is equal to: (a) optimum inventory balance; (b) economic order quantity; (c) both of the above; (d) neither of the above.

____13. The optimum safety-stock level would minimize: (a) stockout costs; (b) inventory carrying costs; (c) the sum of the above; (d) the difference between (a) and (b).

____14. The "two-bin" inventory system is designed to: (a) identify responsibility for inventory; (b) signal reorder of inventory items; (c) both of the above; (d) neither of the above.

____15. When the "ABC method" is used for inventory control, the inventory items with the highest safety stocks would be: (a) type A; (b) type B; (c) type C.

____16. The increasing computerization of inventory control systems promises to eradicate completely the need for the use of human judgment in inventory control: (a) true; (b) false.

____17. Making choices between the FIFO and LIFO inventory methods will affect the transfer of: (a) specific inventory *units* to production or to customers; (b) inventory *costs* to production or sales; (c) both of the above; (d) neither of the above.

____18. Compared to the FIFO method, LIFO tends to: (a) leave the inventory valuation closer to current replacement costs; (b) match current costs more closely with current sales.

____19. During a period of rising prices, the use of the LIFO method, in comparison to FIFO, will tend to produce: (a) lower reported net income; (b) higher reported cost of goods sold; (c) both of the above; (d) neither of the above.

____20. The effects of price changes are automatically isolated for managerial use by: (a) the FIFO method; (b) the LIFO method; (c) the weighted-average method; (d) a standard-cost system.

(B) Complete each of the following statements:

1. The optimum level of inventory would minimize____
____.

2. The optimum size of a normal purchase order for replenishing materials is called________________
____.

3. The interval between placing an order and receiving delivery is called____________________________.

4. The estimated minimum inventory quantity needed as a buffer or cushion against reasonable expected maximum usage is called____________________
____.

5. In general the inventory reorder point is the sum of
____
________________and________________
____________.

6. The "ABC method" ranks inventory items in
____
order of____________________________________
________________ and divides all the items into
________________groups.

7. During a period of rising prices, the use of the average method of costing inventories would tend to produce inventory costs above ______ cost and below ____ cost.

(C) Given for Material AOK of Precision Puzzle Company:

Total annual requirements	3,000 units
Carrying costs per unit per year	$5
Costs per purchase order	$300
Inventory level when each order arrives	zero

1. Using the form below, compute the total costs associated with ordering one, two, five, ten, and twenty times per year:

Number of orders per year	One	Two	Five	Ten	Twenty
Order size					
Average inventory in units					
Annual carrying cost					
Annual purchase-order cost					
Total annual relevant costs					

2. Check one blank for least-cost order size ____ ____ ____ ____ ____

3. Using the formula, compute the economic order quantity (EOQ):

4. Using the formula, compute the total annual relevant costs:

(D) Given for Material PDQ of Enigma, Incorporated:

Maximum daily usage	80 units
Average daily usage	70 units
Minimum daily usage	60 units
Lead time	22 days

1. Compute the safety stock ________ units

2. Determine the reorder point ________ units

(E) Given for Material RPM of Acceleration Manufacturing Company:

April 1 inventory: 40 units at $20 cost each	$800
Purchases:	
April 13, 50 units at $21 each	
April 20, 80 units at $22 each	
April 27, 30 units at $24 each	
April 30 inventory: 60 units	

Compute the following total costs:	FIFO	LIFO	Weighted Average
Cost of April 30 inventory	$_____	$_____	$_____
Cost of materials used in April	$_____	$_____	$_____
Total	$_____	$_____	$_____

Cost Allocation: An Introduction

15

Costs must often be assigned to such cost objectives as periods, processes, programs, products, departments, and divisions. This is an identification or tracing procedure that may be called cost allocation, apportionment, assignment, or distribution. Important purposes of cost allocation include predicting effects of decisions, determining income and asset valuations, arriving at a product price, and obtaining desired motivation.

Cost allocation is not a standard process that can be simply applied under all circumstances; it is a rather broad and complex matter that involves a variety of intriguing conceptual ideas and challenging implementation problems. This chapter serves as an introduction to some of the theoretical and practical aspects of cost allocation.

REVIEW SUMMARY

A. Let's look at the general approach to cost allocation.

1. There are three main facets to cost allocation:

a. Determining the *cost objective*; for example, products, processes, or departments, all of which represent *actions.*

b. Identifying and accumulating (*pooling*) the costs that pertain to the cost objective; for example, selected manufacturing and nonmanufacturing costs.

c. Choosing a *base* for allocating costs to objectives; for example, direct-labor hours or machine-hours.

2. Because it is often not practicable to use the ideal cost-allocation base that would relate cost to its most causal factor, the preferable cost-allocation base is one that *facilitates the prediction of changes* in total costs, one that *accurately depicts persistent relationships*, whether either the cost objective or the cost incurrence is regarded as cause or effect.

B. You should become familiar with some important cost-allocation terminology:

1. *Cost pools* are groupings of individual cost items to facilitate allocation, such as pools of factory service or producing-department costs, pools of fixed or variable costs, and pools of costs related to materials or people.

2. Cost objectives may be *intermediate,* such as a manufacturing department, or *final*, such as the finished product to which all manufacturing costs may eventually be allocated.

3. Costs may have a *direct relationship* to an intermediate cost objective but an *indirect relationship* to the final cost objective in the allocation process. (For example, a stores clerk's salary is directly related to the stores department, but indirectly related to the product.)

4. The key to cost allocation is the *cost-allocation base*, such as direct-labor hours or machine-hours, which can provide a systematic means for linking a given cost or cost pool with a cost objective.

C. Management planning and control can be aided by cost allocation.

1. *Dual allocation* of costs is usually appropriate; for example:

a. The *variable costs* of a service department would be allocated on the basis of the *actual short-term usage.*

b. The *fixed costs* of the same department would be allocated on the basis of the *long-term capacity to serve.*

2. *Full reallocation of actual costs* would have two basic faults:

a. The resultant charges of a service department's costs to an operating department would depend on the quantity of services consumed by *other* operating departments.

b. The amounts of service-department costs charged to operating departments would depend on factors *not directly subject to control* of the operating managers; for example, the efficiency of the service activities.

3. General guidelines for allocating costs include:

a. Use *flexible* budgets, not *static* budgets.

b. Distinguish between *variable* and *fixed* costs.

c. Allocate variable costs of services rendered with *predetermined* rates instead of *actual* rates.

d. Allocate fixed costs by assigning lump-sum amounts of *budgeted* costs of long-term capacity to serve, not portions of *actual* costs on the basis of actual consumption of services.

D. Often, cause-and-effect relationships cannot be readily identified for purposes of allocating individual costs:

1. The use of *sales dollars* as indicative of *ability to bear* costs would usually ignore cause-and-effect relationships and could lead to dangerously misleading reports of segment operating results.

2. When *fairness* or *equity* is specified as a criterion for allocating indirect costs, it is such a broad ethical standard that it does not really furnish any operational guidelines for allocating costs.

3. Some writers maintain that indirect costs should be assigned to operations and products according to the *relative benefits received*, but this criterion also seems not to be of any practical value to cost allocation.

E. *Motivation* should be a major criterion in designing systems for cost allocations.

1. Generally, it may be thought that cost allocations that reflect causal relationships are most likely to produce information leading to optimum decisions.

2. However, there is much controversy concerning the ways to apply this concept and the motivational effects of various cost-allocation ideas and methods.

3. For example, some accountants and managers favor the *full allocation* of costs so that all managers will become more aware of the costs incurred and benefits offered by other parts of the organization.

4. However, others maintain that such costs as central corporate costs should *not be allocated at all*, because there is no measurable cause-and-effect relationship and managers would have no direct influence over the amounts allocated to their departments.

SELF-TEST AND PRACTICE EXERCISES

(A) For each of the following multiple-choice and true-false statements, select the single most appropriate answer and enter its identification letter in the space provided:

____ 1. An example of a cost objective would include: (a) direct materials purchased; (b) finished products; (c) both of the above; (d) neither of the above.

____ 2. A cost pool is a collection of: (a) cost objectives; (b) costs that have been allocated to a cost objective; (c) costs that are to be allocated to several cost objectives.

____ 3. The preferable cost-allocation base is one that facilitates the prediction of changes in total costs: (a) true; (b) false.

____ 4. Lubricants used in a manufacturing department serve as an example of costs *directly* related to: (a) the department; (b) the product being manufactured; (c) both of the above; (d) neither of the above.

____ 5. The key to cost allocation is: (a) determining cost objectives; (b) pooling costs; (c) selecting the cost-allocation base.

____ 6. *Variable costs* of a service department are best allocated to operating departments on the basis of: (a) actual short-term usage based on *predetermined* rates; (b) actual short-term usage based on *actual* rates; (c) the service department's *budgeted costs* of long-term capacity to serve; (d) the service department's *actual costs* on the basis of actual consumption of services.

____ 7. *Fixed costs* of service departments are best allocated to operating departments on the basis of: (a) actual short-term usage based on *predetermined* rates; (b) actual short-term usage based on *actual* rates; (c) the service department's *budgeted costs* of long-term capacity to serve; (d) the service department's *actual costs* on the basis of actual consumption of services.

____ 8. If a service department's actual costs were fully reallocated to operating departments: (a) the charges to a particular department would be affected by the quantity of services consumed by other operating departments; (b) the charges would be affected by factors not directly subject to the control of the operating managers; (c) both of the above; (d) neither of the above.

____ 9. It is usually feasible and reasonable to allocate most costs to segments of an organization on the basis of dollar sales: (a) true; (b) false.

____ 10. Fairness and equity are usually: (a) broad ethical standards; (b) operational guidelines for allocating costs; (c) both of the above; (d) neither of the above.

____ 11. Relative benefits received are usually of practical value as a basis for allocating indirect costs to operations and products: (a) true; (b) false.

____ 12. Some accountants and managers feel that: (a) full allocation of costs will help all managers become more aware of the costs incurred and benefits offered by other segments of an organization; (b) some central costs should not be allocated at all; (c) both of the above; (d) neither of the above.

____ 13. The major criterion in designing systems for cost allocations should be: (a) accuracy; (b) expediency; (c) motivation; (d) income tax effects.

(B) Complete each of the following statements:

1. The preferable cost-allocation base is one that accurately depicts ____________.

2. Costs may have a direct relationship to ____________ ____________ cost objective, but an indirect relationship to ____________ cost objective.

3. A systematic means for connecting costs with cost objectives is called ____________.

4. In allocating the costs of such services as repairs and computers, it would be more accurate to use, instead of a single basis, one basis for the ____________ ____________ cost element and another basis for the ____________ cost element.

5. In order to prevent the charges to a specific operating department from depending on the quantity of services consumed by other operating departments, a ____________ rate should be used for charging service-department costs.

6. The use of sales dollars as a basis for allocating indirect costs to operations and products ignores ____________ relationships and could lead to ____________ reports of segment operations.

(C) Desert Products Company's power plant provides electricity for its two producing departments, A and B. The 19_6 budget for the power plant shows:

Budgeted fixed costs	$80,000
Budgeted variable costs per kilowatt-hour (KWH)	$ .05

Additional data for 19_6:

	Long-Run Demand (KWH)	Budgeted for 19_6 (KWH)	Actual for 19_6 (KWH)
Producing Dept. A	300,000	250,000	230,000
Producing Dept. B	200,000	180,000	190,000

Actual power plant costs for 19_6 are :

Fixed costs	$81,000
Variable costs	$22,000

Compute the 19_6 allocation of power plant costs to A and B:	Dept. A	Dept. B
1. Fixed costs	$______	$______
2. Variable costs	$______	$______

A Closer Look at Cost Allocation

16

This chapter continues our study of cost allocation introduced in the preceding chapter. Here we examine some important practical applications that illustrate how cost allocation can be used to help management evaluate the performance of individual segments of an organization and make better-informed decisions for planning and controlling all operations.

Four main topics are included: the contribution approach to cost allocation, service-department cost allocation, determining the number of cost pools, and choosing cost-allocation bases.

REVIEW SUMMARY

A. A useful framework for understanding and applying cost-allocation principles is provided by the *contribution approach*, as illustrated by a key example in the textbook, Exhibit 16-1, a model income statement by segments.

1. In addition to responsibility centers and products, cost objectives may include segments of the organization such as divisions, sections, or product lines.

2. A cost-contribution approach by segments can be valuable because it emphasizes the cost behavior patterns that are generally useful for evaluating performance and making decisions.

3. If a cost cannot be allocated to certain segments on a meaningful basis, it should be included in the income statement and be clearly identified as unallocated with respect to those segments.

4. The *segmented contribution margins* (excess of revenues over allocable variable costs) are helpful in predicting the impact on income of short-run changes in volume.

5. The *contribution controllable by segment managers* may be computed as the excess of the divisional contribution margins over the fixed costs controllable by division managers (discretionary fixed costs), but the performance of a division (or other segment) as an economic investment is measured only after a further deduction for allocable fixed costs controlled by others.

6. Although the nonsegmented figure for income before income taxes may be helpful in estimating the long-run earning power of the entire company, it could be quite misleading in many cases to use some arbitrary basis for breaking it down into segment figures.

B. The factory-overhead costs that are allocated to service departments must be reallocated to producing departments so that the combined overhead of service and producing departments may then be applied by predetermined rates to the products that flow through the producing departments.

1. The most widely used reallocation method is the *direct method*, which reallocates each service department's total costs directly to producing departments, thus ignoring services rendered to other service departments. See Exhibit 16-2.

2. A widely used reallocation method is the *step method*, which reallocates costs of service departments to both producing and service departments.

a. The sequence of reallocation usually begins with the service to the greatest number of other service departments and progresses in descending order to the one rendering service to the least number of other departments.

b. Once a service department's costs have been reallocated, no subsequent service-department costs are recirculated back to it.

c. Exhibit 16-3 in the textbook illustrates the scheduling and computation techniques for the step method. The exhibit also shows the computation of predetermined rates for applying overhead costs from producing departments to products.

3. The most accurate overhead-reallocation method would recognize *reciprocal services* among service departments, and this approach can be facilitated by the use of linear algebra. See Exhibit 16-4.

C. Because it is often not feasible to allocate individual cost items directly to cost objectives, they are usually aggregated or pooled to produce an average cost-allocation rate.

1. If an average rate produces the same cost allocations as produced by the individual rates, such average rate is said to be *perfectly homogeneous.*

2. An average plant-wide rate for applying factory-overhead costs to jobs could be quite inaccurate compared to the more homogeneous departmental overhead rates, as demonstrated in Exhibit 16-5.

3. Lack of a sufficient degree of homogeneity in cost-allocation rates could be caused by combining costs with different purposes to obtain a numerator or by using a denominator that has no direct causal relationship to the costs being allocated.

4. In order to achieve a reasonable degree of accuracy on a feasible basis, three intermediate aggregations or poolings of costs have been suggested:

a. Responsibility centers (departments)

b. Fixed- and variable-cost groups

c. Functionally oriented classes of costs (people, payroll, materials, machines, etc.)

5. Cost-allocation results can also be improved by choosing appropriate rate bases for different kinds of overhead costs.

6. General guidelines regarding homogeneity include:

a. Begin with the most detailed cost data that are economically feasible to collect.

b. Start to form cost pools only if they are justified by savings in clerical and other costs.

c. To achieve better homogeneity, establish additional cost pools.

D. In practice, attempts are made to apply each pool of factory-overhead costs to products by using an appropriate allocation base.

1. The choice of bases for allocating pools of factory-overhead costs should depend on the factors obviously associated with individual jobs or products, related clerical costs, and the differences in final results.

2. Four bases are widely used as denominators in calculating rates for applying factory-overhead costs to products.

a. Direct-labor hours result in the application of overhead on a time-expiration basis, the factor to which most overhead costs are most closely related.

b. Machine-hours may be a more accurate base than direct-labor hours if overhead costs result largely from the use of machines instead of people.

c. Direct-labor cost rates would produce about the same results as direct-labor hour rates when wage rates are fairly uniform for each type of labor.

d. Direct-material cost or quantity would not usually be valid for rate bases except for factory-overhead costs associated with material storage and handling.

SELF-TEST AND PRACTICE EXERCISES

(A) For each of the following multiple-choice and true-false statements, select the single most appropriate answer and enter its identification letter in the space provided:

____ 1. The contribution margin by segments is the excess of net sales over: (a) variable cost of sales and variable selling and administrative expenses by segments; (b) allocable fixed costs controllable by segment managers; (c) both of the above; (d) neither of the above.

____ 2. If a cost cannot be allocated to certain segments on a meaningful basis, it should be: (a) excluded from the income statement; (b) allocated to segments on the basis of segment sales; (c) clearly identified as unallocated with respect to those segments.

____ 3. Most helpful in predicting the impact on income of short-run changes in volume is: (a) contribution margin; (b) contribution controllable by division managers; (c) contribution by segments; (d) income before income taxes.

____ 4. The performance of a division as an economic investment is best measured by: (a) income before income taxes; (b) income after income taxes; (c) contribution margin; (d) contribution margin less fixed costs controllable by division managers; (e) contribution controllable by division managers less allocable fixed costs controllable by others.

____ 5. It is usually quite helpful for management planning and control purposes to show in a segmented income statement the income of each segment before income taxes: (a) true; (b) false.

____ 6. Discretionary fixed costs controllable by division managers would ordinarily include: (a) sales promotion; (b) management consulting; (c) both of the above; (d) neither of the above.

____ 7. The most widely used method for reallocating service-department costs to producing departments is: (a) the reciprocal method; (b) the step method; (c) the direct method.

____ 8. The step method reallocates costs of service departments to: (a) other service departments; (b) producing departments; (c) both service and producing departments.

____ 9. Once a service department's costs have been reallocated by the step method, no other service-department costs are to be charged back to it: (a) true; (b) false.

____ 10. The most accurate overhead-reallocation method is: (a) the direct method; (b) the step method; (c) the reciprocal method.

____ 11. In the application of factory-overhead costs to jobs, the more accurate rates would be: (a) departmental overhead rates; (b) plant-wide rates.

____ 12. Higher homogeneity of cost-allocation rates may be achieved by: (a) increasing the number of cost pools; (b) decreasing the number of cost pools.

____ 13. In the application of factory-overhead costs to products, the two rate bases that are most fundamentally related to the cause of most overhead costs are: (a) direct-labor cost and direct-material cost; (b) direct-labor hours and direct-material quantity; (c) machine-hours and physical units produced; (d) physical units produced and direct-material quantity; (e) direct-labor hours and machine-hours.

(B) Complete each of the following statements:

1. The contribution controllable by division managers is the excess of the ____________ margin over the fixed ____________________________________.

2. The contribution by segments is the excess of the contribution ____________________________ over the allocable fixed costs ____________________.

3. In the step method of cost allocation, the sequence usually begins with the service department that renders service to the ____________ number of other service departments and progresses in descending order to the one rendering service to the ________ number of other departments.

4. If an average rate for applying cost pools to cost objects produces the same cost allocations as produced by separate rates for individual cost items, the average rate is said to be "perfectly ____________."

5. In the application of factory-overhead costs to products, the two bases that would produce about the same results are ____________________ and ____________________.

(C) From the following data for General Omnibus Company, prepare a contribution-approach income statement by segments:

(In thousands)	Company Total	Alpha Division	Omega Division
Net sales	$900	$500	$400
Fixed costs:			
Controllable by division managers	140	60	80
Controllable by others	70	30	40
Variable costs:			
Manufacturing cost of sales	450	300	150
Selling and administrative expenses	130	60	70
Unallocated costs	75	–	–

(D) From the following data for Easy Escalator Corporation, use the step method to prepare a budget schedule showing the reallocation of factory-overhead costs to production departments and the computation of predetermined direct-labor hour rates for applying overhead to products:

(In thousands)	Service Departments			Production Departments		
	A	B	C	X	Y	Z
Overhead costs before reallocation	300	210	240	160	110	105
Proportions of service to be furnished by:						
Department A to other departments	–	10%	20%	30%	15%	25%
Department B to other departments	20%	–	10%	30%	10%	30%
Department C to other departments	–	10%	–	30%	30%	30%
Total direct-labor hours	–	–	–	300	100	190

(In thousands)	Service Departments			Production Departments		
	A	B	C	X	Y	Z
Overhead costs before reallocation						

Joint-Product Costs and By-Product Costs

17

There are many manufacturing processes that produce two or more products from a single raw material; for example, petroleum refining, meat-packing, flour milling, and copper mining. The output from such processes may be called joint products or by-products. These multiple-product situations create the accounting problem of allocating to the individual products the direct-material costs and other manufacturing costs incurred prior to the point at which the separate products can be identified.

Various ways for allocating such prior costs to the different products are examined in this chapter. However, the idea emphasized here is that any method for assigning prior costs to joint products and by-products is useful *only for purposes of product costing*. Such cost assignments are useless for management decision, planning, or control purposes.

REVIEW SUMMARY

A. When two or more individual products are simultaneously produced, with each product having significant relative sales values, the outputs are usually called *joint products.*

1. The *split-off point* is the stage of production at which the different individual products can be identified.

2. *Joint costs* include all manufacturing costs incurred prior to the split-off point.

B. For the purposes of product costing, several methods are used for allocating joint costs to the different units produced.

1. Joint costs may be allocated to products on the basis of *physical measures* at the split-off point; for example: pounds, gallons, yards.

a. However, this basis ignores the revenue-producing properties of the separate products, which could vary widely in unit values at the split-off point.

b. As a result, the physical-measures method of allocation could show unrealistically large profits for some joint products while showing unrealistically large losses for others.

2. Joint costs may be allocated to products on the basis of their *net realizable values.*

a. If there are zero costs of completion and disposal because all products are sold upon split-off at no incremental costs, the net realizable values would simply be their sales values: the quantities multiplied by unit selling prices at the split-off point.

b. If there is no market for joint products at the split-off point and they must be further processed individually before they are salable, their sales values at the split-off point may be *approximated* by deducting costs beyond that point from their respective expected sales values on a fully processed basis.

c. The allocation of joint costs on the basis of net realizable values implicitly recognizes the different abilities of joint products to generate revenue.

d. In effect, this method allocates costs in proportion to a product's ability to absorb the costs, and as a result, all end products usually show some profit margin under typical marketing conditions.

e. However, such allocated costs are useful *only for product-costing purposes* and should not be used for sell-or-process-further decisions, for judging the performance of either the joint or the separable processes, or for product-pricing decisions.

3. Some companies ignore the joint-cost allocation approach and carry their joint-product inventories on a *non-cost basis.*

a. The use of *net realizable values* (ultimate sales values less estimated separable costs to complete and sell) results in the recognition of profit before sales are made, which is not a generally acceptable accounting concept.

b. The use of *net realizable values less normal profit margins* avoids the criticism of profit recognition before the goods are sold.

C. The allocation of joint costs to different products is useful *only for purposes of product costing.*

1. When a product is an inherent result of a joint process, the decision to process further should not be influenced by either the size of the total joint costs or the portions of the joint costs assigned to particular products.

2. The only costs that are relevant to further processing decisions are the costs *beyond* the split off point.

a. Such costs are the incremental costs, including implicit costs (opportunity costs) as well as explicit costs.

b. It is profitable to process beyond the split-off point if these incremental costs are exceeded by the incremental revenue produced by such processing.

3. Product-pricing decisions should not be influenced by allocation of joint costs.

a. Circular reasoning would be involved: prices used to set costs, and costs used to set prices.

b. As an example, the textbook pointed out the distorting effects on natural gas prices (page 556).

D. *By-products* are products with relatively minor sales value that are simultaneously produced in the manufacture of the main product(s).

1. In general, by-products have relatively more sales value than *scrap materials* and are often processed beyond the split-off point.

2. The basic accounting for both by-products and scrap materials is the same; two leading methods are described.

3. As illustrated by textbook Exhibit 17-2, both methods recognize that by-products reduce the cost of the major products—and they show the same net income over a period that has no beginning or ending inventories.

4. In the first method, the net revenue from the by-product *sold* is deducted from the cost of the major product(s) *sold.*

a. Unsold by-product is inventoried at zero value.

b. This method has practical appeal, but conceptually it fails to match the value of the by-product with the cost of the major related products.

5. In the second method, the net realizable value of the by-product *produced* is deducted from the cost of the major product(s) *produced.*

a. The by-product inventory is carried forward at net realizable value (plus separable manufacturing costs incurred, if any).

b. This method is more precise about the timing of the cost reductions from the major related products.

6. When by-products are used internally as fuel or materials, they are frequently accounted for at net realizable values or replacement values, the cost of the main product being reduced by such values.

7. In the petroleum industry, many products are produced.

a. Gasoline is viewed as the sole major product for product-mix decisions even though a by-product method may not be followed for costing the inventories of all the other products.

b. Linear programming models are used to determine the optimal product mix between the by-products and gasoline.

SELF-TEST AND PRACTICE EXERCISES

(A) For each of the following multiple-choice and true-false statements, select the single most appropriate answer and enter its identification letter in the space provided:

___ 1. Joint products are: (a) two or more products that are combined to make one finished product; (b) a finished product that is made jointly by two or more companies or divisions of a company; (c) products that can be used for more than one purpose; (d) none of the above.

___ 2. Ordinarily, joint costs include: (a) direct-material costs; (b) direct-labor costs; (c) indirect manufacturing costs; (d) all of the above; (e) none of the above.

___ 3. The allocation of joint costs to products is useless for: (a) cost-planning and control purposes; (b) product-costing purposes; (c) both of the above; (d) neither of the above.

___ 4. Joint costs are incurred after the split-off point: (a) true; (b) false.

___ 5. For cost-planning and control purposes, it is useful to identify processing costs after the split-off point with units produced: (a) true; (b) false.

___ 6. Unrealistically large profits for some joint products and unrealistically large losses for others would most likely be shown by: (a) the use of net realizable values for joint products; (b) allocating joint costs on the basis of relative sales values at the split-off point; (c) allocating joint costs on the basis of physical measures at the split-off point.

___ 7. The different abilities of joint products to produce revenue would be recognized by allocating joint costs on the basis of: (a) physical measures; (b) net realizable values; (c) both of the above; (d) neither of the above.

___ 8. The most widely used basis for allocating joint costs to products is relative: (a) physical measures; (b) net realizable values; (c) further processing costs; (d) gross profit; (e) net profit.

___ 9. The recognition of profit before the goods are sold results from carrying joint-product inventories on the basis of: (a) net realizable values; (b) net realizable values less normal profit margins; (c) both of the above; (d) neither of the above.

___ 10. Using selling prices or variations thereof as bases for inventory valuation would have a greater degree of justification when: (a) inventory turnover is high; (b) differences between costs and selling prices are small; (c) both of the above; (d) neither of the above.

___ 11. When a product is an inherent result of a joint process, the decision to process further should be influenced partly by: (a) the size of the total joint costs; (b) the portions of the joint costs allocated to particular products; (c) both of the above; (d) neither of the above.

___ 12. The costs beyond the split-off point that are relevant to further processing decisions include: (a) opportunity costs (implicit costs); (b) explicit costs; (c) both of the above; (d) neither of the above.

___ 13. In making managerial decisions regarding whether a joint product should be sold or processed further, it is useful to compare the incremental costs of further processing with: (a) the incremental revenue derived from such processing; (b) the net sales value at split-off point; (c) the net sales value after further processing; (d) none of the above.

___ 14. The allocations of joint costs to products can generally be useful in making valid product-pricing decisions: (a) true; (b) false.

___ 15. In general, by-products: (a) are often processed beyond the split-off point; (b) have relatively less sales value than scrap materials; (c) both of the above; (d) neither of the above.

___ 16. The accounting for scrap materials and by-products is basically the same: (a) true; (b) false.

___ 17. When the net revenue from by-product sold is deducted from the cost of the major product sold, the unsold by-product is inventoried at: (a) zero value; (b) net realizable value.

___ 18. Conceptually, the better of the two leading methods of accounting for by-products is to treat the net realizable values of by-products produced as deductions from production costs: (a) true; (b) false.

___ 19. Expediency is usually a major factor influencing the selection of the by-product accounting method: (a) true; (b) false.

(B) Complete each of the following statements:

1. When two or more individual products are simultaneously produced, with each product having significant relative sales values, the outputs are usually called ____________________.

2. The split-off point is defined as ____________________ ____________________ ____________________.

3. When joint costs are allocated to products on the basis of physical measures at the split-off point, this basis ignores ____________________ .

4. A uniform gross-margin percentage would tend to be produced for joint products if the ____________________ approach for allocation of joint costs were used.

5. If there is no market for joint products at the split-off point and they must be further processed individually before they are salable, their approximate sales values at the split-off point may be estimated by deducting ____________________ from the ____________________ .

6. The allocation of joint costs to different products is useful only for purposes of ____________________ .

7. The only costs that are relevant to further processing decisions are ____________________ .

8. Products with relatively minor sales value that are simultaneously produced in the manufacture of the main product(s) are called ____________________ .

(C) The Steer Wheeling Corporation produced the following two products from a joint process at a joint cost of $4,000:

	Product REV	Product ROL
Quantities produced and processed beyond split-off point	150 yd	300 yd
Total processing costs beyond split-off point	$1,500	$1,500
Unit selling prices of completely processed products	$ 40	$ 10

1. Compute the amount of joint costs allocated to each of the products by using selling prices and processing costs beyond the split-off point and working back to find approximate sales values at split-off for use in allocating joint costs.

2. On the basis of your allocation of joint costs, determine the gross profit that would be realized from Product REV sales, Product ROL sales, and total sales.

3. If the selling prices *at the split-off point* were known to be $32 per yard for Product REV and $4 per yard for Product ROL, what would your decisions be regarding further processing of each product? Show supporting calculations.

4. On the basis of your further processing decisions, determine the total gross profit that would be realize *total* sales.

5. Would the allocation of joint costs be relevant to your further processing decisions? Why?

(D) The N. C. Dental Products Company presents the following data:

Gross production costs of main product and by-product	$50,000
Total sales of main product	$75,000
Net realizable value of by-product produced (including ending inventory of by-product)	$ 2,000
Beginning inventories	none
Ending inventory of main product is 10% of production.	

Determine the gross margin on sales of main product by using Method Two of accounting for by-products.

Process Costing: A Type of Product Costing

18

When there is a continuous mass production of like product units, process-costing methods are appropriate for product-costing purposes. This chapter covers three widely used unit-cost computation techniques: the weighted-average method, the first-in, first-out method, and the standard-cost approach. The key to these calculations is the concept of equivalent units produced, which is the measure of the amount of work done in a manufacturing process.

Although you can gain a general understanding of process-costing concepts and methods by merely studying the explanations and examples in the textbook, you can obtain a useful working knowledge of such concepts and methods only by also thoughtfully solving several problems. For this activity, the chapter exhibits provide helpful models that should be followed carefully, step by step, before you attempt to solve the assigned textbook problems and the problems in this student guide.

REVIEW SUMMARY

A. Process costing, like all product costing, is an *averaging process.*

a. Basically, average unit costs for each process are calculated by dividing cost totals by the number of units processed.

2. The key concept is *equivalent units produced.*

a. This measures the amount of work done by each process in terms of units fully processed by it during a given period.

b. Equivalent units are divided into the appropriate cost totals of each process to arrive at unit costs within the process for a given period.

c. Textbook Exhibits 18-1 and 18-4 illustrate the computation of equivalent units when there is a beginning inventory in process. You should study these two exhibits very carefully, because a thorough understanding of them is absolutely essential to your success in applying the main concepts presented in this chapter.

3. A systematic approach that is helpful in making process-cost calculations involves five steps:

a. Summarize in terms of units the *physical quantities* of production inflows and outflows.

b. Compute equivalent units of production.

c. Summarize the total costs to be accounted for.

d. Choose a *cost-flow assumption* and compute the appropriate unit costs.

e. Use these unit costs to compute and reconcile the total costs of goods completed and work in process.

4. When goods are transferred out of a manufacturing process, their total cost is credited to that process (a departmental work-in-process control account) and is debited to the next process or to the finished-goods control account.

B. Three alternative *cost-flow assumptions* are available for computing unit costs: weighted-average; first-in, first-out (FIFO); and standard costing.

1. The *weighted-average method* treats the beginning inventory of work in process as though it were begun and finished during the current period, as illustrated in Exhibits 18-2 and 18-5.

a. Beginning-inventory costs for each type of cost are mingled with the respective current costs. These costs include *transferred-in costs* (or *previous-department costs*), as well as the present department's costs of material, labor, and overhead.

b. Therefore, the *divisor* for computing unit costs is the *total work done*; that is, the equivalent units that include the previous work on the beginning inventory as well as the current work.

c. Thus, monthly unit costs actually represent *weighted averages* of beginning-inventory costs and current costs.

2. The *first-in, first-out method* treats the beginning inventory of work in process as though it were a batch of goods separate and distinct from goods started and finished by a process within the same period, as illustrated in Exhibits 18-3 and 18-6.

a. Thus, in contrast to the weighted-average method, beginning-inventory costs are *not* mingled with current costs.

b. Therefore, the *divisor* for computing unit costs includes only the *new equivalent units* for the current period and *not* the equivalent units of work done on the beginning inventory in previous periods.

c. As a result, monthly unit costs represent only the work that was actually done during the *current period.*

d. However, when costs are transferred out of one process to the next process or to finished-goods inventory, a *single unit cost* is used that is a weighted average of beginning-inventory costs and currently incurred costs.

3. Generally, the weighted-average and FIFO methods arrive at about the same product costs.

a. However, if material prices are volatile, there may be significant differences in results between these two methods.

b. For purposes of cost control, neither of the methods is as effective as standard process costing.

C. Instead of actual costs, *standard costs* may be used for product-costing purposes, as illustrated in Exhibit 18-7.

1. The standard cost is the predetermined cost per equivalent unit.

2. Thus, when standard costs are used, the process-cost calculations are relatively much simpler than those of the weighted-average and first-in, first-out methods.

a. The standard cost of goods completed is the actual quantity completed multiplied by the standard cost per unit.

b. The standard cost of ending goods in process is determined by multiplying the equivalent units for each cost element by the respective standard cost per unit.

3. Standard costing of production is especially useful where there are numerous combinations of materials, operations, and product sizes, as in steel mills, textile manufacturing, and paint production.

4. In addition, a standard-costing approach facilitates management control.

SELF-TEST AND PRACTICE EXERCISES

(A) For each of the following multiple-choice and true-false statements, select the single most appropriate answer and enter its identification letter in the space provided:

___ 1. A product-costing system that is appropriate for dealing with individual batches of products, each receiving different degrees of attention and skill, is: (a) the job-order system; (b) the process-cost system.

___ 2. Product costing is an averaging process: (a) when a process-costing system is used; (b) when a job-order system is used; (c) both of the above; (d) neither of the above.

___ 3. Typically, the number of equivalent units produced for a given period is calculated to measure: (a) the actual number of product units completed and transferred out of a process; (b) the estimated amount of work done by a process in terms of product units fully processed by it; (c) the number of product units that could have been finished by a process under optimum conditions.

___ 4. In process-cost calculations, the cost of the ending inventory of work in process is calculated: (a) before the computation of equivalent units; (b) after the computation of equivalent units.

___ 5. The unit-cost method that treats the beginning inventory of work in process as though it were begun and finished during the current period is: (a) weighted average; (b) first-in, first-out; (c) both of the above; (d) neither of the above.

___ 6. Beginning inventory costs are mingled with current costs in making unit-cost calculations by the weighted-average method: (a) true; (b) false.

___ 7. When the FIFO unit-cost method is used, the divisor for computing unit costs for a period should exclude the equivalent units for work done on the beginning inventory in previous periods: (a) true; (b) false.

___ 8. Monthly unit costs represent only the work that was actually done during the current period, if the unit costs are calculated by: (a) the weighted-average method; (b) the first-in, first-out method; (c) both of the above; (d) neither of the above.

___ 9. When costs are transferred into a process from the preceding process, a single unit cost is used if unit costs are computed by: (a) the weighted-average method; (b) the first-in, first-out method; (c) either of the above; (d) neither of the above.

___ 10. In general, about the same product costs are determined by the weighted-average and first-in, first-out methods: (a) true; (b) false.

___ 11. For cost-control purposes, the standard process-costing method is generally superior to: (a) the weighted-average method; (b) the first-in, first-out method; (c) both of the above; (d) neither of the above.

___ 12. When standard costs are used in process-type operations, product costing is relatively more complex than when the weighted-average or first-in, first-out method is used: (a) true; (b) false.

___ 13. When standard costs are used in process-type operations, equivalent units need not be used: (a) true; (b) false.

(B) Complete each of the following statements:

1. When there is a continuous, mass production of like product units, ____________________ methods are appropriate for product-costing purposes.

2. The key concept in process-costing calculations is ____________________.

3. For goods that are transferred out of the *final* manufacturing process or production step, an entry should be made debiting ____________________ and crediting ____________________ ____________________.

4. When there are beginning inventories in a process and actual costs are to be used instead of standard costs, the two alternative unit-cost methods that are available are ____________________ method and ____________________ method.

5. The unit-cost method that is conceptually closer to the job-order costing method is ____________________ ____________________.

6. Where there are numerous combinations of materials, operations, and product sizes, a process-costing method that is especially useful is ____________________ ____________________.

(C) Given for the EQ manufacturing process for November:

	Units
Inventory in process, November 1, 70% completed	200
Transferred into process in November	700
Completed and transferred out of process in November	600
Inventory in process, November 30, 60% completed	300

Materials are added at the beginning of the process.

1. Find the equivalent units for computing unit costs by the *weighted-average* method:

Material Costs	Conversion Costs

2. Find the equivalent units for computing unit costs by the *first-in, first-out* method:

Material Costs	Conversion Costs

(D) Given for the WA manufacturing process for January:

Inventory in process, January 1, 40% completed	300 units
Transferred into process in January	600 units
Completed and transferred out of process in January	700 units
Inventory in process, January 31, 50% completed	200 units
January 1 inventory costs:	
Transferred-in costs	\$3,000
Conversion costs	\$2,000
Current costs charged in January:	
Transferred-in costs	\$5,100
Conversion costs	\$3,600

No materials are added in this process.

Using the *weighted-average* unit-cost method, calculate the cost of work transferred out in January and the cost of the January 31 inventory of work in process:

Step 1—Units of Physical Flow

Step 2–Equivalent Units

	Transferred-in Costs	Conversion Costs

Step 3–Summary of Total Costs to Account for

	Transferred-in Costs	Conversion Costs	Total Costs

Step 4–Unit Costs

	Transferred-in Costs	Conversion Costs	Total Costs

Step 5–Total Costs of Work Completed and in Process

(E) Given for the FI manufacturing process for February:

Inventory in process, February 1, 75% completed	200 units
Transferred into process in February	600 units
Completed and transferred out of process in February	500 units
Inventory in process, February 28, 50% completed	300 units
February 1 inventory costs:	
Transferred-in costs	$2,200
Conversion costs	$1,300
Current costs charged in February:	
Transferred-in costs	$6,000
Conversion costs	$4,000

No materials are added in this process.

Using the *first-in, first-out* unit-cost method, calculate the cost of work transferred out in February and the cost of the February 28 inventory of work in process:

Step 1—Units of Physical Flow

Step 2—Equivalent Units	Transferred-in Costs	Conversion Costs

Step 3–Summary of Total Costs to Account for

	Transferred-in Costs	Conversion Costs	Total Costs

Step 4–Unit Costs

	Transferred-in Costs	Conversion Costs	Total Costs

Step 5–Total Costs of Work Completed and in Process

Spoilage, Waste, Defective Units, and Scrap

19

In almost every manufacturing operation, there are some outputs that either do not meet established production standards or otherwise appear in some undesirable form or state. Such outputs may be called spoilage, waste, defective units, or scrap. This chapter describes them, emphasizing the accounting implications of the distinction between the normal and the abnormal causes of these outputs.

Specifically, we examine various conceptual and practical ways of accounting for spoilage, waste, defective units, and scrap—both for management control purposes and for product-costing purposes. Various techniques appropriate for process, job-order, and standard costing systems are explained and demonstrated. Particularly helpful in quickly gaining a useful perspective of some key relationships are textbook Exhibit 19-1 and the summary of job-order journal entries on page 617.

REVIEW SUMMARY

A. Although some of the terms and accounting procedures in this area are often vague and inconsistent, we recognize certain basic definitions:

1. *Spoilage* is production that falls below quality or dimensional standards and is sold for *disposal value*, or *salvage value.*

2. *Net spoilage cost* is the excess of costs accumulated to the point of rejection over the disposal value of the spoiled goods.

3. *Defective units* are substandard outputs that are feasible to rework and sell as firsts or seconds.

4. *Waste* is manufacturing residue that has no measurable recovery value.

5. *Scrap* is manufacturing residue that has measurable but relatively minor recovery value.

B. The most economical production method or process usually includes some allowance for spoilage.

1. *Normal spoilage* occurs under *efficient* processing conditions that *are* inherent parts of planned operations.

a. Thus, such spoilage is *uncontrollable* in the short run.

b. In general, the net cost of normal spoilage should be *included* as a necessary part of the cost of good (unspoiled) production.

2. *Abnormal spoilage* is due to *inefficient* processing conditions that are *not* inherent parts of planned operations.

a. Thus, such spoilage is usually regarded as *controllable.*

b. In general, the net cost of abnormal spoilage should be *excluded* from the cost of good production and should be charged to a special loss account for abnormal spoilage because it is not an inventoriable cost of good production.

c. Thus, the net cost of abnormal spoilage would be appropriately isolated for management control purposes.

3. Textbook Exhibit 19-1 provides a helpful summary of the general accounting for spoilage.

a. Note the distinction between normal and abnormal spoilage.

b. Compare the conceptual and practical accounting approaches.

C. Exhibits 19-2 through 19-4 demonstrate the accurate methods for dealing with spoilage in process-cost computations.

1. You should study these helpful exhibits very carefully.

2. Note especially that both normally spoiled units and abnormally spoiled units are *included* in the computation of equivalent units used for finding unit processing costs.

3. Costs applicable to spoiled units may then be easily determined and accounted for.

a. The cost of abnormally spoiled units would be charged to a special loss account for abnormal spoilage.

b. No normal spoilage costs of the current process would be allocated to the ending inventory of work in process, if—as in the textbook example—these units have not yet reached the inspection point.

c. Thus, if the ending inventory of work in process has not reached the inspection point, *all* of the cost of normally spoiled units would be included in the cost of good units completed—as in the textbook examples.

4. A *spoilage random fluctuations account* may be used as an accounting device to permit the recognition of abnormal spoilage only when actual spoilage exceeds the top of a normal range.

D. The accounting treatment of *net spoilage costs* in a *job-costing system* depends upon the general cause of the spoilage.

1. If the spoilage is *normal and is common to all jobs*, the net cost of spoilage may be applied to production through a predetermined overhead rate that anticipates this net cost. The net cost of such normal spoilage actually incurred would therefore be charged to Factory Overhead, Stores being debited with disposal value and Work in Process being credited with the gross spoilage cost.

2. If the spoilage is *normal but is directly attributable to the nature of a particular job*, Stores may be debited and Work in Process credited only with the disposal value of the spoiled goods, thus leaving in Work in Process the net cost of such normal spoilage actually incurred as part of the cost of the particular job.

3. If the spoilage is *abnormal* its net cost actually incurred should be charged to a special loss account for abnormal spoilage, Stores being debited with disposal value and Work in Process being credited with the gross spoilage cost.

E. The accounting treatment of the material, labor, and overhead costs of reworking *defective units* in a *job-costing system* depends upon the same set of general causes described above for spoilage and therefore parallels that accounting treatment. In each case, of course, credits would be made to the usual cost-originating accounts: Stores, Accrued Payroll, Factory Overhead Applied.

1. The cost of normal defective work common to all jobs would be charged to *Factory Overhead.*

2. The cost of normal defective work due to the nature of particular jobs would be charged to *Work in Process.*

3. The cost of abnormal defective work would be charged to *a special loss account for abnormal defective work.*

F. The accounting treatment of *scrap* value recovered in a *job-costing system* depends upon certain circumstances in addition to the general causes of the scrap.

1. When the dollar value of scrap is significant and there is a prolonged time lag between the recovery and sale of scrap, a *debit* to Stores should be made for the value of the scrap at the time of recovery; otherwise, the accounting recognition of scrap value may be postponed to the time of sale, when a *debit* would be made to Cash or Accounts Receivable.

2. The account to be *credited* when scrap value is recognized depends on the general cause of the scrap.

a. The value of *normal scrap common to all jobs* may be used to reduce the cost of all jobs through a predetermined overhead rate that anticipates this value. The actual value of such scrap recovered or sold would therefore be credited to Factory Overhead.

b. The value of *abnormal scrap due to the nature of particular jobs* may be used to reduce the cost of those jobs. The actual value of such scrap recovered or sold would therefore be credited to Work in Process.

3. Summarizing the job-order accounting entries for spoilage, defective work, and scrap is the helpful set of examples on textbook page 617.

G. When a *standard-costing system* is used, allowances for shrinkage, waste, scrap, and spoilage are often included in the standard costs for direct material, direct labor, and factory overhead.

1. Shrinkage and waste in excess of standard cause a material usage or quantity variance.

2. The excess is usually revealed through excess-materials requisitions or by comparing actual-yield percentages with standard-yield percentages.

3. Normally spoiled units are credited to Work in Process at standard costs and charged to Factory Overhead.

4. Periodic comparisons of budget allowances with actual spoilage provide summary information for managerial control.

SELF-TEST AND PRACTICE EXERCISES

(A) For each of the following multiple-choice and true-false statements, select the single most appropriate answer and enter its identification letter in the space provided.

____ 1. Problems of spoilage, waste, defective units, or scrap are found in: (a) very few manufacturing businesses; (b) a moderate proportion of manufacturing businesses; (c) most manufacturing businesses.

____ 2. There is very little distinction between normal spoilage and abnormal spoilage: (a) on a conceptual basis; (b) for management control purposes; (c) both of the above; (d) neither of the above.

____ 3. Substandard outputs that are feasible to rework and sell as firsts or seconds are known as: (a) scrap; (b) waste; (c) spoiled units; (d) defective units; (e) all of the above; (f) none of the above.

____ 4. Manufacturing residue that has no measurable recovery value is called: (a) waste; (b) scrap; (c) either of the above; (d) neither of the above.

____ 5. The most economical combination of production factors usually results in some spoilage: (a) true; (b) false.

____ 6. Normal spoilage is: (a) controllable in the short run; (b) uncontrollable in the short run.

____ 7. Normal spoilage occurs under efficient processing conditions that are inherent parts of planned operations: (a) true; (b) false.

____ 8. Generally, abnormal spoilage: (a) is uncontrollable; (b) should be excluded from cost to good production; (c) both of the above; (d) neither of the above.

____ 9. Spoilage that is due to inefficient processing conditions includes: (a) normal spoilage; (b) abnormal spoilage; (c) both of the above; (d) neither of the above.

____ 10. When spoilage is actually incurred that is normal and is common to all jobs, Work in Process should be credited with: (a) nothing; (b) the disposal value of the spoiled goods; (c) the net spoilage cost; (d) the gross spoilage cost.

____ 11. The predetermined overhead rate used in a job-costing system should include an element for the anticipated net cost of: (a) normal spoilage; (b) abnormal spoilage; (c) both of the above; (d) neither of the above.

____ 12. When abnormal spoilage occurs in a job-costing system, the Work-in-Process account should be credited with: (a) nothing; (b) the disposal value of the spoiled goods; (c) the net spoilage cost; (d) the gross spoilage cost.

____ 13. In a job-costing system, Work in Process would ordinarily be charged with the cost of defective work that is: (a) abnormal; (b) normal and common to all jobs; (c) normal and due to the nature of particular jobs.

____ 14. In a job-costing system, a special loss account should be charged for: (a) the net cost of abnormal spoilage; (b) the cost of remedying abnormal defective work; (c) each of the above; (d) neither of the above.

____ 15. When the dollar value of scrap is significant and there is a prolonged time lag between the recovery and sale of scrap, the accounting recognition of scrap value should be made: (a) at the time of scrap recovery; (b) at the time of scrap sale on account; (c) at the time of cash collection from scrap sale.

____ 16. The value of normal scrap common to all jobs would be: (a) debited to Work in Process; (b) credited to Work in Process; (c) debited to Factory Overhead; (d) credited to Factory Overhead.

____ 17. When a standard-costing system is used, allowances for shrinkage, waste, scrap, and spoilage are included in the standard costs for direct material, direct labor, and factory overhead: (a) often; (b) seldom; (c) never.

(B) Complete each of the following statements:

1. ______________ is defined as production that does not meet dimensional or ______________ standards and that is sold for ______________________________ ______________.

2. Net spoilage cost is defined as the excess of ________ ____ over the ________________________________.

3. Scrap is defined as manufacturing residue that has ____ recovery value.

4. The ______________________ spoilage should be included as part of the costs of good production.

5. The net cost of normal spoilage expected to be common to all jobs would usually be budgeted as part of ____.

6. When spoilage is normal but is directly attributable to the nature of a particular job, the Work-in-Process amount should be credited with ______________.

7. The cost of normal defective work common to all jobs would ordinarily be charged to ______________ ________________________.

8. The value of abnormal scrap attributable to the nature of particular jobs would be credited to the ________________________ account.

9. When a standard costing system is used, normally spoiled production may be charged to ______________ ________________________ at standard costs and credited to ______________________________.

10. A ____ account may be used as an accounting device to permit the recognition of abnormal spoilage only when actual spoilage ________________________ a normal range.

(C) Given for the Batch-Parcel Company, which uses a job-costing system:

Spoiled work:
- Gross cost incurred $900
- Disposal value $200

Cost incurred to remedy defective work $600
Scrap material value recovered $150

Enter selected dollar amounts in the following table to indicate the appropriate journal entries for each of the listed items. Use the dollar amounts above for both normal and abnormal items listed below.

Item	Entry	Stores	Work in Process	Factory Overhead	Special Loss
1. Normal spoilage common to all jobs:	Debit				
	Credit				
2. Normal spoilage due to the nature of particular jobs:	Debit				
	Credit				
3. Abnormal spoilage:	Debit				
	Credit				
4. Normal defective work common to all jobs:	Debit				
	Credit*	–	–	–	–
5. Normal defective work due to the nature of particular jobs:	Debit				
	Credit*	–	–	–	–
6. Abnormal defective work:	Debit				
	Credit*	–	–	–	–
7. Normal scrap common to all jobs:	Debit				
	Credit				
8. Abnormal scrap due to the nature of particular jobs:	Debit				
	Credit				

*Credit Stores, Accrued Payroll, and Factory Overhead Applied, Total $600.

(D) Given for the Anti-Gravity Process of Negative-Weight Products, Inc., which uses the weighted-average method of process costing:

Beginning work in process, 3/5 completed .... 100 units
Transferred in .... 620 units
Lost from normal spoilage .... 40 units
Lost from abnormal spoilage .... 60 units
Good units transferred out .... 540 units
Ending work in process, 3/4 completed .... 80 units
Conversion costs in beginning inventory $2,000
Current conversion costs $9,200
Spoilage is detected upon completion of the process.

Find by the weighted-average method:

1. Equivalent units for conversion costs .... ______units

2. Unit conversion cost . . . . $________

3. Total conversion costs of normal spoilage . . . . $________

4. Total conversion costs of abnormal spoilage . . . . $________

5. Total conversion costs transferred out to the following process . . . . $________

6. Total conversion costs in the ending inventory of work in process . . . . $________

Accounting for Payroll

20

Accounting for payroll involves employees' earnings and related fringe-benefit costs, payroll taxes, and government requirements for keeping records and filing tax returns. This chapter presents the main accounting concepts and procedures for dealing with these matters and the accompanying payroll deductions and liabilities. The nature and cost effects of each type of payroll tax are explained, and the accounting treatment of each principal payroll transaction is described.

Textbook Exhibits 20-1 and 20-2 serve as useful summaries and checklists of the main payroll-tax matters: tax assessments, requirements for filing tax returns, and deadlines for making tax payments. The extended textbook illustration of typical payroll accounting entries can be quite helpful to you in tying together and understanding the main payroll transactions.

REVIEW SUMMARY

A. Today, many subtractions must be made by employers from employees' *gross earnings* to arrive at their *net earnings* or *take-home pay*.

1. These subtractions, usually called *payroll deductions* or *withholdings*, are merely parts of an employee's gross earnings that are being transferred to third parties.

2. The main withholdings are two kinds of taxes levied on employees and deducted from their earnings by employers, who serve in effect as tax-collection agents.

a. Government schedules show the amounts of estimated *individual federal income taxes* on employees that should be withheld for the many different combinations of gross earnings and dependents.

b. The Social Security tax, or Federal Insurance Contributions Act tax (*F.I.C.A. tax* or *F.O.A.B. tax*), on employees, designed primarily to provide retirement pensions, is computed by applying a specified percent to gross earnings, the 1977 rate being 5.85% of the first $16,500 of gross earnings per employee in the calendar year. (These figures increase almost yearly.)

3. In addition to the two tax deductions described above, there are many other payroll withholdings not required by law, such as employee contributions to group life insurance plans, group hospitalization insurance plans, pension funds, and employee savings plans; payment of union dues; and donations to charities.

4. The accounting for payroll deductions may be accomplished in three steps:

a. When the employer records labor costs incurred, debit the appropriate cost accounts (for example, the accounts for work in process, factory overhead, selling and administrative expense) with gross earnings, which, of course, include all payroll deductions. Credit Accrued Payroll for the total gross earnings owed to employees.

b. Debit Accrued Payroll and credit the separate liability accounts for the various items deducted from gross earnings.

c. When the employer pays each payroll-related liability, debit the appropriate liability account and credit the cash account.

B. Labor costs incurred *by employers* include, in addition to the gross earnings of employees, two other kinds of costs (*fringe labor costs*) that typically amount to a large fraction of total employment costs:

1. Payroll taxes are assessed against employers.

a. *Federal and state unemployment taxes* apply only to the first $4,200 earned by each employee each calendar year.

b. *Federal F.I.C.A. taxes* apply only to the first $16,500 earned by each employee each calendar year. This is *in addition* to the equal amount of F.I.C.A. taxes assessed against employees and deducted from their gross earnings.

2. Other labor costs are borne by employers.

a. These include workmen's compensation insurance, vacations and paid holidays, and employers' contributions to pension funds and to health and life insurance plans.

b. These costs are in addition to those borne by employees through payroll deductions.

3. When these fringe labor costs accrue, debits are made to appropriate cost accounts and credits are made to the related liability accounts.

a. *In theory*, these fringe costs should be charged to the *same accounts* to which the gross earnings are charged; for example, the Work-in-Process account for direct-labor costs.

b. *In practice*, however, the fringe labor costs for *all* factory labor, both direct and indirect, are usually charged to the *Factory Overhead Control account.*

4. Each liability account is, of course, debited when paid in cash.

C. In use today are a wide variety of *incentive wage plans* that provide additional compensation to employees for part of the cost savings that employees make possible by increasing their rates of production.

1. Although these plans generally add to clerical costs and may tend to increase spoilage costs, they often produce favorable net results.

2. In no event, however, would an incentive wage plan automatically substitute for adequate management as the most effective way of controlling labor costs.

3. The accounting for incentive wage plans vary according to their details and application.

D. A separate payroll bank account facilitates the control, preparation, and reconciliation of huge numbers of payroll checks.

SELF-TEST AND PRACTICE EXERCISES

(A) For each of the following multiple-choice and true-false statements, select the single most appropriate answer and enter its identification letter in the space provided.

____ 1. Accounting for payroll is significantly involved with: (a) payroll taxes; (b) employment fringe benefits; (c) both of the above; (d) neither of the above.

____ 2. Typically, there is little difference between an employee's gross earnings and his net earnings after payroll deductions: (a) true; (b) false.

____ 3. Payroll withholdings for taxes should be charged to tax-expense accounts: (a) true; (b) false.

____ 4. The Social Security tax is also called: (a) the F.I.C.A. tax; (b) the F.O.A.B. tax; (c) both of the above; (d) neither of the above.

____ 5. Payroll taxes that are ordinarily borne by both employees and their employers include: (a) the F.I.C.A. tax; (b) the Federal Unemployment Insurance tax; (c) both of the above; (d) neither of the above.

____ 6. Deductions for payroll taxes are the only deductions that are allowed to be made from the gross earnings of employees: (a) true; (b) false.

____ 7. In general, there is no upper limit to the annual amount of employees' earnings subject to: (a) F.I.C.A. taxes; (b) Federal Unemployment taxes; (c) both of the above; (d) neither of the above.

____ 8. Fringe labor costs of employers would generally include part of the: (a) F.I.C.A. taxes; (b) individual federal income taxes; (c) both of the above; (d) neither of the above.

____ 9. The fringe labor costs incurred by employers could include: (a) part of the cost of life insurance on lives of employees; (b) all of the federal unemployment taxes; (c) both of the above; (d) neither of the above.

____ 10. The amounts of fringe labor costs in relation to gross earnings of employees are typically: (a) quite large; (b) very small.

____ 11. Most companies treat fringe costs on direct labor as overhead costs: (a) true; (b) false.

____ 12. Federal and state unemployment taxes apply to no more than the statutory maximum of earnings paid to the employee in a calendar year: (a) true; (b) false.

____ 13. In effect, equal amounts of taxes are assessed against employees and employers for: (a) federal unemployment taxes; (b) state unemployment taxes; (c) both of the above; (d) neither of the above.

____ 14. In practice, employer payroll taxes are usually allocated by employers over the year, using a leveled rate: (a) true; (b) false.

____ 15. Theoretically, employers' payroll taxes should be accrued as wages are earned by employees: (a) true; (b) false.

____ 16. Incentive wage plans automatically substitute for adequate management as the most effective way of controlling labor costs; (a) always; (b) often; (c) occasionally; (d) never.

____ 17. The make-up pay for piecework in a common incentive wage plan would ordinarily be charged as factory-overhead cost: (a) true; (b) false.

____ 18. The accounting for incentive wage plans is generally: (a) fairly uniform; (b) quite varied.

(B) Complete each of the following statements:

1. The subtractions made from the gross earnings of employees are usually called ____________________ ____________.

2. The two kinds of taxes ordinarily deducted from the gross earnings of employees are the____________ ____________________ tax and the ____________ ____________________ tax.

3. Under the textbook accounting method, when an employer records labor costs incurred, he should credit the ____________________ account for the ____________ earnings owed to employees.

4. The labor costs incurred by employers in addition to the gross earnings of employees are called ________ ____________________.

5. The two kinds of *federal* payroll taxes typically assessed against employers are ____________ ________ taxes and ____________taxes.

6. Theoretically, the fringe costs pertaining to direct labor should be charged to the____________ ____________________account.

7. Usually, equal amounts of taxes are assessed against employees and employers for ____________ taxes.

8. The usual practice in accounting for payroll taxes tends to result in a ratio of payroll taxes to employee earnings that is ____________ in the earlier months than in the later months of the ____________ year.

(C) Scrooge and Cratchit Clerical Supplies uses for its payday the last day of each month. The firm's labor summary for a month included the following data:

Gross earnings of employees:	
Direct labor	$20,000
Indirect labor	5,000
Selling expense	3,000
Administrative expense	2,000
Total	$30,000
Vacation pay	5.0%
F.I.C.A. tax	6.0
Federal unemployment tax	0.5
State unemployment tax	2.5
Total	14.0%

All earnings are subject to the above rates.

Employee's income taxes withheld	$4,000

1. Prepare the journal entry to record the *incurrence of all payroll costs* for the month:

Calculations:

2. Prepare the journal entry to record the *payment of the payroll* for the month:

Calculations:

Accounting Systems and Internal Control

21

Internal control, which is aimed at increasing an organization's operational efficiency and effectiveness, involves a number of accounting techniques presented in previous chapters, such as budgets, standards, and responsibility accounting. This chapter, therefore, does not contain a comprehensive treatment of internal control systems in general. Nor do we emphasize here special features applicable to specific types of businesses. Rather, this chapter is limited mainly to an explanation of certain principles designed to minimize errors, fraud, and waste—principles that are widely applicable to many different kinds of operations.

REVIEW SUMMARY

A. Definitions of *internal control* vary considerably in scope.

1. In the broadest sense, internal control consists of systems and procedures that promote the operational efficiency and effectiveness of an organization (budgets, standards, responsibility accounting).

2. In the narrowest sense, internal control (often called *internal check*) consists only of those procedures that are designed to minimize errors, fraud, and waste.

B. Although no internal control system can prevent fraud completely or result in operating perfection, there are some general principles and procedures that can help an organization move toward these ideals. A ten-item checklist is provided:

1. Use the *cost-benefit* approach, avoiding procedures with monetary or psychological costs in excess of benefits.

2. Assign all employees to supervisors for directing and appraising performance, a management function.

3. Select employees with adequate qualifications for their jobs.

4. Assign recordkeeping and physical handling of assets to separate persons instead of combining the two functions in a job for one person.

5. Establish uniform routines for repetitive procedures in order to permit specialization of effort, division of duties, and automatic checks.

6. Systematize the handling of transactions, especially sales, to help ensure that they are recorded on documents immediately, adequately, and in a tamper-proof manner (*document control*).

7. Identify responsibilities for actions with individuals as far down in the organization as feasible.

8. Observe certain precautions for key personnel: bonding, vacations, rotation of duties.

9. Provide for independent checks through periodic reviews of the system by both internal and external auditors.

10. Use physical safeguards: safes, locks, watchmen, and limited access.

C. Certain aspects of internal control systems deserve special mention or illustration.

1. In the infamous McKesson & Robbins fraud case of the 1930s, cash in excess of $3 million was embezzled.

a. The company president headed a conspiracy involving the use of dummy companies and false documents to support fictitious transactions.

b. As a consequence of this case, independent accountants adopted as a standard auditing procedure the *physical testing of inventories.*

c. This case also dramatized the truth that no economically feasible system can be devised for verifying all the innumerable and complex transactions of a large organization.

2. The solution to a CPA examination problem was used to illustrate how the ten-item checklist (see B above) can serve as a useful starting point in designing or judging an internal control system.

a. Employees' duties should be assigned so that one individual does not have sole control over all recordkeeping and physical handling for any single transaction.

b. Such a division of jobs limits chances for fraud and furnishes some automatic checks on efficiency and accuracy.

3. Reliable reports from many sources point to an alarming increase in retail *inventory shrinkage or shortage.*

a. These merchandise losses, which are due primarily to shoplifting by customers and embezzling by employees, can make disastrous inroads on slim profit margins.

b. Although the best deterrent is an alert employee at the point of sale, other methods are increasingly being used to cope with such thefts; for example, surveillance by television cameras and placing sensitized tags on merchandise.

4. The *retail inventory method* is widely used as a control device, especially in situations of wide merchandise variety, high sales volume, and low unit values of products (food stores, for example).

a. The retail inventory method is helpful in measuring the inventory shortages for which store managers bear prime responsibility.

b. Best results from this method are obtained when it is used in conjunction with close supervision and spot checks by branch managers.

c. The method is also used to obtain an inventory valuation for financial-statement purposes.

5. Electronic computers have important implications for internal control.

a. Although electronic data systems can have high degrees of reliability, efficiency, and effectiveness, they are less flexible than manual systems.

b. The ten-item checklist for internal control (see B above) also applies to electronic computer systems, particularly such items as rotation of employees' duties, careful selection of employees, and separation of recordkeeping and cash-handling responsibilities.

D. Two useful techniques for accumulating accounting data are described in an appendix to this chapter.

1. The classification and coding of accounts can increase the speed and accuracy of recordkeeping.

2. The use of branch ledgers tied to home-office ledgers by *reciprocal control accounts* helps to integrate all company accounts in a manner that minimizes duplications, omissions, and other errors.

SELF-TEST AND PRACTICE EXERCISES

(A) For each of the following multiple-choice and true-false statements, select the single most appropriate answer and enter its identification letter in the space provided:

___ 1. In general, a good internal control system for a given company would need little modification over the years: (a) true; (b) false.

___ 2. In the broadest view, internal control includes: (a) budgets; (b) standards; (c) responsibility accounting; (d) all of these; (e) none of these.

___ 3. In a large organization, it is feasible for an internal control system to: (a) prevent fraud completely; (b) provide verification of all transactions; (c) both of the above; (d) neither of the above.

___ 4. In general, internal control systems involve, in addition to accounting procedures and the processing of business documents: (a) employee selection; (b) physical safeguards; (c) both of the above; (d) neither of the above.

___ 5. If an internal control system is properly designed, there should be no need for: (a) internal auditors; (b) external auditors; (c) both of the above; (d) neither of the above.

___ 6. The McKesson & Robbins Company was bilked of millions of dollars by: (a) outsiders; (b) insiders.

___ 7. In general, it is desirable that only one employee should have sole control over the recordkeeping and physical handling for the individual transactions that are assigned to him: (a) true; (b) false.

___ 8. In a certain company, one employee maintains both the cash-receipts journal and the accounts-receivable ledger. For a good system of internal control, this would be: (a) an undesirable combination; (b) an acceptable combination.

___ 9. Retail inventory shortages seem to be: (a) increasing; (b) decreasing; (c) remaining about the same.

___ 10. In general, shoplifting has a significant effect on profits: (a) true; (b) false.

___ 11. The retail inventory method is useful: (a) as a control device; (b) for obtaining an inventory valuation for financial-statement purposes; (c) both of the above; (d) neither of the above.

___ 12. Use of the retail inventory method automatically eliminates merchandise thefts by employees: (a) true; (b) false.

___ 13. Electronic computer systems: (a) can have high degrees of reliability, efficiency, and effectiveness; (b) are more flexible than manual systems; (c) both of the above; (d) neither of the above.

___ 14. In general, the ten-item checklist for internal control would be applicable to: (a) electronic computer systems; (b) manual systems; (c) both of the above; (d) neither of the above.

___ 15. The classification and coding of accounts in a large organization is intended primarily to: (a) protect confidential information; (b) increase the speed and accuracy of recordkeeping.

___ 16. When reciprocal control accounts are used for a factory ledger and the home-office ledger as described in the chapter appendix, the purchase of direct materials would require: (a) a credit to Factory Ledger Control; (b) a debit to Home Office Ledger Control; (c) a credit to Home Office Ledger Control; (d) all of the above; (e) none of the above.

(B) Complete each of the following statements:

1. In its narrowest sense, internal control may be called __________ and is designed to minimize __________, __________, and __________.

2. A desirable feature of an internal control system is the assignment of the functions or duties of __________ and __________ __________ to separate persons.

3. Systematizing the handling of transactions to help ensure that they are recorded on documents immediately, adequately, and in a tamper proof manner is called __________ __________.

4. As a consequence of the McKesson & Robbins case, the standard auditing procedures used by __________ __________ were changed to include __________ __________.

5. Typically, large retail inventory shrinkages and shortages are caused primarily by __________ __________ and __________.

6. The retail inventory method is particularly useful as a control device in situations of wide merchandise variety, high __________, __________ and low __________.

7. When reciprocal control accounts are used to tie a branch factory ledger to the home-office ledger, the Home Office Ledger Control account is included in

the ______________________ ledger and normally has

a ______________________ balance.

(C) For each of the following pairs of employee functions, indicate whether it is an acceptable combination (A) or an unacceptable combination (U) for one employee to perform in a good system of internal control:

___ 1. Maintaining general ledger; handling and depositing cash receipts.

___ 2. Maintaining general ledger; reconciling bank account.

___ 3. Handling and depositing cash receipts; issuing credits on returns and allowances.

___ 4. Handling and depositing cash receipts; preparing checks for signature.

___ 5. Maintaining accounts-payable ledger; maintaining accounts-receivable ledger.

___ 6. Maintaining cash-disbursements journal; maintaining accounts-payable ledger.

___ 7. Reconciling bank account; handling and depositing cash receipts.

___ 8. Issuing credits on returns and allowances; maintaining accounts-receivable ledger.

(D) Given for Neeman-Markups Company:

	Retail Prices
Beginning merchandise inventory (physical count)	$ 8,000
Merchandise purchases	77,000
Merchandise sales	72,000
Markups	3,000
Markdowns	6,000
Allowable inventory shrinkage	2,600
Ending merchandise inventory (physical count)	6,500

Using the retail method of inventory control, determine the amount of the inventory shortage (in excess of allowable inventory shrinkage) . . . . $______

22

Decentralization and Transfer Pricing

As organizations increase in size, work tends to increase in both volume and scope, and it must be divided among a larger number of subunits such as departments, cost centers, profit centers, and divisions. As a result, the power to make decisions may be distributed more widely among managers (*decentralization*).

Decentralized operations often involve exchanges of goods and services among the subunits of an organization. *Transfer prices* are the monetary values assigned to these exchanges or transfers.

Ideally, transfer prices should motivate managers to make decisions that maximize the profits of the organization as a whole. However, there is rarely a single type of transfer price that will accomplish this goal. In this chapter, we examine the main types of transfer prices and their impacts on three major problems involved in designing or judging accounting control systems: goal congruence, incentive, and subunit autonomy.

REVIEW SUMMARY

A. The decentralization of an organization's management is a matter of degree.

1. The essence of decentralization is the *freedom of managers to make decisions.*

2. Certain claimed advantages of decentralization are supposed to benefit the company through increased profits.

a. Decisions are better and more timely because of the manager's proximity to local conditions.

b. Top managers have more time for strategic planning.

c. Managers' incentives increase because they have more control over results.

d. Greater latitude of managerial action develops more frequent comparison of outside market prices with prices used for internal transfers.

e. Increased decision making provides better training for managers.

f. The profit-center structure has a more desirable motivational effect.

3. The largest cost of decentralization is probably *dysfunctional decision making,* which produces a net negative benefit to the subunits affected.

a. This can be caused by lack of goal congruence, insufficient information, or increased costs of obtaining sufficient information.

b. Dysfunctional decision making is most likely when there is a high degree of *interdependence* among subunits.

4. It is difficult to determine thee optimal degree of decentralization, the maximization of the *net benefit* (excess of benefits over costs).

a. When the organizational subunits are *independent* (self-contained), decentralization is likely to be most beneficial and least costly.

5. A *profit center* is any subunit of an organization that is assigned both revenues and expenses.

a. The profit center is normally the major organizational device used to maximize decentralization.

b. However, various segment labels used by different companies (for example, "cost center" and "profit center") are sometimes deceptive indicators of the actual degrees of decentralization.

c. The degree of decentralization within a given company (General Electric, for example) depends not only on the number of subunits and their size, but also on the way they are managed.

B. In designing or judging accounting control systems, one should consider how they relate to three major problems:

1. Inducing *goal congruence*, the harmonizing of managers' goals with organization goals.

2. Maintaining an appropriate level of *incentive* through evaluation of management performance.

3. Preserving *autonomy*, the freedom of managers to operate their subunits as decentralized entities.

C. Transfer pricing necessarily results from interactions among decentralized subunits, typically a profit center supplying a product or service to another profit center.

1. The transfer price will affect not only the reported profit of each center, but will also affect the allocation of an organization's resources.

2. The basic purpose of transfer pricing is to induce *optimal decision making* in a decentralized organization; i.e., to maximize the profit of the organization as a whole.

3. Transfer-pricing methods should be evaluated in the light of the same three major problems identified above: goal congruence, incentive, and autonomy.

D. Under some conditions, *market prices* are the most appropriate transfer prices because they help solve the three major problems.

1. Favorable conditions for using market prices include *minimal interdependencies of subunits* and the existence of a *competitive intermediate market* with dependable market-price quotations.

2. There are three principal guidelines for using market prices for transfer prices:

a. Use a market price or a negotiated market price.

b. The selling subunit should have the option of not selling internally.

c. An arbitration procedure should be available for settling disputes among subunit managers.

3. Generally, the outside market price would be a *ceiling* not to be exceeded by the internal transfer price.

4. The main difficulty with the use of market prices for transfer prices is the frequent lack of a market that is perfectly competitive or that contains the exact product or service subject to transfer.

5. If there is idle capacity in a supplying division and no market for the intermediate product, the extent of top management's interference in a transfer-pricing dispute between independent divisions can create a dilemma.

a. To benefit the organization as a whole, the supplying division should transfer the intermediate product at a price equal to its variable cost only.

b. However, if the manager of the supplying division were forced by top management to forego a profit by accepting such a low price, there would be a natural lessening of both incentive and subunit autonomy.

6. If there are only some isolated price quotations reflecting temporary distress or dumping prices, they may be appropriate in general for monitoring short-term performance but not for making long-range plans.

E. There is no general rule for transfer pricing that will lead toward optimal economic decisions.

1. However, there is a general rule that serves as a helpful first step in reaching an optimal economic decision in a particular situation. This rule is that the minimum transfer price should be the sum of two elements:

a. One element is composed of the *additional outlay costs* incurred to the point of transfer: cash outflows that are directly associated with the production and transfer of the goods or services (sometimes approximated by variable costs).

b. The other element consists of *opportunity costs* for the firm as a whole: the maximum contribution to profits foregone by the firm as a whole if the goods are transferred internally (often quite difficult to measure).

2. Transfer pricing is often complicated by imperfect, ill-structured, or nonexistent intermediate markets.

a. *Imperfect competition* occurs when a single buyer or seller can influence the market price.

b. If imperfect competition exists in the intermediate market, additional volume can be obtained only if selling prices are lowered, thus causing transfer-price analyses to be exceedingly complex.

3. Again, when heavy interdependencies exist among organization subunits and intermediate markets, transfer-pricing analyses can become quite complex.

a. An economic analysis might dictate variable cost to be used for the transfer price, but this would seldom be appropriate for solving all three problems: goal congruence, incentive, and autonomy.

b. Therefore, as a practical solution, different kinds of transfer prices (for example, market prices and cost prices) may be assigned to different classes of transactions.

F. Although nearly every version of a transfer price has some drawbacks, there are several useful bases other than market prices for setting transfer prices.

1. There is a widespread use of *full cost* as a transfer price.

a. Because full *actual* costs can include inefficiencies, this basis for transfer pricing often fails to provide an incentive to control such inefficiencies.

b. Although the use of full *standard* costs may minimize the inefficiencies mentioned above, suboptimal decisions can result from the natural inclination of the manager of an autonomous buying division to view such *mixed costs* of a selling division as *variable costs* of his buying division.

c. Despite the above defects of the full-cost basis, it is commonly used for transfer prices because of its clarity and convenience and because it is often viewed as a satisfactory approximation of outside market prices.

2. Top management may want buying-division managers to make purchasing decisions based on the variable costs of supplying divisions.

a. In such cases, the transfer could be made at standard variable cost for the purpose of motivating buying-division managers toward the desired purchasing decisions.

b. However, the buying divisions would be charged periodically with lump-sum amounts to cover the supplying divisions' related fixed costs and to provide them with a profit margin.

3. Managers can negotiate a single transfer price so that the overall contribution to corporate profit from a given internal transfer would be *prorated* between the buying and selling divisions on some mutually agreeable basis (for example, variable cost).

4. *Dual transfer prices* can be devised.

a. For the purpose of motivating the manager of the buying division to make the *optimal economic decision,* the transfer price would be *variable cost.*

b. For the purpose of fairly *evaluating performance* of the supplying division, the transfer price would be a *synthetic market price* allowing for a normal profit margin to the supplying division.

c. However, a disadvantage of this scheme is that both managers may tend to relax cost controls within their divisions.

G. A given company may well use different transfer prices for different purposes.

1. Various purposes related to *internal* problems could include:

a. To induce goal congruence
b. To maintain management incentive
c. To preserve subunit autonomy

2. Various purposes related to *external* problems could include:

a. To minimize tariffs and income taxes
b. To observe certain legal restrictions on selling prices

H. Despite the weaknesses of profit centers and control systems in improving goal congruence and incentive in an economically feasible way, profit centers provide the formal device that is so often the most persuasive means of communicating top management's goals and improving incentives.

I. If intracompany transfers are accounted for at prices in excess of cost, appropriate elimination entries should be made for external reporting purposes. When consolidated financial statements are prepared, items to be eliminated include:

1. Intracompany receivables and payables
2. Intracompany sales and cost of goods sold, and
3. Intracompany gross profit in inventories

SELF-TEST AND PRACTICE EXERCISES

(A) For each of the following multiple-choice and true-false statements, select the single most appropriate answer and enter its identification letter in the space provided.

___ 1. The degree of decentralization in a business depends primarily on: (a) the number of profit centers; (b) the size of profit centers; (c) the freedom of profit-center managers to make decisions.

___ 2. The claimed advantages of decentralization include: (a) improved management incentives and motivation; (b) decreased costs of gathering and processing information; (c) both of the above; (d) neither of the above.

___ 3. The costs of decentralization can include: (a) poorer training for managers; (b) dysfunctional decision making; (c) both of the above; (d) neither of the above.

___ 4. Included among the causes of dysfunctional decision making are: (a) lack of goal congruence; (b) insufficient information; (c) both of the above; (d) neither of the above.

___ 5. Decentralization is likely to be most beneficial and least costly when the organization's subunits are: (a) independent; (b) interdependent.

___ 6. A profit center is: (a) an organization subunit that is assigned both revenues and expenses; (b) normally the prime organizational device for maximizing decentralization; (c) both of the above; (d) neither of the above.

___ 7. The three major problems of goal congruence, incentive, and subunit autonomy should be considered in designing or judging: (a) accounting control systems; (b) transfer-pricing methods; (c) both of the above; (d) neither of the above.

___ 8. Subunit autonomy means the freedom of each individual member of the organization to define his own job or function: (a) true; (b) false.

___ 9. Transfer pricing deals primarily with the problems of determining appropriate transportation charges for goods exchanged or traded between two companies: (a) true; (b) false.

___10. The fundamental objective of a transfer-pricing system is to: (a) minimize income taxes; (b) minimize clerical and bookkeeping costs; (c) maximize a company's assets; (d) maximize a company's profits.

___11. The dominant idea behind the use of transfer prices is: (a) income taxation; (b) customer satisfaction; (c) stockholder information; (d) management motivation.

___12. The transfer-pricing problem is most difficult in organizations that are: (a) highly *centralized* with *many interdependencies* among subunits; (b) highly *decentralized* with *many interdependencies* among subunits; (c) highly *centralized* with *few interdependencies* among subunits; (d) highly *decentralized* with *few interdependencies* among subunits.

___13. A floor for transfer prices is typically established when market prices are used for transfer prices: (a) true; (b) false.

___14. A principal difficulty with the use of market prices for transfer prices is the frequent lack of a perfectly competitive intermediate market: (a) true; (b) false.

___15. If there is idle capacity in a supplying division and no intermediate market, a transfer price dictated by top management would tend to cause: (a) decreased incentive; (b) decreased subunit autonomy; (c) both of the above; (d) neither of the above.

___16. There is no general rule for transfer pricing that will lead toward optimal economic decisions: (a) true; (b) false.

___17. A helpful general way to determine a transfer price that will lead toward optimal economic decisions is to determine the relevant opportunity costs for the firm as a whole and to add: (a) fixed costs incurred to the point of transfer; (b) market prices in the intermediate market; (c) additional outlay costs incurred to the point of transfer; (d) all of the above.

___18. When many interdependencies exist among organizational subunits and markets, the use of dependable market prices alone would often fail to indicate directly the optimum buying decision: (a) true; (b) false.

___19. Transfer prices based upon full cost are widely used: (a) true; (b) false.

___20. When full costs are used as transfer prices, an incentive to control the inefficiencies that might increase such costs would be provided by using: (a) full actual costs; (b) full standard costs.

___21. When a buying division pays transfer prices based upon the full cost of the selling division, such prices are: (a) mixed costs of the company as a whole; (b) inclined to be viewed as variable costs by the manager of the buying division; (c) both of the above; (d) neither of the above.

___22. Some of the objections of supplier divisions to the use of marginal or variable costs for transfer prices could be overcome by: (a) prorating to buying and selling divisions the overall contribution to company profits; (b) using a dual transfer-pricing approach; (c) both of the above; (d) neither of the above.

____23. The purposes for using transfer prices include: (a) to improve management motivation; (b) to minimize tariffs and income taxes; (c) both of the above; (d) neither of the above.

(B) Complete each of the following statements:

1. Dysfunctional decision making is most likely to occur in an organization with a high degree of____________________________________.

2. The harmonizing of manager's goals with the organizational goals is called _____________________________.

3. Transfer prices are the monetary values assigned to exchanges of__________________ among ________________________.

4. The three major problems to be considered in judging the effectiveness of transfer prices are __________, ____________________, and ____________________.

5. For routine use where the intermediate market is __________________, the most desirable transfer price is market price if the interdependencies of subunits are ____________________.

6. The use of transfer prices based only on some simple rule such as a price to cover the full costs of a supplier division would tend to cause __________________________ decision making.

7. When there is no intermediate market and when marginal or variable cost is used as a transfer price, this would tend to please the manager of the _____________ division.

8. Although total decentralization implies complete freedom for organizational subunits to make decisions in their best interests as though they were ____________________, a major cost of such decentralization would be ________________________________.

9. If intracompany transfers are accounted for at prices in excess of ____________, appropriate elimination entries must be made when consolidated financial statements are prepared for _________________ reporting purposes. Items to be eliminated include intracompany: receivables and ________________, sales and ________________, and ________________________________.

(C) Given for the Quotient Division of Abacus Calculator Equipment, Inc:

Costs of manufacturing 5,000 units of a certain part:

	Total	Per Unit
Variable costs	$200,000	$40
Fixed costs.	$ 40,000	$ 8

1. Find the total benefit (or detriment) to the company if there *are no alternative uses* for Quotient Division's facilities, and if the Subtrahend Division of the same company purchases 5,000 units of this part from an outside supplier at a market price of:

   (a) $43 per unit . . . . $__________

   (b) $36 per unit . . . . $__________

2. Find the total benefit (or detriment) to the company if there *is an alternative use* for Quotient Division's facilities by other Abacus operations that would otherwise require an additional outlay of $26,000, and if Subtrahend Division of the same company purchases 5,000 units of this part from an outside supplier at a market price of:

(a) $43 per unit . . . . $__________

(b) $36 per unit . . . . $__________

Segment Performance Measurement

23

In the preceding chapter, we saw how decentralization highlights the problems of goal congruence, management incentive, and subunit autonomy. Here we consider the measurement of segment performance in developing management incentives toward the achievement of organizational goals.

Earlier chapters have shown how responsibility accounting helps measure the performance of managers of cost centers by focusing on the cost objects subject to an individual's control. This chapter extends the basic ideas of responsibility accounting beyond cost centers to investment centers. We examine the nature of these business segments and the principal problems of measuring both segment performance and managerial performance. Special emphasis is placed upon the widely used measure called *rate of return on investment (ROI).*

REVIEW SUMMARY

A. Large business organizations may have at least three kinds of subunits or segments:

1. A *cost center,* typically a department, is the smallest segment of activity or area of responsibility for which costs are accumulated.

2. A *profit center,* often called a division, is a segment responsible for both revenues and expenses.

3. An *investment center* is a segment responsible for its invested capital and the related income. ("Investment center," not a widely used term, is usually also described by the terms "profit center" and "division.")

B. The basic matters to be considered by control system designers include:

1. Making some critical choices concerning:

a. Measures of accomplishment that reflect organization goals.

b. Definitions of key terms such as "income" and "investment."

c. Bases for measuring various items: historical cost, present value, etc.

d. Standards of performance to be required.

e. Timing of performance reports.

2. Assessing the feasibility of the system in solving certain broad problems:

a. Goal congruence

b. Management incentive

c. Subunit autonomy

C. The measures of accomplishment that best represent the objectives of top management usually relate profits to invested capital.

1. One widely used measure is the *rate of return on investment (ROI).*

a. ROI is the ratio of *net income* to *invested capital.*

b. ROI can also be computed by multiplying *capital turnover* by the *net income percentage of sales:*

$$\frac{\text{Sales}}{\text{Invested Capital}} \times \frac{\text{Net Income}}{\text{Sales}} = \frac{\text{Net Income}}{\text{Invested Capital}}$$

$$= \text{ROI}$$

c. Management's understanding and use of ROI can be aided by thus breaking it down into its basic components.

2. *Residual income* is another measure of accomplishment that relates profit to invested capital.

a. This is the excess of an investment center's *net income over the imputed interest on the invested capital used by the center.*

b. This approach induces a desirable expansion of an investment center as long as it earns a rate in excess of the charge for invested capital (the minimum desired rate of return).

c. In contrast to the results of the residual-income approach, using the maximization of ROI as an investment criterion would sometimes result in the rejection by division managers of projects that, from the viewpoint of the organization, should be accepted because they promise an ROI in excess of the minimum desired rate of return.

D. In measuring performance by whatever means, one should make a distinction between the performance of the *division manager* and the performance of the *division* as an investment by the corporation.

1. To measure divisional performance, division income would be compared with the total division investment.

2. On the other hand, a division manager's performance would be measured by comparing the controllable contribution of his division with the investment controllable by him.

3. Because operating conditions vary so widely, performances should be compared only with extreme caution among divisions or among managers.

a. Actual performances of both divisions and managers are more appropriately judged against *budget targets*, rather than against competing divisions or managers.

E. In designing performance measures, one should be aware of different definitions of key elements and their implications for appraising performance and motivating managers.

1. The definitions of income, investment, etc., should be agreed on within an organization.

2. The method of allocating assets to divisions can significantly affect the motivation of managers.

a. The aim, of course, should be to allocate in a way that tends to be goal-congruent, provides management incentives, and recognizes subunit autonomy.

b. In general, if managers perceive that they are being treated uniformly, they tend to accept asset allocations as fair.

c. However, many managers feel it is better not to allocate assets to divisions than to use an arbitrary basis for allocation.

3. Different bases are available for measuring invested capital.

a. In general, for evaluating the operating performance of managers, it is appropriate to use as a base an asset total *not* reduced by any long-term debt, such as *total assets available, total assets employed,* and *net working capital plus other assets.*

b. On the other hand, the use of *stockholders' equity* as an investment base is more appropriate for evaluating owners' returns under a particular capital structure, which might involve a significant degree of *financial leverage,* or *trading on the equity.*

F. Of crucial importance in evaluating performance and making decisions is the selection of appropriate alternatives for the measurement of investments and the related performance of managers and divisions.

1. For the routine measurement of assets included in the investment base, the most frequently used valuation is

net book value, but this is not necessarily conceptually correct.

2. In choosing between the disposal of an asset and its continuance, one should compare the asset's highest *current disposal value* (exit value) with its *total present value* (present value of expected cash inflows).

3. If expansion of assets is also an available alternative, one should compare the additional asset's *total present value* with its *acquisition cost* (the required investment).

4. In order to make valid productivity comparisons among executives as managers and among divisions as economic investments, one should measure the related assets on a *uniform* basis.

a. Using *historical cost* of assets would usually involve different acquisition dates and therefore would not provide an appropriate common denominator.

b. Although many theorists claim that *total present value* is the ideal investment measure for the evaluation of performance, its use is rarely feasible.

c. However, a practical substitute for the "ideal" present value is *replacement cost*, for which it is often quite feasible to obtain reasonably objective approximations at given dates.

5. Although historical cost has defects as an investment measure, it is often used because it is generally believed that its routine use for this purpose may be more economical on a regular basis than the use of replacement cost and current disposal values, which are often viewed as feasible to obtain only for special decisions.

a. Some companies are experimenting with the use of historical cost adjusted for general price-level changes.

6. When historical cost is used as an investment measure, some users prefer *gross cost* (undepreciated cost) because it facilitates comparisons among divisions, but others prefer *net cost* (net book value) because it is consistent with conventional reporting of assets and net income.

G. It is naturally important to be *consistent* in the use of models for decisions and for the evaluation of their implementation.

1. Dysfunctional decisions may be induced by the inconsistent practice of using *discounted cash-flow models (DCF models) for making investment decisions* and the traditional *accrual accounting models* for evaluating the performance resulting from those decisions.

2. Unless formal methods are adopted for reconciling DCF planning models with accrual accounting control models, the follow-up of investment decisions must be done by one of two methods:

a. Gather samples of actual cash flows for comparison with the previously predicted cash flows.

b. At the time DCF decisions are made, translate them into predicted rates of return on the accrual accounting basis for later comparison with the actual rates of return on the same basis.

H. Another important matter is the choice of desired rates of return for decision making and performance evaluation.

1. Most practitioners use *uniform rates* of return for all divisions because of the widespread view that it would be unfair to use different rates for different divisions.

2. However, financial theorists advocate the use of *different rates* for different divisions in order to reflect *different risks.*

SELF-TEST AND PRACTICE EXERCISES

(A) For each of the following multiple-choice and true-false statements, select the single most appropriate answer and enter its identification letter in the space provided.

___ 1. The name for the segment of a business organization that is responsible for both income and invested capital is: (a) investment center; (b) asset center; (c) profit center; (d) cost center.

___ 2. The critical test of the profitability of an organization is: (a) the absolute amount of profit; (b) the relationship of profit to sales; (c) the relationship of profit to the number of employees; (d) the relationship of profit to invested capital.

___ 3. ROI may be computed by dividing invested capital by net income: (a) true; (b) false.

___ 4. Capital turnover is computed by dividing invested capital into: (a) sales; (b) total assets; (c) stockholders' equity; (d) none of the above.

___ 5. A measure of accomplishment that induces a desirable expansion of an investment center as long as it earns a rate in excess of the charge for invested capital is: (a) the ROI measure; (b) the residual income measure; (c) each of the above; (d) neither of the above.

___ 6. To use the maximization of ROI as an investment criterion could result in the rejection by division managers of projects that, from the viewpoint of the organization, should be accepted: (a) true; (b) false.

___ 7. In general, it is desirable to use different criteria in evaluating the performance of the division manager and the performance of the division as an investment by the corporation: (a) true; (b) false.

___ 8. Actual performances of divisions and managers should be judged against: (a) competing divisions or managers; (b) budget targets.

___ 9. Many managers: (a) tend to accept asset allocations as fair if they believe they are being treated uniformly; (b) think it is better not to allocate assets to divisions than to use an arbitrary basis for allocation; (c) both of the above; (d) neither of the above.

____10. In evaluating owners' returns under a particular capital structure, the most meaningful investment base to which an appropriate income figure should be related would be: (a) total assets; (b) total liabilities; (c) stockholders' equity.

____11. For the routine measurement of assets included in the investment base, the most frequently used valuation is: (a) total present value; (b) current disposal value; (c) net book value.

____12. It is generally desirable to use DCF models for making investment decisions and the traditional accrual accounting models for evaluating the performance resulting from those decisions: (a) true; (b) false.

____13. When desired rates of return are used for decision making and performance evaluation, it is conceptually more correct to use: (a) the same rates of return for different divisions; (b) different rates of return for different divisions.

(B) Complete each of the following statements:

1. ROI is equal to ____________________ multiplied by ____________________.

2. Residual income is the excess of an investment center's net income over ____________________ ____________________.

3. It would be appropriate to evaluate a division manager's performance by comparing the controllable contribution of his division with ____________________ ____________________.

4. In choosing between the disposal of an asset and its continuance, one should compare the asset's ____________________ value with its ____________________value.

5. A practical substitute for the "ideal" present value as the investment measure for the evaluation of performance is ____________________.

(C) Given:

	Capover Company	Investurn Company	Marsales Company
Invested capital	$200,000	$300,000	*
Sales	$900,000	*	$600,000
Net income	$ 27,000	*	$ 24,000
Capital turnover	*	*	5 times
Net income percentage of sales	*	4%	*
Return on investment	*	10%	*

*To be computed

1. Find for Capover Company:
   (a) Capital turnover .... __________ times
   (b) Net income percentage of sales .... __________ %
   (c) Return on investment .... __________ %

2. Find for Investurn Company:

(a) Net income . . . . $ ________

(b) Sales . . . . $ ________

(c) Capital turnover . . . . ________ times

3. Find for Marsales Company:

(a) Invested capital . . . . $ ________

(b) Net income percentage of sales . . . . ________ %

(c) Return on investment . . . . ________ %

(D) Given for Key Division of Hard Lock Company:

Invested capital.	$450,000
Net income	99,000

1. What is Key Division's ROI? . . . . ________ %

2. If interest is imputed at 18%, what is Residual Income? . . . . $ ________

3. If an available project promises a 20% ROI, would it tend to be accepted if:

(a) ROI were used to evaluate performance? ____________ Why?

(b) Residual Income were used to evaluate performance? ________ Why?

(E) Given for a special project of Astute Computer Company:

Investment in special equipment	$200,000
Annual net cash inflows from operations	$ 38,344
Useful life of equipment	10 yr
Time-adjusted rate of return	14%

(The 14% rate was determined by dividing $200,000 by $38,344 and entering the annuity present value table with the quotient at the 10-year line, as explained in Chapter 12.)

1. Assuming that the traditional accrual accounting model is used as a basis for performance evaluation, compute the ROI as follows (use straight-line depreciation with no terminal salvage value):

	First Year	Sixth Year
(a) Using gross cost as the investment base	________ %	________ %
(b) Using net book value at the beginning of the year as the investment base	________ %	________ %

2. What would be the objection to using the traditional accounting model as a basis for performance evaluation in this case?

3. If the traditional accrual model is used as a basis for performance comparisons among divisions, which cost basis would be preferable, gross cost or net book value? ____________ Why?

Decision Models, Uncertainty, and the Accountant

24

Business decisions are made by managers, not by accountants per se. However, accountants participate in the management function of an organization by providing the main source of the quantitative information needed for making decisions. Therefore, accountants, who design and operate accounting information systems, must understand the entire managerial decision process. An important part of this process is the *decision model*, a method for systematically aiding managers to make decisions. Decision models help business managers by providing them with the means for measuring the effects of different actions that might be chosen to obtain a particular objective.

In this chapter, we study formal decision models expressed in mathematical form: the nature of their basic elements, the selection of appropriate models, and the relationship of information to these models. A considerable part of the chapter deals with the use of mathematical decision models under conditions of *risk and uncertainty.*

REVIEW SUMMARY

A. Mathematical decision models typically have five principal elements:

1. A *choice criterion,* or *objective function,* which is a maximization (or minimization) of some form of profit (or cost) for the purpose of evaluating courses of action and thus assisting in the selection of the best alternative.

2. A set of *alternative courses of action* that are collectively exhaustive and mutually exclusive.

3. A set of *events*, also called *states* or *states of nature*, that are also collectively exhaustive and mutually exclusive.

4. A set of *probabilities* of occurrence of the various events.

5. A set of *payoffs* that measure the *outcomes* of various possible combinations of actions and events.

B. Decisions may be classified as being made under certainty, risk, or uncertainty.

1. When decisions are made under *certainty,* this means that for each action there is only one event, and therefore only one outcome or payoff for each action.

a. The decision consists of choosing the action that will produce the most desirable outcome.

b. However, this could be quite difficult if there is a great number of possible actions to consider.

2. There are many situations where for each action there are *several* events, each with its probability of occurrence.

a. Decisions are made under *risk* when these probabilities can be determined with a high degree of confidence because of mathematical proofs or actual experience.

b. Decisions are made under *uncertainty* when probabilities can be assessed only on a *subjective* basis.

c. However, risk and uncertainty are used as interchangeable terms in the textbook.

C. When decisions are to be made under risk or uncertainty, it is often helpful to make some selected computations.

1. The *expected value* of each action is the average of the outcomes (payoffs) of each of its events (states of nature) weighted by their probabilities of occurrence (the sum of the products of payoffs and probabilities). Be sure you understand how such calculations are made, as shown in the textbook examples for the two proposals on pages 754 and 755.

2. The *standard deviation,* which is the common measure of the *dispersion* of a probability distribution, is the square root of the mean of the squared deviations from the expected value.

3. The *coefficient of variation,* which is a relative measure of *risk or uncertainty,* is the standard deviation divided by the expected value.

D. The measurements of almost all accounting data are subject to uncertainty.

1. This is true *whether we are estimating historical costs or predicting future costs.*

2. Because of inadequacies in representing probability distributions by single amounts, accountants will probably begin to provide decision makers with more complete data such as the summary measures described above in C.

E. It is sometimes feasible to compute the *value of additional information* that may be available to the decision maker at some cost.

1. The first step is to prepare a *decision table* or *payoff table* for arriving at the *expected value with existing information* (the expected value of the action that would maximize payoff under conditions of uncertainty). See textbook Exhibit 24-2.

2. Second, compute the *expected value with perfect information* (the total of the expected values of actions selected on the assumption of perfect information). See Exhibit 24-3.

3. Third, subtract (1) from (2) to arrive at the *expected value of perfect information* (the maximum amount that should be paid for perfect advance information).

4. A similar approach can sometimes be used to estimate the *expected value of imperfect information.* See Exhibit 24-4 and the accompanying computations.

5. These textbook examples illustrate the *cost-benefit* aspect of getting information relevant to decision making. The *cost* of information (including alternative accounting systems for providing the information) should be compared with its *value* in arriving at management decisions.

F. When relatively large amounts of money are involved in decisions, expected monetary profits may not be effective determinants of decisions.

1. For psychological reasons, different people faced with the same situation may use personal money evaluations that are quite different from the actual dollar amounts involved.

2. These different expressions of personal preference reflect different *utility values* of money that in turn may produce different decisions.

3. The main idea here is illustrated by the textbook example, which in essence is like tossing a fair coin where "heads" wins $25,000 and "tails" loses only $10,000.

a. This would indeed be an attractive proposition to a person with sufficient cash to rely on these probabilities.

b. However, there are many more persons who could simply not afford the 50% probability of losing $10,000 on the first toss of the coin.

SELF-TEST AND PRACTICE EXERCISES

(A) For each of the following multiple-choice and true-false statements, select the single most appropriate answer and enter its identification letter in the space provided.

___ 1. The sets of probabilities in mathematical decision models pertain to the likelihood of occurrence of: (a) courses of action; (b) outcomes; (c) events; (d) the objective function; (e) none of the above.

___ 2. Used as synonyms in formal decision models are: (a) outcomes and events; (b) states and payoffs; (c) events and actions; (d) payoffs and outcomes.

___ 3. Certainty exists when there is absolutely no doubt about which: (a) action will occur; (b) event will occur.

___ 4. When the relevant probabilities can be determined with a high degree of confidence, decisions are said to be made under: (a) certainty; (b) uncertainty; (c) risk; (d) all of the above; (e) none of the above.

___ 5. When decisions are made under certainty, there is: (a) only one event; (b) only one outcome for each action; (c) both of the above; (d) neither of the above.

___ 6. When decisions are determined under risk, the relevant probabilities can usually be determined: (a) by mathematical proofs; (b) by actual experience; (c) either of the above; (d) neither of the above.

___ 7. The coefficient of variation is a relative measure of: (a) efficiency; (b) profitability; (c) accuracy or reliability; (d) risk or uncertainty.

___ 8. If two probability distributions have the same expected values, they would not necessarily also have the same standard deviations: (a) true; (b) false.

___ 9. Accounting-data measurements that are subject to uncertainty include: (a) historical costs; (b) future costs; (c) both of the above; (d) neither of the above.

___ 10. The expected value of perfect information is the difference between the expected value with perfect information and the expected value with existing information: (a) true; (b) false.

___ 11. Utility values of money: (a) are determined by well-known formulas; (b) are usually equal to the actual monetary amounts; (c) are the same for persons facing the same decisions; (d) reflect different personal preferences in a given situation.

(B) Complete each of the following statements:

1. The choice criterion of a mathematical decision model is also called the ________________ .

2. The choice criterion of a mathematical decision model is often expressed as a maximization of ________________ or a minimization of ________.

3. A mathematical decision model contains a set of events, which are also called ________________ or ________________ .

4. Typically, mathematical decision models include sets of alternative courses of action, which are collectively ________________ and mutually ________________ .

5. The payoffs in a mathematical decision model indicate the possible outcomes of ________________ ________________ for ________________ .

6. A mathematical decision model may include ________________ costs.

7. When the relevant probabilities can be determined only by subjective means, decisions are said to be made under ________________ .

8. Decisions are said to be made under risk or uncertainty when there are several ________________ ________________, each with its ________________ of occurrence.

9. The common measure of the dispersion of a probability distribution is called ________________ ________________ .

10. The expected value of a particular action is the sume of ________________ each multiplied by ________ ________________ .

11. The coefficient of variation is ________________ ________________ divided by ________ ________________ .

(C) Given for Kismet Fortune Cookies, Inc.:

		A	B	C	D
Event or state of nature		A	B	C	D
Probability of occurrence		.1	.4	.3	.2
Outcomes or payoffs for actions:	1	$10	$ 5	-0-	−$10
	2	$15	$10	$5	−$ 5
	3	$20	$15	-0-	-0-
	4	$30	$10	-0-	−$15

1. What is the expected value of action 1? . . . . . . $ ________

2. What is the expected value of action 2? . . . . . . $ ________

3. What is the expected value of action 3? . . . . . . $ ________

4. What is the expected value of action 4? . . . . . . $ ________

5. What is total expected value with perfect information? . . . . . . $ ________

6. What is the action that would maximize the payoff? . . . . . . $ ________

7. What is the total expected value of perfect information? . . . . . . $ ________

Determination of Cost Behavior Patterns

25

As other chapters have emphasized, management decisions can be significantly influenced by predicted costs of the alternative actions being considered. Cost predictions rest in turn on the manner in which costs behave under certain conditions. Therefore, managerial accountants need to know how to determine various cost-behavior patterns (*cost functions*).

This chapter deals with the important and complex problem of searching for cost-behavior patterns that are useful for predicting costs under different circumstances. Managers can choose from a variety of methods for determining cost functions. We briefly examine the most widely used of these along with their principal limiting assumptions and management implications. Special attention is given to the role of *regression analysis*, a well-known mathematical technique for measuring relationships among variables.

REVIEW SUMMARY

PART ONE—GENERAL APPROACH

A. Some accountants and statisticians distinguish between two terms that others might use interchangeably:

1. *Cost estimation* is the measurement of historical costs to aid in determining predicted costs for decision purposes.

2. *Cost prediction* is the forecasting of expected future costs.

B. Cost predictions are based upon cost-behavior patterns (*cost functions*).

1. The cost function may be either linear or non-linear. The general formula for a straight line is:

$$y = a + bx$$

a. The variable to be predicted is y the *dependent variable;* for example, power cost.

b. The other variable is x, the *independent variable, controllable variable,* or *decision variable*; for example, machine-hours.

c. The *intercept* is a, the value of y when x is zero.

d. The *slope* of the line is b, the amount of increase in y for each unit of increase in x.

e. The values of a and b are called *coefficients.*

2. The cost-behavior analyst attempts to identify the independent variable likely to have the most influence on the total cost (the dependent variable), typically some kind of input such as material, labor, or machine-hours.

3. The analyst seeks *plausible relationships* between actions and costs incurred.

4. The preferable cost function is one that *facilitates the prediction of changes in costs, that accurately depicts persistent relationships, whether or not cause and effect can be linked together.*

5. The best evidence of such a relationship is probably based upon physical observation, when it is possible.

6. *Scatter diagrams* are often used to determine cost functions.

a. These show the *past* behavior of individual costs at different volumes.

b. For example, see textbook Exhibit 25-1, which pictures the typical relationships between cost and volume for fixed costs, variable costs, and mixed costs.

c. Scatter diagrams should be used with caution for *predicting future costs*, for there may be changes in conditions affecting the relationships between cost and volume.

C. In determining cost functions, cost accountants have developed feasible methods by making tradeoffs between accuracy and simplicity. As a result, two common assumptions are usually made concerning cost behavior:

1. *Only one independent variable* (for example, labor hours or machine-hours) is needed for an adequate explanation of the behavior of a particular cost.

2. *Linear approximations* to cost functions are satisfactory reflections of the actual behavior, which is more likely to be non-linear.

a. Note, as Exhibit 25-2 shows, that the linearity assumption is valid only within the *relevant range* of output.

D. However, not all costs are simply fixed or variable, and some costs are *non-linear:*

1. Exhibit 25-3 shows the function of an upward-sloping supply curve for a scarce raw material that increases in price as demand increases.

2. Exhibit 25-4 shows the effects of quantity discounts on material costs.

3. Exhibit 25-5 shows the step-like cost behavior of labor services that cannot be obtained in the small fractional quantities needed for use.

a. The cost steps may be so narrow that they approach a proportionately variable cost-behavior pattern, such as the cost of part-time employees.

b. In other cases, the cost steps could be so wide that they approach costs classified as step-fixed costs or fixed costs (Exhibit 25-6).

E. The first of several approaches to determining cost functions, which are described in this chapter, is the *industrial engineering approach*: a normative, forward-looking approach that aims at discovering the *most efficient means* of achieving the desired outputs.

1. It emphasizes the use of time and motion studies and physical measures of inputs and outputs, and it de-emphasizes reliance on historical cost functions.

2. Although the industrial engineering approach becomes less satisfactory when costs cannot be traced to inputs and outputs, its use has increased in recent years.

3. This is the most complete approach, and it may be used with one or more of the six other methods described in this chapter.

F. The simplest of these six other methods for approximating cost functions is to *analyze each cost account* and classify it into one of three categories: *variable, fixed,* and *mixed* (or semi-variable).

1. The time periods over which the account balances have been accumulated should be *long enough* to link costs incurred with related outputs, but *short enough* to avoid the deceptive effects of averaging meaningful intraperiod fluctuations in costs and outputs.

2. Separate identification should be given to any specific factors that have significantly influenced costs (for example, prices of inputs, changes in technology, and seasonal differences).

3. The analyst should beware of *fixed costs* allocated to accounts on an ouput-unit basis. These costs may falsely appear to be *variable costs.*

G. The next three methods of approximating cost functions have significant shortcomings and therefore are not generally recommended:

1. The *high-low* method described in Chapter 8 in volves the danger of relying on two extreme points of cost that often represent abnormal situations.

2. The method that computes *representative marginal or incremental cost* is regarded as too subjective for general use.

3. The *visual-fit* method (simply drawing a straight line through the points on a scatter diagram) provides no objective test for assuring that the line is the most accurate representation of the underlying data.

H. The other two methods are examined in Part Two of the textbook and Part Two of this student guide: simple regression and multiple regression.

PART TWO–REGRESSION ANALYSIS, INCLUDING APPENDIX

A. An important technique for approximating cost functions is *regression analysis.*

1. *Simple regression analysis* measures the average amount of change in one variable that is associated with unit increases in another variable.

2. *Multiple regression analysis,* which uses more than one independent variable, can sometimes substantially improve predictions of cost made by simple regression analysis.

3. Part Two and the appendix to this textbook chapter deal almost exclusively with simple regression analysis.

B. For a helpful introduction to simple regression analysis, see the chapter appendix example of the historical sampling data regarding the relationship of direct-labor costs to batch size.

1. The first step is to select two variables and plot them on a *scatter diagram* to detect any unusual features that need further investigation:

x: batch size, the independent variable
y: direct labor costs, the dependent variable

2. Second, use the mathematical *method of least squares* (if the function seems to be linear) as an objective way to determine the equation for the particular regression line.

3. The regression line is the line that will *most precisely fit* the data plotted for the two variables.

4. However, this line represents only an estimation of the *average* values of y for different x values.

5. A useful statistic that should be computed is the *coefficient of correlation,* a measure of the extent to which the independent variable accounts for the variability in the dependent variable.

6. In order to determine the accuracy of the regression line for prediction purposes, one may compute the *standard error of estimate,* a measure of the scatter of the actual observations about the regression line.

7. Digital computer programs are widely available for regression analysis and for the routine computations of such tests as the above, including *confidence intervals,* so that the accountant can more easily choose the most appropriate independent variable in a given instance.

C. As pointed out by Part Two of the textbook chapter, managers and accountants should be aware of certain limitations and pitfalls in the use of regression analysis to predict costs.

1. Guidelines should be followed in choosing from various possible regressions that use different independent variables.

2. Three main criteria should be met in order for regression analysis to be useful:

a. Economic plausibility and correlation
b. Goodness of fit
c. Specification analysis

3. *Economic plausibility:* The regression should make economic sense to the manager and the accountant.

a. Physical relationships that can be implicitly determined through logic and a knowledge of operations are useful in meeting the plausibility test.

b. *A high correlation between two variables merely indicates that the two variables move together and does not prove a cause-and-effect relationship* (for example, church attendance and beer consumption!).

4. *Goodness of fit:* This criterion involves steps that help measure the degree of plausibility of the cost function.

a. Useful statistical tests include r-square (coefficient of determination) and the t-value for the slope of the regression line.

b. The "fixed-cost" part of the cost function must be interpreted cautiously, because the regression line is not necessarily valid in its extensions beyond the *relevant range.*

5. *Specification analysis:* This criterion deals with various statistical pitfalls to be guarded against or allowed for.

a. The use of canned computer programs without professional help from statisticians might result in the application of statistical tools inappropriate to the particular circumstances.

b. Regression analysis inherently assumes that the relationships will persist, and therefore it should not be used for *nonrepetitive* operations.

c. The validity of inferences from sample data about population relationships depends on four conditions, all of which must be satisfied:

Linearity between x and y in the population. This can be easily checked by a scatter diagram.

Constant variance (*homoscedasticity*), the uniform and random scattering of deviations around the regression line. Again, the scatter diagram furnishes the easiest proof.

Independence from each other of the deviations from points about the regression line.

Normal distribution of points around the regression line.

SELF-TEST AND PRACTICE EXERCISES

(A) For each of the following multiple-choice and true-false statements, select the single most appropriate answer and enter its identification letter in the space provided:

___ 1. The term *cost functions* refers to: (a) the objective of costs; (b) the role of costs; (c) the behavior of costs; (d) none of the above.

___ 2. The main purpose for determining cost functions is to: (a) prove the validity of management decisions; (b) improve the accuracy of cost predictions; (c) correct errors in recording historical costs; (d) develop precise mathematical equations.

___ 3. In the general formula for a straight line, $y = a + bx$, y is: (a) the dependent variable; (b) the independent variable; (c) the intercept; (d) the slope of the line.

___ 4. In the general formula for a straight line, $y = a + bx$, a is: (a) the dependent variable; (b) the independent variable; (c) the intercept; (d) the slope of the line.

___ 5. The dependent variable in a cost function is typically some kind of: (a) input; (b) output.

___ 6. In determining cost functions, the cost analyst aims at predicting persistent relationships between actions and the cost incurred: (a) true; (b) false.

___ 7. In general, our search for appropriate cost functions places primary emphasis on the establishment of cause-and-effect relationships between actions and the cost incurred: (a) true; (b) false.

___ 8. Observations of physical relationships between inputs and outputs are generally: (a) of little use in identifying cost behavior; (b) quite useful in identifying cost behavior.

___ 9. Scatter diagrams: (a) show past behavior of costs; (b) can be used to predict costs; (c) both of the above; (d) neither of the above.

___ 10. Managerial accountants commonly assume that an adequate explanation of cost behavior requires: (a) only one independent variable; (b) several independent variables.

___ 11. In general, managerial accountants assume that cost behavior can be reflected satisfactorily: (a) by linear cost functions; (b) only by non-linear cost functions.

___ 12. Step-variable costs are more often represented by: (a) material costs; (b) labor costs.

___ 13. In step-function costs, as the cost steps become wider, the cost behavior approaches the behavior of: (a) fixed costs; (b) variable costs; (c) mixed costs.

___ 14. The industrial engineering approach to the determination of cost functions: (a) aims at discovering the most efficient means of obtaining a desired output; (b) is the most complete attack on the problem of determining cost behavior; (c) both of the above; (d) neither of the above.

___ 15. The industrial engineering approach: (a) traces costs to inputs and outputs; (b) de-emphasizes dependence on historical cost functions; (c) both of the above; (d) neither of the above.

___ 16. Methods with significant shortcomings for approximating cost functions include: (a) the high-low method; (b) the visual-fit method; (c) both of the above; (d) neither of the above.

___ 17. Regression analysis is used in cost accounting for the primary purpose of: (a) increasing the precision of cost measurements; (b) determining cause-and-effect relationships; (c) aiding in cost prediction; (d) assisting in the assignment of cost responsibilities.

___ 18. The regression line determined by the least-squares method is: (a) straight; (b) curved.

___ 19. The first step that should be taken in a simple regression-analysis approach is: (a) to calculate the coefficient of correlation; (b) to make the least-squares computations; (c) to plot two variables on a scatter diagram; (d) to find the standard error of estimate.

___ 20. For making regression-analysis computations, digital computer programs are: (a) usually available; (b) seldom available.

___ 21. Canned computer programs for regression analysis can generally be used quite safely without professional help from statisticians: (a) true; (b) false.

___ 22. In cost accounting, regression analysis is appropriate for: (a) repetitive operations; (b) nonrepetitive operations; (c) both of the above; (d) neither of the above.

___ 23. A high correlation between two variables is proof of a cause-and-effect relationship: (a) true; (b) false.

(B) Complete each of the following statements:

1. A rather technical term often used in referring to cost-behavior patterns is ______________________ ______________________.

2. The ______________________ variable may be expressed as a function of the ______________________ variable.

3. One method for approximating cost functions is to analyze each account and classify it into one of three categories: ______________________, ______________, and ____________.

4. The method of approximating cost functions by simply drawing a straight line through the points on a ______________________ is called the ______________________ method.

5. A mathematical technique that measures the average amount of change in one variable that is associated with unit increases in another variable is called ______________________.

6. In the formula for a straight line, $y = a + bx$, b measures ______________________ and is called ______________________.

7. The mathematical method for determining the equation for a particular regression line is called ______________________.

8. The uniform and random scattering of deviations around the regression line is called ______________________.

9. The regression line is not necessarily valid in its extensions beyond ______________________.

(C) The Verity Statistical Equipment Company uses a least-squares equation for predicting its direct labor costs for different batch sizes in its Veneering Process: $y = \$200 + \$50\,x$.

1. Identify or determine the symbol or amount that represents each of the following ideas or amounts:

   (a) The dependent variable . . . . ______________

   (b) The independent variable . . . . ______________

   (c) The slope of the regression line . . . . ______________

   (d) The total labor cost for a batch size of 12 . . . . $ ______________

   (e) The mathematical value of the dependent variable when the independent variable is zero . . . . $ ______________

2. See (e) above.

   (a) Is this the expected cost at zero activity? . . . . ________ Why?

   (b) Is this a valid estimate of fixed cost? . . . . ________ Why?

Variances: Mix, Yield, and Investigation

26

We have studied cost variances for price and efficiency in relatively simple situations that involve the use of labor, overhead, and one kind of material to make a single type of product. However, variance analysis is usually more complicated, because most companies produce several types of products in different combinations or mixes and also utilize different mixes of materials in manufacturing a given type of product. For convenience in dealing with these and related problems, the chapter is divided into three major parts, each of which can be studied independently.

The first part of the chapter explains and demonstrates how computations of *sales-mix variances* can be included in the analysis of the total difference between actual and budgeted *contribution margins.* The second part describes procedures for including *yield variances* in the analysis of the difference between actual and budgeted *manufacturing costs.* The third part of the chapter distinguishes between variances or deviations due to chance (*random deviations*) and those due to other causes. This part also includes an approach to investigating variances that uses probabilities and predictions for comparing expected costs and benefits.

REVIEW SUMMARY

PART ONE

A. For management control purposes, it is useful to analyze the difference between the actual and budgeted amounts of a company's *contribution margin* (sales minus variable costs).

1. The simplest approach to explaining the total variance between budgeted and actual operations is to make a product-by-product analysis having three components: price, efficiency, and volume variances.

a. The central example for this part of the chapter (textbook Exhibit 26-1) shows variances that are due only to the *volume component.*

b. Note in this example that there are no changes from the budget in product selling prices or variable costs per unit, and thus the unit contribution margin is unchanged for each of the two products, A and B.

2. As the example shows, the *total volume* in units did not change from the budget, but there were changes in the *physical proportions* of the two products, and hence a *mix variance.*

a. Observe that the total contribution margin was $60,000 more than budgeted because a larger proportion of the higher-margin Product B was actually sold than was specified in the original mix.

b. Although the *volume* variance in a situation like this could be subdivided into *quantity* and *mix* variances, a more straightforward analysis of the volume variance shows that the $60,000 improvement in total contribution margin was simply the excess of the $70,000 favorable variance in Product B's contribution margin over the $10,000 unfavorable variance in the contribution margin of Product A.

3. The profit-volume graph in Exhibit 26-2 (called a P/V chart) shows the relationships for the textbook example.

a. The main point this illustrates is that in using cost-volume-profit analysis, one must be aware of the effects of underlying assumptions, particularly as to the product mix.

b. For example, if the specified proportions of Products A and B are maintained at various volume levels, the *average* contribution margin per unit would not be affected by volume changes.

PART TWO

B. Manufacturing processes often involve different mixes of materials to make a specific product.

1. *Mix* means the relative proportion or combination of the various ingredients of direct materials or of the components of a finished product line.

2. *Yield* means the quantity of finished output produced from a predetermined or standard combination and amount of inputs such as direct material or direct labor.

3. Changes in the specified mix of inputs will, of course, affect yield or output.

4. The usual analysis can be made of the difference between actual inputs at actual prices and standard inputs allowed at standard prices, as shown by the textbook example of material costs:

a. The *price variance* would be the difference between the actual inputs at actual prices and the actual inputs at standard prices.

b. The *efficiency variance* would be the difference between actual inputs at standard prices and standard inputs allowed at standard prices.

5. However, if the manager wants a more exhaustive analysis, beginning from his initial expectations, he could make the type of analysis summarized in Exhibit 26-4.

a. The *yield variance* would be the difference between the standard combination of inputs for actual output at standard prices and the "adjusted expectations."

b. The *order-adjustment variance* would be the difference between the "adjusted expectations" and the "initial expectations."

c. Note that these two variances account for the usual *volume variance.*

d. Exhibit 26-4 shows all these variances for both direct materials and direct labor.

6. You should especially try to understand the yield variance.

a. This variance assumes that the standard combination of inputs is not changed.

b. Thus, the yield variance is defined as the anticipated change in expected cost because output deviated from that expected for the total actual inputs.

PART THREE

C. Usually, of course, the actual costs of any process differ from the expected, budgeted, or standard costs.

1. The variances or deviations from standards may be classified into five types on the basis of their *causes*, or *sources*, each type involving different management decisions for corrective actions:

a. An *implementation deviation* is a human or mechanical failure to achieve a specific obtainable action. This is largely the *traditional concept* of cost variances.

b. A *prediction deviation* is an error in predicting a parameter value in the decision model.

c. A *measurement deviation* is an error in measuring the actual cost of operating a process.

d. A *model deviation* is an error in the functional representation or formulation of the decision model.

e. A *random deviation* is a difference between actual cost and expected cost due to chance, which by definition is a deviation that calls for no corrective action.

2. When deviations from standards are reported in manufacturing processes, management must decide whether to investigate them.

a. Unfortunately, such deviations are often quite difficult to analyze, because *interdependencies* typically exist among the different kinds of processes, deviations, and investigations.

b. Conceptually, the decision to investigate performance deviations would be made if the expected benefits from the investigation exceeded the expected costs of the investigation.

c. The textbook example (see Exhibit 26-5) describes mathematical models that use probabilities and predicted costs in developing three critical figures that can aid the decision maker:

(1) The expected cost of the decision to investigate,

(2) The expected cost of the decision not to investigate,

(3) The level of the probability of being out of control that would equalize the expected costs of investigating and the expected costs of not investigating (*point of indifference*, or *breakeven point*).

d. The rules of thumb or intuition often used in practice are models that are simpler than these mathematical models, but they nevertheless implicitly recognize the same variables used in the mathematical models.

3. *Statistical quality control* (SQC) techniques are often used to distinguish between random deviations and other deviations as a first step in deciding whether to investigate deviations or variations from standards.

a. In practice, actual performance may vary from a *single* standard and yet fall within a *band*, or *range*, of acceptable results.

b. SQC offers means for distinguishing between deviations falling within the acceptable band (*random variances*) and those falling outside the band (*nonrandom variances*).

c. Random variances are due to chance, and they do not need investigation.

d. Nonrandom variances are due to other causes, and they do require investigation.

e. However, traditional SQC has certain weaknesses, and therefore, limited usefulness in an accounting setting.

SELF-TEST AND PRACTICE EXERCISES

(A) For each of the following multiple-choice and true-false statements, select the single most appropriate answer and enter its identification letter in the space provided;

PART ONE

____ 1. Most companies produce more than one product or service: (a) true; (b) false.

____ 2. Volume variance is the difference between some initial or original budgeted or expected output and the actual output, multiplied by: (a) actual price; (b) standard price.

____ 3. A sales-mix variance is due to changes in: (a) total volume of product units sold; (b) prices of product units sold; (c) proportions of product units sold.

____ 4. If the original sales mix of products was maintained, but the physical volume decreased by 10%, there would be: (a) a quantity variance; (b) a sales-mix variance; (c) both of the above; (d) neither of the above.

____ 5. There is only one way to compute the volume variance: (a) true; (b) false.

____ 6. The vertical axis of a P/V chart is: (a) net income in dollars; (b) volume of sales dollars or product units; (c) neither of the above.

PART TWO

____ 7. In the context of this chapter, yield means: (a) budgeted net income; (b) proportions of inputs; (c) quantity of outputs from a standard combination of inputs.

____ 8. Yield can be affected by changes from the specified mix of inputs: (a) true; (b) false.

____ 9. Efficiency variance is the standard price multiplied by the difference between actual inputs and standard inputs allowed: (a) true; (b) false.

____ 10. A favorable order-adjustment variance is the excess of: (a) initial expectations over adjusted expectations; (b) adjusted expectations over initial expectations; (c) neither of the above.

____ 11. The yield variance: (a) assumes that the standard combination of inputs is not changed; (b) is defined as the anticipated changes in expected cost because output deviated from that expected for the total actual inputs; (c) both of the above; (d) neither of the above.

PART THREE

____ 12. The traditional concept of cost variances from standard is represented by: (a) prediction deviations; (b) random deviations; (c) implementation deviations; (d) model deviations; (e) measurement deviations.

____ 13. A deviation in predicting a parameter value in the decision model is conceptually: (a) a model deviation; (b) a prediction deviation; (c) both of the above; (d) neither of the above.

____ 14. A random deviation of actual costs from standard costs: (a) is due to chance; (b) requires no corrective action; (c) both of the above; (d) neither of the above.

____ 15. The textbook mathematical models for determining whether to investigate performance deviations use: (a) probabilities; (b) predicted costs; (c) both of the above; (d) neither of the above.

____ 16. If the probability of being out of control exceeds the point of indifference, investigation of the deviation is generally: (a) desirable; (b) not desirable.

____ 17. In practice, the actual performance of manufacturing processes is usually acceptable: (a) only if it meets the single standard of performance; (b) if it falls within a predetermined band or range.

____ 18. The main objective of statistical quality control (SQC) is: (a) to classify products according to their quality; (b) to measure the total difference between standard costs and actual costs; (c) to distinguish between random and nonrandom variances from standard performance; (d) to measure individual variances from standard performance.

____ 19. It would not be necessary to seek causes for observations that fall within the normal band determined by SQC techniques: (a) true; (b) false.

(B) Complete each of the following statements:

PART ONE

1. Contribution margin is __________ minus __________ ____________________.

2. The combination in which a company sells different products is called ____________________.

3. The total variance in contribution margin is the difference between the actual contribution margin and ____________________.

PART TWO

4. The material price variance is the difference between actual and standard unit price multiplied by __________ ____________________.

5. The yield variance is the difference between the standard combination of inputs for actual output at standard prices and ____________________.

PART THREE

6. When the difference between actual cost and expected cost is due to chance, it is called __________ ____________________.

7. Conceptually, the management decision to investigate performance deviations would be made if the ____________________ exceeded the ____________________.

8. A useful first step in deciding whether to investigate variances from standard performances is to distinguish between ____________________ __________ and __________ __________.

9. ____________________ is a general approach that relies on classical statistics techniques for identifying random deviations and for deciding when to investigate deviations.

(C) This problem is based on the textbook case presented in Exhibit 26-1. However you need to use only the following data in working the problem:

Product	Unit Contribution Margin	Budgeted Unit Sales	Actual Unit Sales
A	$1.00	120,000	130,000
B	7.00	40,000	38,000
Weighted Average	2.50		

Assume that actual contribution margins for Products A and B are the same per unit as budgeted: $1.00 and $7.00.

1. Compute the following amounts:

(a) Total budgeted contribution margin .... $__________

(b) Total actual contribution margin .... $__________

(c) Total variance to be accounted for .... $__________

2. Prepare a detailed analysis of the volume variance:

Product A: .... $__________

Product B: .... $__________

Total volume variance .... $__________

3. Break the volume variance into these two subparts:

(a) Quantity variance:

Product A: .... $__________

Product B: .... $__________

Total quantity variance .... $__________

(b) Sales-mix variance:

Product A: .... $__________

Product B: .... $ ________

Total sales-mix variance .... $ ________

4. a) Which of the analyses above seems more helpful in understanding what happened: 2 or 3? ________

   b) Give reasons to support your answer:

PART TWO

(D) Intricate Electronics Inc. presents the following data concerning its materials costs:

Initial expectations: standard combination of inputs for scheduled outputs	$63,000
Adjusted expectations: standard combination of actual outputs	$57,500
Actual output:	
Actual inputs at actual prices........	$59,100
Actual combination of inputs at standard prices	$60,200
Standard combination of inputs at standard prices	$58,800

Compute the following:

1. Price variance: .... $ ________

2. Efficiency variance: .... $ ________

3. Volume variance: .... $ ________

4. Order-adjustment variance: .... $ ________

5. Yield variance: .... $ ________

(E) Given for the Balancing Process of the Candid Scales Company:

Cost of investigation (C)	$ 2,400
Cost of correcting the deviation (M)	$10,000
Present value of costs that could be saved by correcting the deviation (L)	$40,000
Probability of being out of control	.05

1. **Summarize these data in a decision table.**

2. Compute the expected cost of the decision to investigate . . . . . $______

3. Compute the expected cost of the decision not to investigate . . . . . $______

4. Compute the out-of-control probability at the point of indifference (breakeven point) . . . . . ______

Cost Accounting and Linear Programming

27

Cost accounting today is not a narrow field, separate and distinct from other areas; it is an important part of the information system needed for executive decision making. For example, as we have seen in other chapters, management decisions are often facilitated by various kinds of *mathematical models* that typically depend on accounting data for their usefulness.

This chapter deals with the fundamentals of another widely known mathematical decision model, *linear programming* (*LP*). This is a formal approach to the short-run assignment of limited productive resources for use in an optimal manner. As a modern management accountant, you should be able to recognize the situations for which LP would be feasible, to construct the appropriate models, to deal with computer programmers in solving LP problems, and to understand the principal implications for managers and accountants.

REVIEW SUMMARY

A. *Linear programming* is a mathematical search procedure for finding the optimum solution to certain types of short-run problems.

1. The objective of LP is to determine, for a fixed set of available resources, the combination of products or services that maximizes profits or minimizes costs.

a. For example, a typical problem is the determination of the optimal quantity of two or more products to process through a series of manufacturing operations.

b. The basic idea was described in Chapter 11: to determine these quantities on the basis of the maximum contribution per unit of the *scarce resource* or *constraining factor,* such as total available machine-hours.

c. However, in practice there is usually more than one constraint—often many—and it is these situations for which the LP model is appropriate.

2. The most crucial step in solving an LP problem is to build the LP model.

a. Essentially this means the formulation of the *simultaneous linear equations* to express the relationships of numerous variables.

b. Most LP problems have so many variables that these equations must be solved by digital computers (typically with the aid of computer programmers).

c. The formulation of the equations is, of course, the most crucial step, not the mechanics of the solution.

3. Your most helpful key to understanding how to set up the LP equations is the textbook example on which most of the chapter is based.

a. The first step is to construct an equation to express the objective. This equation is an *objective function* to be maximized or minimized.

b. The second step is to determine the basic relationships: to construct in mathematical form the *inequalities* to reflect the applicable *constraints* imposed by scarce resources.

c. Your understanding of these constraints can be greatly aided if you trace them to the graph in textbook Exhibit 27-1.

4. The textbook refers to three different ways for solving an LP problem:

a. The graphic approach (Exhibit 27-1) is practicable only in the simplest of situations, but it is used here mainly to help you grasp the principal idea that the optimal solution is typically at a corner of the "area of feasible production combinations," the polygon bounded by straight lines representing constraints.

b. Manual trial-and-error computations can be used to arrive at the optimal solution in a simple case like the textbook example. You should carefully follow these computations and trace them to the graphic solution in Exhibit 27-1.

c. However, the solution to most LP problems requires digital computers for performing an *iterative* (step-by-step) process called the *simplex method.*

d. Accountants and managers should concentrate on a careful and accurate construction of the LP model, because solutions obtained through linear programming are, of course, no more reliable than the data used in formulating the LP equations.

B. All approaches to solving LP problems are based, in essence, on the *substitution of the scarce resource* (productive capacity) among two or more products that can be processed through a particular operation.

1. Moving from one corner of the polygon of feasible solutions to another corner involves giving up the contribution margin of one product and adding the contribution margin of another product.

2. You should be certain to understand this key concept. See the related corners in the graph (Exhibit 27-1).

C. LP problems have important implications for managers and accountants.

1. It is, of course, impossible to predict (or measure) accurately all relevant revenues, costs, and technical coefficients in an LP model.

a. Thus, managers and accountants need to know the possible effects on the optimal solutions that may be due to errors of prediction (or measurement).

b. These effects can be determined by making a *sensitivity analysis* in order to find the *cost of the prediction error* for selected differences in predicting certain data.

c. In some cases, although the total contribution margin will be affected by prediction errors, there may be no change in the selection of the optimal combination of products to make.

d. Sensitivity analysis can also reveal how much prediction error can be tolerated before the optimal choice would change.

2. Prediction errors can often be reduced by spending more money to obtain better information or to implement predictions; thus, a *cost-benefit approach* is often appropriate.

3. The determination of possible changes in contribution margins by expanding capacity can be facilitated by computations of *shadow prices.*

a. These are opportunity costs that measure contributions foregone by failing to have an additional unit of a scarce resource in a particular situation.

b. Shadow prices are customarily provided by LP computer programs.

4. The use of LP techniques requires at least two basic assumptions, and these are important limitations that managers must face in deciding whether to use an LP approach in a given case:

a. All relationships between capacity and production are *linear.*

b. All data used in the equations for the LP model are *stated in certain terms.* (Probability factors do not *appear* in the equations, although probabilities may have been *used* to forecast the data appearing in the equations.)

SELF-TEST AND PRACTICE EXERCISES

(A) For each of the following multiple-choice and true-false statements, select the single most appropriate answer and enter its identification letter in the space provided:

____ 1. The most widespread use of the LP model is for: (a) short-run decisions; (b) long-run decisions.

____ 2. Accountants and managers should be able at least to: (a) help construct LP models; (b) understand the mathematics of LP problems; (c) work with computer programmers; (d) all of these.

____ 3. A typical objective of linear programming is: (a) to measure the quality of production; (b) to control the quality of production; (c) to forecast completion dates for special projects; (d) to determine the best combination of resources to use in production.

____ 4. Most LP problems have such a large number of variables that they must be solved by digital computers: (a) true; (b) false.

____ 5. The most critical phase of linear programming is: (a) solving the simultaneous linear equations; (b) building the LP model.

____ 6. LP models typically have: (a) no constraints; (b) only one constraint; (c) several constraints.

____ 7. In an LP model there is usually only one: (a) objective function; (b) feasible alternative; (c) both of these; (d) neither of these.

____ 8. All of the equal total-contribution-margin lines on an LP graph show the slope of the objective function: (a) true; (b) false.

____ 9. Manual trial-and-error computations are feasible to use in arriving at the optimal solution of an LP problem in: (a) all situations; (b) no situations; (c) simple situations only.

____10. Sensitivity analysis can be used in LP situations to: (a) find the cost of the prediction error; (b) determine how much prediction error can be tolerated before the optimal choice would change; (c) both of these; (d) neither of these.

____11. The assumptions or requirements that underlie the use of LP techniques include: (a) non-linear relationships between capacity and production; (b) statement of equations in probabilistic terms; (c) both of the above; (d) neither of the above.

____12. In practice, the optimum solution to an LP problem is usually determined by: (a) a graphic approach; (b) the simplex method.

____13. In LP problems, there are typically several: (a) feasible alternatives; (b) constraints; (c) both of the above; (d) neither of the above.

____14. Solutions to most LP problems require: (a) digital computers; (b) an iterative process; (c) both of the above; (d) neither of the above.

(B) Complete each of the following statements:

1. A mathematical search procedure for finding the best solution to short-run problems for the allocation of resources is called ____________.

2. The equation that expresses the objective in an LP problem is called ____________ ____________.

3. The mathematical expressions of inequalities for an LP problem represent ____________ ____________.

4. The coefficients of the constraints are often called ____________.

5. Alternative LP solutions that are technically possible are called ____________.

6. In the graphic solution to an LP problem, the optimal combination of resources generally lies at a polygon corner through which an ____________ ____________ line can be drawn that is furthest from the origin.

7. Opportunity costs that measure contributions foregone by failing to have an additional unit of a scarce resource in a particular situation are called ____________.

(C) Effortless Perfume Company, which can produce either of two kinds of perfume called Explore and Encore, furnishes the following data:

Product	Daily Capacity in Product Units Process Q	Process T	Contribution Margin per Product Unit
Explore (X)	200	400	\$ 7.00
or			
Encore (Y)	400	160	\$ 8.00

Severe material shortages for Encore will limit its production to a maximum of 150 per day. Assuming that daily capacities in *total machine-hours* are 200 for Process Q and 400 for Process T compute:

1. Process Q machine-hours required per Y product unit: .... ________ hr

2. Process T machine hours required per Y product unit: .... ________ hr

Developing the relevant equations for a linear programming solution:

3. Maximum total contribution margin = ________________________________

4. Process Q constraint: ________________________________

5. Process T constraint: ________________________________

6. Material shortage constraint: ________________________________

7. Negative production constraints: ________________________________

Cost Accounting in Professional Examinations

28

The many readers of the textbook who plan to become Certified Public Accountants or Certified Management Accountants are interested, of course, in the content of the CPA and CMA examinations Because cost accounting is one of the two most important topics in the Practice section of the CPA examination, many of the previous chapters in this book can be quite useful for study and review. This is especially so now because of the increasing emphasis by the CPA examination upon mathematical and statistical methods of analysis and upon the management-decision aspects of cost accounting. The CMA examination also emphasizes these and related topics.

However, the accounting terminology in these professional examinations is not uniform, and some problem situations appear somewhat strange to candidates. Moreover, alternative solutions are acceptable for some problems. Candidates who understand and anticipate these differences are better prepared for the examinations. Therefore, we take up in this chapter several of the alternative terms, accounting procedures, and solution approaches for examination problems dealing with cost accounting.

REVIEW SUMMARY

A. Because the professional examinations include problems from many sources and are given on a nationwide basis, they have two characteristics that should be recognized by candidates:

1. A meaning may be expressed by different terms; for example:

a. *Factory overhead* may be called *factory burden, manufacturing expenses, indirect manufacturing costs,* or *manufacturing overhead.*

b. *Cost of goods sold* and *cost of sales* are used interchangeably.

c. *Direct materials* are often referred to as *raw materials.*

d. *Denominator volume* is our textbook term for the level of activity used for computing predetermined overhead rates, but this is most often called *normal* or *standard volume.*

e. *Efficiency variance* may be called *usage* or *quantity variance.*

f. *Price variance* may be called *rate variance.*

2. Alternative solutions may be acceptable for full grading credit in some cases.

a. When solving problems, candidates should always use terminology that is *consistent* with the problem terminology.

b. In general, candidates should interpret problem requirements *literally.*

c. If a candidate thinks it is desirable to make an assumption—and this is *rarely necessary*—he should state the assumption clearly and support it with adequate reasons.

B. As shown by textbook Exhibit 28-1, several alternative methods are used for accumulating manufacturing costs in general-ledger accounts.

1. When direct materials are issued for production or direct-labor costs are incurred, they may be charged immediately to the Work in Process account, or they may be carried first through intermediate accounts called Direct Materials Used or Direct Labor, respectively.

2. The materials-efficiency variance and the direct-labor price variance may be recognized either when costs are charged to the Work in Process account or when costs are transferred to the Finished Goods account.

3. When factory-overhead costs are incurred, they may be charged directly to a single control account, or they may be carried first through several intermediate accounts for functional types of costs, such as Depreciation, Repairs, and Power.

C. Alternative procedures for standard costs are in use:

1. The Work in Process account can be charged on any of three different bases:

a. Actual quantities at actual prices

b. Actual quantities at standard prices

c. Standard quantities at standard prices

2. Overhead variances are computed in different ways:

a. The recommended approach described in Chapter 9 breaks the total variance into a volume variance and a budget variance, the latter being subdivided into a spending variance and an efficiency variance (Alternative 1 in Chapter 28).

b. Three other methods for analyzing variances are sometimes used, but they have the serious shortcomings described in this textbook chapter (Alternatives 2, 3, and 4 in Chapter 28).

D. Alternative methods of accounting for spoilage in process costing are sometimes used in published examination solutions.

1. Some of these methods ignore the computations of equivalent units for spoilage, shrinkage, or waste.

2. However, the conceptually superior method described in Chapter 19 includes computations of equivalent units for spoilage, shrinkage, and waste, and thus does not improperly charge spoilage costs to goods that have not yet reached the stage where spoilage occurs.

SELF-TEST AND PRACTICE EXERCISES

(A) For each of the following multiple-choice and true-false statements, select the single most appropriate answer and enter its identification letter in the space provided:

____ 1. CPA examinations seem to be placing decreasing emphasis upon (a) the management-decision aspects of cost accounting; (b) quantitative methods and techniques; (c) measurements of inventory and income; (d) all of the above; (e) none of the above.

____ 2. In the professional accounting examinations: (a) alternative solutions may be acceptable; (b) terminology may not be uniform; (c) both of the above; (d) neither of the above.

____ 3. An acceptable alternative term for factory overhead is manufacturing expenses: (a) true; (b) false.

____ 4. In general, it would not be unwise to use acceptable alternative terminology in solving CPA and CMA problems, even though such terminology is inconsistent with that used in the problem: (a) true; (b) false.

____ 5. When solving CPA and CMA problems, candidates should make assumptions: (a) always; (b) frequently; (c) rarely; (d) never.

____ 6. When direct-labor costs are incurred, they may be charged first to: (a) the Work in Process account; (b) Direct Labor; (c) either of the above; (d) neither of the above.

___ 7. The materials-efficiency or usage variance may be recognized when costs are charged to: (a) the Work in Process account; (b) the Finished Goods account; (c) either of the above; (d) neither of the above.

___ 8. The charges to the Work-in-Process account under a standard cost accounting system may be made on the basis of: (a) standard quantities at standard prices; (b) standard quantities at actual prices; (c) either of the above; (d) neither of the above.

___ 9. Published solutions to CPA exams have included some unsound methods for analyzing overhead variances: (a) true; (b) false.

___ 10. Equivalent units for spoilage, shrinkage, and waste: (a) would be computed under the conceptually superior method; (b) would not be computed under the conceptually superior method.

(B) Complete each of the following statements:

1. An acceptable alternative term for cost of goods sold is ______________________.
2. An acceptable alternative term for denominator volume is ______________________.
3. When direct materials are issued for production, debits may be made either to the ______________ account or to ______________ account.
4. The direct-labor price or rate variance may be recognized either when costs are charged to the ______________ account or when costs are transferred to the ______________ account.
5. In the recommended approach for analyzing overhead variances, the budget variance is subdivided into ______________ variance and ______________ variance.

Solutions to Self-Tests and Practice Exercises

CHAPTER 1

(A) 1c, 2b, 3b, 4d, 5b, 6a, 7b, 8e, 9b, 10c, 11c, 12a, 13b, 14d, 15d, 16c, 17a

(B) 1 management or managerial; 2 alternative actions, objectives, or goals; 3 decision model; 4 feedback; 5 objectives or goals, decision; 6 cost-benefit; 7 the controller; 8 watchdog, helper.

(C) 1L, 2N, 3S, 4L, 5S, 6N, 7N, 8L, 9S, 10L

(D) 1S, 2S, 3P, 4P, 5S, 6S, 7P, 8S, 9S, 10P

CHAPTER 2

(A) 1a, 2c, 3d, 4b, 5a, 6c, 7b, 8e, 9b, 10b, 11d, 12b, 13a, 14a, 15c, 16a

(B) 1 a cost objective; 2 cost accumulation; 3 cost functions; 4 direct-material, direct-labor; 5 conversion; 6 indirect materials (or supplies); 7 gross margin (or gross profit); 8 inventoriable; 9 finished-goods, work-in-process, materials and supplies; 10 payroll fringe; 11 the cost of goods sold (or cost of sales); 12 the cost of goods available for sale.

(C) 1 F N, 2 F I, 3 F N, 4 V I, 5 F N, 6 V N, 7 V I, 8 F I, 9 V I, 10 V I

(D) 1.

Perfect Square Domino Manufacturing Company
Schedule of Cost of Goods Manufactured
For Year Ended December 31, 19_2

Direct materials:		
Inventory, December 31, 19_1	$ 22,000	
Purchases of direct materials	88,000	
Cost of direct materials available for use	$110,000	
Inventory, December 31, 19_2	20,000	
Direct materials used		$ 90,000
Direct labor		70,000
Factory overhead:		
Indirect labor	$ 28,000	
Supplies	2,000	
Heat, light, and power	3,000	
Depreciation, machinery	4,000	
Rent, factory building	12,000	
Miscellaneous	1,000	50,000
Manufacturing costs incurred during 19_2		$210,000
Add work-in-process inventory, December 31, 19_1		18,000
Manufacturing costs to account for		$228,000
Less work-in-process inventory, December 31, 19_2		12,000
Cost of goods manufactured (to Income Statement)		$216,000

2.

Perfect Square Domino Manufacturing Company
Income Statement
For Year Ended December 31, 19 _2

Sales		$350,000
Less cost of goods sold:		
Finished goods, December 31, 19 _1	$ 39,000	
Cost of goods manufactured (see schedule)	216,000	
Cost of goods available for sale	$255,000	
Finished goods, December 31, 19 _2	45,000	
Cost of goods sold		210,000
Gross margin		$140,000
Less selling and administrative expenses (detailed)		120,000
Net income		$ 20,000

CHAPTER 3

(A) 1d, 2b, 3c, 4a, 5b, 6c, 7a, 8d, 9a, 10b, 11b, 12a, 13b, 14e, 15a, 16b

(B) 1 contribution margin; 2 activity volume (or level of activity); 3 relevant range; 4 activity volume (or level of activity); 5 sensitivity analysis; 6 increase; 7 sales mix.

(C) Adjustable Products, Inc.:

1. Unit contribution margin is unit selling price less unit variable expenses: $40 – $30 = $10.
2. Breakeven sales in units is total fixed expenses divided by unit contribution margin: $600 ÷ $10 = 60 units.
3. Unit sales to produce a target net income would be the sum of the total fixed expenses and the target net income divided by the unit contribution margin: ($600 + $250) ÷ $10 = $850 ÷ $10 = 85 units.
4. If the target net income is 15% of sales, the target net income per product unit would be: (15%) ($40) = $6 per unit. Therefore, the dollars per product unit available for coverage of the total fixed expenses would be the unit sales price less the unit net income less the unit variable costs: $40 – $6 – $30 = $4 per unit. Dividing this into the total fixed expenses gives us the required sales in units: $600 ÷ $4 = 150 units.
5. Each unit would contribute $10 toward total fixed expenses. Therefore, net income would be: ($10) (80) – $600 = $800 – $600 = $200.
6. The new unit contribution margin would be $40 – ($30 + $3) = $7 per unit. The new total fixed expenses would be: $600 – $110 = $490. Therefore, the new breakeven sales in units would be: $490 ÷ $7 = 70 units.

7. The necessary unit contribution margin to cover *both* the target net income and the total fixed expenses would be: (\$200 + \$600) ÷ 100 = \$800 ÷ 100 = \$8 per product unit. Therefore, the selling price per unit would be the variable cost per unit plus this unit contribution margin: \$30 + \$8 = \$38.

(D) Aggregate Sales Company:

1. Sales less fixed and variable expenses: \$60,000 – \$12,000 – \$42,000 = \$6,000.
2. Contribution-margin ratio: (\$60,000 – \$42,000) ÷ \$60,000 = \$18,000 ÷ \$60,000 = 30%.
3. Breakeven sales are total fixed expenses divided by the contribution-margin ratio: \$12,000 ÷ 30% = \$40,000.
4. Divide the sum of the fixed expenses and the desired net income (target net income) by the contribution-margin ratio: (\$12,000 + \$9,000) ÷ 30% = \$21,000 ÷ 30% = \$70,000.
5. These sales would be total fixed expenses divided by the excess of the contribution-margin ratio (or percent) over the net-income ratio (or percent): \$12,000 ÷ (30% – 20%) = \$12,000 ÷ 10% = \$120,000. Another approach would be to set up an equation with *S* for the required sales and using the 70% variable-expenses percentage and the 20% net income percentage:

$$S = \$12{,}000 + 70\%\,S + 20\%S = \$12{,}000 + 90\%\,S$$
$$10\%S = \$12{,}000$$
$$S = \$12{,}000 \div 10\% = \$120{,}000$$

6. The new total fixed expenses would be: \$12,000 – \$2,000 = \$10,000. The new variable-cost percentage (*to total dollar sales*) would be: \$42,000 ÷ (\$60,000 – 10% of \$60,000) = \$42,000 ÷ \$54,000 = 7/9. Therefore, the new contribution-margin ratio would be 2/9. The new breakeven sales would then be the new total fixed expenses divided by the new contribution-margin ratio: \$10,000 ÷ 2/9 = \$10,000 X 9/2 = \$45,000.

(E) 1.

Dual-View Lens Corporation
Income Statement
For the Year Ended December 31, 19_8

Sales		\$365,000
Less manufacturing cost of goods sold		200,000
Gross profit (or gross margin)		\$165,000
Less selling and administrative expenses:		
Selling expenses	\$100,000	
Administrative expenses	40,000	140,000
Operating income		\$ 25,000

2.

Dual-View Lens Corporation
Income Statement
For the Year Ended December 31, 19_8

Sales		\$365,000
Less variable expenses:		
Manufacturing	\$120,000	
Selling	80,000	
Administrative	10,000	210,000
Contribution margin		\$155,000
Less fixed expenses:		
Manufacturing	\$ 80,000	
Selling	20,000	
Administrative	30,000	130,000
Operating income		\$ 25,000

3.

Operating income, as above	\$ 25,000
Add 10% of contribution margin: 10% X 155,000	15,500
Operating income after a 10% increase in sales volume	\$ 40,500

CHAPTER 4

(A) 1b, 2c, 3b, 4b, 5c, 6b, 7a, 8a, 9b, 10b, 11a, 12a, 13b, 14e, 15a, 16a, 17b

(B) 1 job-order, process; 2 cost centers or departments; 3 cost sheets for uncompleted jobs; 4 the stores requisition; 5 Work-in-Process, job-cost sheets; 6 budgeted factory-overhead, budgeted direct-labor (or budgeted machine); 7 the predetermined overhead rate, the actual (or historical) amount of the rate base; 8 credit, Cost of Sales, Finished Goods, Work-in-Process.

(C) Forward Calendar Company:

1. The predetermined overhead rate is budgeted factory-overhead cost divided by budgeted direct-labor hours: $220,000 ÷ 200,000 = $1.10 per hr.

2. Applied factory-overhead cost is actual direct-labor hours times the predetermined overhead rate: (210,000) ($1.10) = $231,000.

3. Overapplied factory-overhead cost is applied overhead cost minus actual overhead cost: $231,000 – $226,000 = $5,000.

(D) Great Works Producing Corporation:

1. (e)

April 1 balance of stores	$ 32,000
Add materials purchased (b)	42,000
Materials available for use	$ 74,000
Less April 30 balance of stores	30,000
Materials used in April	$ 44,000
Less direct materials used (c)	39,000
Indirect materials used in April	5,000

(f)

Factory payroll paid (1)	$ 22,000
Add accrued payroll, April 30	3,000
Total payroll incurred in April	$ 25,000
Less direct factory labor incurred (d)	16,000
Indirect factory labor incurred in April	9,000

(j)

Direct factory labor incurred (d)	$ 16,000
Multiply by predetermined overhead rate (j)	125%
Applied factory overhead cost for April	$ 20,000

(m)

April 1 balance of work in process	$ 41,000
Add:	
Direct materials used (c)	$ 39,000
Direct labor incurred (d)	16,000
Factory overhead applied (j)	20,000
Total	$116,000
Less April 30 balance of work in process	47,000
Cost of goods manufactured in April	$ 69,000

(n)

April 1 balance of finished goods	$148,000
Add cost of goods manufactured (m)	69,000
Cost of goods available for sale in April	$217,000
Less April 30 balance of finished goods	152,000
Cost of goods sold in April	$ 65,000

2.

Cash

	Debit		Credit
	10,000	k)	49,000
a)	105,000	l)	22,000

Unexpired Insurance

	Debit		Credit
	1,000	g)	300

Allowance for Depreciation

	Debit		Credit
			70,000
		h)	1,700

Accounts Payable

	Debit		Credit
k)	49,000		27,000
		b)	42,000
		i)	3,000

Accrued Payroll

	Debit		Credit
l)	22,000		-0-
		d)	16,000
		f)	9,000

Stores Control

	Debit		Credit
	32,000	c)	39,000
b)	42,000	e)	5,000

Factory Department Overhead Control

	Debit		Credit
	62,000		
e)	5,000		
f)	9,000		
g)	300		
h)	1,700		
i)	3,000		

Factory Overhead Applied

	Debit		Credit
			63,000
		j)	20,000

Work-in-Process Control

	Debit		Credit
	41,000	m)	69,000
c)	39,000		
d)	16,000		
j)	20,000		

Finished Goods Control

	Debit		Credit
	148,000	n)	65,000
m)	69,000		

Cost of Sales

	Debit		Credit
	200,000		
n)	65,000		

Sales

	Debit		Credit
			310,000
		a)	105,000

CHAPTER 5

(A) 1b, 2c, 3b, 4b, 5c, 6b, 7c, 8a, 9e, 10d, 11a, 12b, 13c, 14e, 15a, 16c

(B) 1 pro forma; 2 plans, plans; 3 continuous; 4 sales; 5 the desired ending inventory of finished goods, the beginning inventory of finished goods; 6 deficiencies, idle; 7 financial planning models (or total models); 8 cost-benefit.

(C) Four-C Company:

	Case 1	Case 2
Expected sales in units	10,000	9,500
Add desired ending inventory	1,800	1,200
Total needs	11,800	10,700
Less beginning inventory	1,300	2,850
Budgeted purchases in units	10,500	7,850

(D) Credit Claim Corporation:

	Case 1	Case 2
Beginning balance of accounts receivable	$ 75,000	$ 42,100
Add expected sales on account	243,000	349,000
Total	$318,000	$391,600
Less expected collections from customers	285,000	324,400
Expected ending balance of accounts receivable	$ 33,000	$ 67,200

(E) **Cash-Plan, Inc.:**

	Case 1	Case 2
Beginning cash balance	$ 4,200	$ 2,700
Add expected cash receipts	98,000	73,600
(a) Total available before current financing	$102,200	$ 76,300
Expected cash disbursements	$ 87,000	$ 80,800
Add minimum ending cash balance desired	8,000	8,500
(b) Total cash needed	$ 95,000	$ 89,300
1. Necessary to borrow (b − a)		$ 13,000
2. Available for repayment of loans and interest (a − b)	$ 7,200	

(F) Summ-Totall Material Company:

	Material A	Material B
1. Number of Product X units to be produced	2,000	2,000
Multiply by number of material units needed per Product X unit	X10	X20
(a) Total	20,000	40,000
Number of Product Y units to be produced	3,000	3,000
Multiply by number of material units needed per Product Y unit	X 15	X 6
(b) Total	45,000	18,000
Total number of material units needed for production of both products (a + b)	65,000	58,000
2. Multiply above by unit purchase prices of materials	X $4	X $6
Cost of materials needed for production	$260,000	$348,000
3. **Number of material units desired in ending inventories**	10,000	8,000
Add number of material units needed for production	65,000	58,000
Total material units needed	75,000	66,000
Less number of material units in beginning inventories	6,000	15,000
Number of materials units to be purchased	69,000	51,000
4. Multiply above by unit purchase prices of materials	X $4	X $6
Cost of materials to be purchased	$276,000	$306,000

CHAPTER 6

(A) 1b, 2a, 3d, 4c, 5a, 6b, 7a, 8c, 9b, 10a, 11b, 12b, 13a, 14b, 15c, 16a, 17d, 18a, 19c, 20b, 21b

(B) 1 goal congruence; 2 cost-benefit; 3 responsibility; 4 variances, exception; 5 controllable; 6 human resources, asset; 7 accepted behavior norms.

(C) Adam Taylor Company:

	Variable Cost	Controllable Cost By Controller	By Punch Press Foreman	By Production Superintendent	By Mfg. Vice-Pres.
1. Direct material used in drill press department	Yes	No	No	Yes	Yes
2. **Salary of personnel vice-president**	No	No	No	No	No
3. **Supplies used by purchasing agent**	Yes	No	No	No	Yes
4. **Straight-line depreciation in punch-press department.**	No	No	No*	No*	No*
5. **Secretary's salary in controller's department**	No	Yes	No	No	No
6. Direct labor used in punch press department	Yes	No	Yes	Yes	Yes

*Perhaps controllable over a longer span of time.

Note: Although each of several executives can often regard a given cost item as being within his control, usually there is only one manager in the whole company who bears primary responsibility for control. This is usually the manager who is closest to overseeing the day-to-day action which influences costs. Nevertheless, all costs which are controllable by him are also regarded as being controllable by his superior line executives.

CHAPTER 7

(A) 1b, 2c, 3a, 4c, 5a, 6a, 7d, 8b, 9b, 10c, 11b, 12d, 13a, 14a, 15a, 16b, 17b, 18a, 19c

(B) 1 standard costs, feedback; 2 actual, standard; 3 efficiency, price; 4 unit, total; 5 basic; 6 actual, standard; 7 purchased, issued (or used); 8 purchasing; 9 standard; first-in, first-out; last-in, last-out; 10 hours, wage rates; 11 learning, standards.

(C) Mustang Saddle Corporation:

1. Analysis Framework

(1) Actual Inputs at Actual Prices	(2) Actual Inputs at Standard Prices	(3) Actual Outputs at Standard Prices
Actual Inputs × Actual Rate: (1,100) ($5.50) = $6,050	Actual Inputs × Standard Rate: (1,100) ($6.00) = $6,600	Standard Hours Allowed × Standard Rate: (200) (5) ($6.00) = (1,000) ($6.00) = $6,000

Price Variance (1)–(2):
$6,600 – $6,050 = $550 F
or (1,100) ($6.00 – $5.50) =
(1,100) ($0.50) = 550 F

Efficiency Variance (2)–(3):
$6,600 – $6,000 = $600 U
or ($6.00) (1,100 – 1,000) =
($6.00) (100) = $600 U

Flexible-Budget Variance (1)–(3):
$6,050 – $6,000 = $50 U
or $600 – $550 = $50 U

2. Journal

	Dr.	Cr.
Work in process	6,000	
Direct-labor efficiency variance	600	
Direct-labor price variance		550
Accrued payroll		6,050

(D) Peruna Medicinal Products, Inc.:

1. Analysis Framework

(1) Actual Inputs at Actual Prices	(2) Actual Inputs at Standard Prices (Purchases)	(2) Actual Inputs at Standard Prices (Usage)	(3) Actual Outputs at Standard Prices
Actual Quantity × Actual Price: (4,000) ($1.80) = $7,200	Actual Quantity × Standard Price: (4,000) ($2.00) = $8,000	Actual Quantity × Standard Price: (3,500) ($2.00) = $7,000	Units Produced × Standard Price: (300) (10) ($2.00) = (3,000) ($2.00) = $6,000

Price Variance:
$8,000 – $7,200 = $800 F
or (4,000) ($2.00 – $1.80)
= (4,000) ($0.20) = $800 F

Efficiency Variance:
$7,000 – $6,000 = $1,000 U
or ($2.00) (3,500 – 3,000)
= ($2.00) (500) = $1,000 U

2. Journal

	Dr.	Cr.
a) Stores	8,000	
Direct-material price variance		800
Accounts payable		7,200
b) Work in process	6,000	
Direct-material efficiency variance	1,000	
Stores		7,000

(A) 1a, 2e, 3b, 4b, 5c, 6a, 7a, 8c, 9a, 10c, 11b, 12b, 13d, 14d, 15c, 16a, 17b, 18b

(B) 1 static (or inflexible), flexible (or variable); 2 the cost rate per unit of product or activity; 3 actual costs incurred, standard hours of work allowed for units produced; 4 price; 5 actual costs incurred, actual hours of work; 6 cost functions; 7 mixed costs; 8 managed, programmed; 9 committed; 10 discretionary; 11 mixed.

(C) Mixed Products Company:

1. Difference in total cost per month: $12,000 – $9,500 = $2,500
   Difference in direct-labor hours: 40,000 – 30,000 = 10,000 hrs.
   Variable cost rate per direct-labor hour: $2,500 ÷ 10,000 = $0.25

2. | | |
|---|---|
| Total cost at 30,000 hours per month | $ 9,500 |
| Less variable cost: (30,000) ($0.25) | 7,500 |
| Fixed cost per month | $ 2,000 |
| or: | |
| Total cost at 40,000 hours per month | $12,000 |
| Less variable cost: (40,000) ($0.25) | 10,000 |
| Fixed cost per month | $ 2,000 |

(D) Longhorn Boot Corporation

1. Inputs at actual rates:	
Actual direct-labor cost incurred (given)	$ 8,800
Outputs at standard rates:	
The budget based on the standard hours of work allowed for units produced:	
200 product units at 7 standard hours at $6 standard wage rate per hour: (200) (7) (6)	8,400
Direct-labor flexible-budget variance	$ 400 U
2. Inputs at actual rates:	
Actual direct labor cost incurred (given)	$ 8,800
Inputs at standard rates:	
The budget based on the actual hours of work:	
1,500 actual labor hours at $6 standard wage rate per hour: (1,500) (6)	9,000
Direct-labor price variance	$ 200 F
3. Inputs at standard rates:	
The budget based on the actual hours of work: (see 2 above)	9,000
Outputs at standard rates:	
The budget based on the standard hours of work allowed for units produced: (see 1. above).	8,400
Direct-labor efficiency variance	$ 600 U
or:	
Actual direct-labor hours used	1,500 hr
Standard direct-labor hours allowed: (200) (7)	1,400 hr
Excess direct-labor hours used	100 hr
Multiply by standard wage rate per direct-labor hour (given)	X $6
Direct-labor efficiency variance	$ 600 U
4. Inputs at actual rates:	
Actual variable overhead cost incurred (given)	$ 5,100
Outputs at standard rates:	
The budget based on the standard hours of work allowed for units produced:	
200 product units at 7 standard hours at $4 variable overhead rate per hour: (200) (7) (4).	5,600
Variable factory-overhead flexible-budget variance	$ 500 F
5. Inputs at actual rates:	
Actual variable-overhead cost incurred (given)	$ 5,100
Inputs at standard rates:	
The budget based on the actual hours of work:	
1,500 actual hours at $4 variable-overhead rate per hour: (1,500) (4)	6,000
Variable factory-overhead spending variance	$ 900 F

6. Inputs at standard rates:

The budget based on the actual hours of work: (see 5 above)	$ 6,000
Outputs at standard rates:	
The budget based on the standard hours of work allowed for units produced: (see 4. above).	5,600
Variable factory-overhead efficiency variance	$ 400 U

or:

Actual direct-labor hours used	1,500 hr
Standard direct-labor hours allowed: (200) (7)	1,400 hr
Excess direct-labor hours used	100 hr
Multiply by standard variable-overhead costs per direct-labor hour (given)	X $4
Variable-overhead efficiency variance	$ 400 U

CHAPTER 9

(A) 1c, 2c, 3a, 4b, 5e, 6d, 7b, 8a, 9c, 10b, 11c, 12b, 13a, 14a, 15a, 16a, 17b, 18a, 19a

(B) 1 variable, fixed; 2 management planning and control, product costing and pricing; 3 debit, Variable Factory Overhead Control; 4 Work-in-Process Control, Variable Factory Overhead Applied; 5 Fixed Factory Overhead Control; Accrued Payroll, Allowance for Depreciation, etc.; 6 spending, efficiency; 7 flexible-budget, favorable; 8 denominator level; 9 budget, denominator; 10 Fixed Factory Overhead Control, Fixed Factory Overhead Applied.

(C) Razorback Coverall Company:

1.

(a)	Actual direct-labor hours used	700 hr
	Multiply by standard overhead rate per hour	X $2
	Actual labor hours used at standard overhead rate	$1,400
(b)	Actual product units made	400 units
	Multiply by standard variable-overhead cost per unit: 1.5 hours @ $2 per hour	X $3
	Actual units made at standard cost (variable overhead cost applied)	$1,200
(c)	Inputs at actual prices: Actual variable-overhead cost incurred (given)	$1,350
	Outputs at standard prices: Variable-overhead cost applied (b)	1,200
	Flexible-budget variance	$ 150 U
(d)	Inputs at standard prices: Actual labor hours used at standard overhead rate (a)	$1,400
	Inputs at actual prices: Actual variable-overhead cost incurred (given)	1,350
	Variable-overhead spending variance	$ 50 F
(e)	Inputs at standard prices: Actual labor hours used at standard overhead rate (a)	$1,400
	Outputs at standard prices: Variable-overhead cost applied (b)	1,200
	Variable-overhead efficiency variance	$ 200 U
	or	
	Actual direct-labor hours used	700 hr
	Standard hours allowed: (1.5) (400)	600 hr
	Excess hours used	100 hr
	Multiply by standard variable-overhead rate per hour (given)	X $2.00
	Variable-overhead efficiency variance	$ 200 U

2.

	Debit	Credit
Variable factory-overhead control	1,350	
Accounts payable, accrued payroll, etc.		1,350
To record actual variable-overhead incurred.		
Work in process	1,200	
Variable factory overhead applied		1,200
To record variable-overhead applied		

(D) Red Raider Exterminator Corporation:

1.

(a)	Budgeted fixed-overhead cost	$1,800
	Divide by denominator level of activity	300 hr
	Standard rate for fixed overhead	$ 6.00 per hr
(b)	Standard hours allowed for work done on product units manufactured	280 hr
	Multiply by standard rate (a)	$ 6.00
	Applied fixed-overhead cost	$1,680

(c) Actual fixed-overhead cost (given)		$1,750
Applied fixed-overhead cost (b)		1,680
Underapplied fixed-overhead cost		$ 70 U
(d) Budgeted fixed-overhead cost (given)		$1,800
Actual fixed-overhead cost (given)		1,750
Fixed-overhead budget variance (always equal to spending variance)		$ 50F
(e) Budgeted fixed-overhead cost (given)		$1,800
Applied fixed-overhead cost (b)		1,680
Fixed-overhead denominator variance		$ 120 U
or:		
Denominator hours used (given)		300 hr
Standard hours allowed (given)		280 hr
Excess hours used		20 hr
Multiply by standard fixed-overhead rate per hour (a)		$ 6.00
Fixed-overhead denominator variance		$ 120 U
2. Fixed factory-overhead control	1,750	
Accrued payroll, allowance for depreciation, etc.		1,750
To record actual fixed overhead incurred.		
Work in process	1,680	
Fixed factory overhead applied		1,680
To record fixed overhead applied.		

CHAPTER 10

(A) 1b, 2b, 3c, 4d, 5a, 6a, 7c, 8b, 9b, 10a, 11b, 12c. 13b, 14b, 15a, 16d, 17b, 18c, 19b, 20a, 21b, 22d, 23b, 24b, 25a

(B) 1 fixed, variable; 2 contribution; 3 direct-material, direct-labor variable-overhead; 4 internal (or management); 5 production, sales; 6 practical capacity (or practical attainable capacity); 7 capacity, master-budgeted; 8 expected annual activity; 9 normal activity; 10 cost of goods sold, gross margin (or gross profit); 11 Work-in-Process, Finished Goods, Cost of Goods Sold; 12 increased.

(C) 1. (a)

Bear Cupboard Manufacturing Company
Income Statement
For the Year Ending December 31, 197 _

Sales: (80,000) (15)		$1,200,000
Less cost of goods sold:		
Beginning inventory: (10,000) (10)	$ 100,000	
Cost of goods manufactured (90,000) (10)	900,000	
Cost of goods available for sale	$1,000,000	
Less ending inventory: (20,000) (10)	200,000	
Cost of goods sold		800,000
Gross margin on sales		$ 400,000
Less total selling and administrative expenses: 200,000 + 100,000		300,000
Net income		$ 100,000

(b)

Bear Cupboard Manufacturing Company
Income Statement
For the Year Ending December 31, 197 _

Sales: (80,000) (15)		$1,200,000
Less variable costs:		
Beginning inventory: (10,000) (8)	$ 80,000	
Variable cost of goods manufactured: (90,000) (8)	720,000	
Available for sale	$ 800,000	
Less ending inventory: (20,000) (8)	160,000	
Variable manufacturing cost of goods sold	$ 640,000	
Add variable selling and administrative expenses	200,000	
Total variable costs charged against sales		840,000
Contribution margin		$ 360,000
Less fixed costs:		
Fixed manufacturing costs: (90,000) (2)	$ 180,000	
Fixed selling and administrative costs	100,000	
Total fixed costs		280,000
Net income		$ 80,000

2. Net income:

Absorption-costing method (a)		$ 100,000
Direct-costing method (b)		80,000
Difference to be accounted for		$ 20,000
Ending inventory		20,000 units
Less beginning inventory		10,000 units
Increase in inventory		10,000 units
Multiply by fixed-overhead cost per unit		$ 2.00
Increase in inventory, as above		$ 20,000
(Current year's addition to the fixed-overhead costs that are carried forward as an asset)		

(D) Aggie Farm Equipment Company:

1. (a) Budgeted fixed factory overhead		$ 72,000
Divide by expected annual activity		12,000 hr
Fixed overhead rate per hour		$ 6.00
(b) Standard hours allowed for work done		13,000 hr
Multiply by predetermined rate (a)		$ 6.00
Fixed overhead applied		$ 78,000
(c) Fixed overhead applied (b)		$ 78,000
Less actual fixed overhead		74,000
Overapplied fixed overhead		$ 4,000
2. (a) Budgeted fixed overhead		$ 72,000
Divide by normal activity		16,000 hr
Fixed-overhead rate per hour		$ 4.50
(b) Standard hours allowed for work done		13,000 hr
Multiply by predetermined rate (a)		$ 4.50
Fixed overhead applied		$ 58,500
(c) Actual fixed overhead		$ 74,000
Less fixed overhead applied		58,500
Underapplied fixed overhead		$ 15,500

(E) Owl Bookend Company:

1. Sales		$ 25,000
Less standard cost of goods sold:		
Standard cost of goods manufactured	$ 20,000	
(Cost per unit: $20,000 ÷ 2,000 = $10)		
Less standard cost of ending inventory: (400) (10)	4,000	
Cost of goods sold: (1,600) (10)		16,000
Gross margin		$ 9,000
Less selling and administrative expenses		6,000
Net income before variances		$ 3,000
2. Unfavorable labor-efficiency variance		$ 1,200
Less favorable labor-rate variance		400
Net unfavorable variance		800
3. (a) Net income before variances (1)		$ 3,000
Less net unfavorable variance (2)		800
Net income		$ 2,200
(b) Standard cost of goods manufactured		$ 20,000
Divide by product units manufactured		2,000 units
Standard cost per product unit		$ 10
Multiply by ending inventory		400 units
Standard cost of ending inventory		$ 4,000
4. (a) Net income before variances (1)		$ 3,000
Less proration of variance to cost of goods sold: (800) (1,600 ÷ 2,000)		640
Net income		$ 2,360
(b) Standard cost of ending inventory (3, b)		$ 4,000
Add proration of variance to inventory: (800) (400 ÷ 2,000)		160
Actual cost of ending inventory		$ 4,160

5. 3 a
6. 4 b

CHAPTER 11

(A) 1c, 2a, 3b, 4b, 5a, 6b, 7c, 8b, 9c, 10a, 11b, 12c, 13c, 14a, 15c, 16b

(B) 1 relevant; 2 expected future (or predicted), will differ (or will be different); 3 Historical (or Past), the decision itself; 4 contribution approach; 5 Robinson-Patman, costs; 6 full manufacturing costs (or a full-costing approach, or the absorption-costing approach), fixed; 7 to profit per unit of constraining factor; 8 opportunity cost.

(C) Bevo Enterprises:

Yes:

Special-order sales: (400) (24)		$ 9,600
Less variable expenses:		
Manufacturing: (400) (18)	$7,200	
Sales commissions: (400) (1)	400	7,600
Addition to company profit		$ 2,000

(D) The Bruin Company:

Cash outflow to buy the new machine	$84,000
Less cash inflow from sale of old machine	9,000
Net cash outflow to change machines	$75,000
Net cash inflow from annual power-expense savings: (10) (6 000)	60,000
Difference in favor of keeping old machine	$15,000

(E) Stan's Cardinal Products Company:

	V	W
Selling price per unit	$10	$15
Less variable expenses per unit	7	9
Contribution margin per unit	$ 3	$ 6
Multiply by number of units that can be manufactured per hour	10	4
Contribution to profit per hour of plant capacity	$30	$24

All 2,400 hours should be devoted to the manufacture of product V because it would make the larger profit contribution per unit of the constraining factor (hours of plant capacity).

(F) 1.

Frog Novelty Manufacturing Corporation
Pro Forma Operating Statement
Giving Effect to Discontinuance of Product T Operations
($000 omitted)

	C	U	Total
Sales	150	180	330
Variable costs and expenses	90	100	190
Fixed costs and expenses:			
Annual salaries of product-line supervisors	20	23	43
Total company-wide fixed costs allocated equally to product lines	45	45	90
Total costs and expenses	155	168	323
Net operating income (loss)	(5)	12	7

2. No, because the company's net operating income would be reduced from $30,000 to $7,000 without any reduction in the total assets used by the company.

CHAPTER 12

(A) 1b, 2b, 3a, 4c, 5c, 6a, 7b, 8a, 9b, 10c, 11b, 12a, 13a, 14c, 15d, 16c, 17a, 18c

(B) 1 capital budgeting; 2 discounted cash flow; 3 less; 4 internal rate of return, net present value; 5 time-adjusted rate of return; 6 negative; 7 sensitivity analysis; 8 will differ between alternatives; 9 initial cash investment, annual cash inflow; 10 future annual net income, required investment, 11 cash-flow differences between the two projects.

(C) Optional Equipment Company:

Annual savings in cash operating expenses	$15,000	
Multiply by present value of $1 annuity	5.197	
1. Present value of annual cash savings		$77,955
Predicted residual value of machine	$ 3,000	
Multiply by present value $1	0.168	
2. Present value of machine residual value		504
3. Total present value of expected net cash inflows		$78,459
Less initial investment		60,000
4. Net present value		$18,459

(D) Auxiliary Products, Inc.:

Payback period is: $\frac{\$120,000 \text{ initial cost}}{\$\ 20,000 \text{ annual cash savings}} = 6.000$

Rates of Return	Present Value Factors	
14%	6.142	6.142
Internal rate		6.000
16%	5.575	
2%	.567	.142

Internal rate: 14% + (2%) (.142 ÷ .567) = 14% + (2%) (.25) = 14% + .5% = 14.5%

(E) Apparatus Control Corporation:

1. Initial cost of proposed new equipment	$80,000
Divide by predicted annual cash savings	16,000
Payback period	5 yr
2. The payback reciprocal is 100% divided by the 5 years payback period	20%
3. Initial cost of equipment	$80,000
Divide by predicted useful life	8 yr
Straight-line depreciation expense per year	$10,000
4. Predicted annual cash savings in operating expenses	$16,000
Less annual depreciation expense	10,000
Predicted increase in future average annual net income	$ 6,000
5. Predicted increase in annual net income	$ 6,000
Divide by initial investment	80,000
Accounting rate of return based on initial investment	7.5%
6. Predicted increase in annual net income	$ 6,000
Divide by one-half of initial investment	40,000
Accounting rate of return based on average investment	15%

CHAPTER 13

(A) 1b, 2c, 3b, 4a, 5a, 6c, 7b, 8d, 9c, 10c, 11b, 12d, 13b, 14a, 15b, 16c, 17c, 18c

(B) 1 depreciation, revenues; 2 depreciation, present value; 3 double-declining-balance, sum-of-the-years' digits; 4 cash flows, after-tax (or net-of-tax); 5 the reinvestment of the cash proceeds at the end of the shorter project life; 6 capital rationing; 7 the cost of capital; 8 the expected cash dividend yield on market price of the stock (the expected cash dividend divided by the current market price of the stock), an expected constant rate of growth.

(C) 1.

Old Guard Company
Income Statement
For Year Ended December 31, 197_
($000 omitted)

Sales		$ 500
Less:		
Depreciation expense	$ 40	
Other operating expenses	410	450
Income before income taxes		$ 50
Less income taxes at 60%		30
Net income after income taxes		$ 20

2. Depreciation expense	$ 40
Less tax reduction effect at 60%	24
After-tax effect of depreciation expense on net income	$ 16
3. Depreciation deduction	$ 40
Multiply by income tax rate	60%
Annual tax savings from the depreciation deduction	$ 24

4. a) Sales		$ 500
Less:		
Other operating expenses	$ 410	
Income taxes	30	440
After-tax net cash inflow from all revenue-producing operations		$ 60
b) Net income after income taxes		$ 20
Add back depreciation expense		40
After-tax net cash inflow from all revenue-producing operations		$ 60
c) Sales		$ 500
Less other operating expenses		410
Cash inflow from operations before taxes and depreciation effects		90
Less income tax outflow at 60%		54
After-tax effects of cash inflow from operations before depreciation effects		$ 36
Add tax savings from depreciation: 60% of $40		24
After-tax net cash inflow from all revenue- producing operations		$ 60

(D) Instant Transit Company:

1. Annual savings in cash operating costs	$30,000	
Less income tax at 60%	18,000	
After-tax effect of annual cash savings		$ 12,000
Annual depreciation ($100,000 ÷ 10 yr)	$10,000	
Multiply by income tax rate	60%	
Annual tax savings from depreciation		6,000
Total annual after-tax net cash inflow		$ 18,000
Cost of special equipment		$100,000
Payback period (100,000 ÷ 18,000)		5.56 yr

2.

	Rate of Return	Discount Factor	Rate of Return	Discount Factor
	12%	5.65	12%	5.65
		-	True rate	5.56
	14%	5.22	-	-
Differences	2%	0.43	?	0.09

By interpolation the true rate, or internal rate of return, is:

12% + (2%) (0.09 ÷ 0.43) = 12% + (2%) (0.2) = 12% + 0.4% = 12.4%

3. See 1 for predicted annual after-tax net cash inflow	$ 18,000
Multiply by present value of an annuity of $1 at 10%	6.15

Total present value of expected after-tax net cash inflows	$110,700
Less cost of the investment	100,000
Net present value of the investment	$ 10,700

(E) Dilemma Unlimited:

Project	Net Present Value	Excess-Present-Value Index
A	$6,000	140%
B	4,000	150
C	2,500	150
D	2,400	160
E	1,500	175
F	900	190

2.

Project	Total Cost	Present Value	Net Present Value	Excess-Present-Value Index
A	$15,000	$21,000	$6,000	140%
C	5,000	7,500	2,500	150
D	4,000	6,400	2,400	160
F	1,000	1,900	900	190
Totals	$25,000	$36,800	$11,800	147%

No other combination within the $25,000 total budget constraint would show as much net present value as the above combination. Note that Project E is not included even though its 175% excess-present-value index is higher than three of the included projects.

3. (a)

Project	Total Cost	Present Value	Net Present Value	Excess-Present Value Index
B	$8,000	$12,000	$ 4,000	150%
C	5,000	7,500	2,500	150
D	4,000	6,400	2,400	160
E	2,000	3,500	1,500	175
F	1,000	1,900	900	190
Totals	$20,000	$31,300	$11,300	156.5%

It is not necessary to utilize the full $24,000 available budget in order to maximize net present value. For example, two combinations that do use the entire $24,000 but which have *lower* net present values are shown below:

(b)

Project	Total Cost	Present Value	Net Present Value	Excess-Present-Value Index
A	$15,000	$21,000	$ 6,000	140%
B	8,000	12,000	4,000	150
F	1,000	1,900	900	190
Totals	$24,000	$34,900	$10,900	145%

(c)

Project	Total Cost	Present Value	Net Present Value	Excess-Present-Value Index
A	$15,000	$21,000	$ 6,000	140%
C	5,000	7,500	2,500	150
D	4,000	6,400	2,400	160
Totals	$24,000	$34,900	$10,900	145%

CHAPTER 14

(A) 1e, 2c, 3a, 4c, 5b, 6b, 7b, 8b, 9c, 10b, 11b, 12d, 13c, 14b, 15c, 16b, 17b, 18b, 19c, 20d

(B) 1 total long-run costs; 2 the economic order quantity; 3 lead time; 4 the safety stock; 5 the average usage during lead time, the safety stock; 6 descending (or decreasing), total consumption costs, three; 7 LIFO, FIFO.

(C) Material AOK of Precision Puzzle Company:

1\. Number of orders per year

	One	Two	Five	Ten	Twenty
Order size (3,000 divided by number of orders per year)	3,000	1,500	600	300	150
Average inventory in units (order size divided by 2)	1,500	750	300	150	75
Annual carrying cost (average inventory multiplied by $5)	$7,500	$3,750	$1,500	$ 750	$ 375
Annual purchase-order cost (number of orders multiplied by $300)	$ 300	$ 600	$1,500	$3,000	$6,000
Total annual relevant costs	$7,800	$4,350	$3,000	$3,750	$6,375
2. Least-cost order size			X		

3\. E = least-cost order size = $\sqrt{\frac{2AP}{S}}$

A = annual quantity used in units	3,000
P = cost per purchase order	300
S = annual cost of carrying one unit one year	5

Substitute in formula:

$$E = \sqrt{\frac{(2)(3{,}000)(300)}{5}} = \sqrt{\frac{1{,}800{,}000}{5}}$$

$$E = \sqrt{360{,}000} = 600 \text{ units, the EOQ}$$

Optimum number of orders per year would therefore be 3,000 ÷ 600 = 5

4\. $C = \sqrt{2APS} = \sqrt{(2)(3{,}000)(300)(5)} = \sqrt{9{,}000{,}000} = \$3{,}000$

(D) Material PDQ of Enigma, Incorporated:

1. Maximum daily usage	80 units
Less average daily usage	70 units
Excess usage per day	10 units
Multiply by lead time	22 days
Safety stock	220 units
2. Safety stock	220 units
Add average usage during lead time: 70 units for 22 days	1,540 units
Reorder point (inventory level at which additional units should be ordered)	1,760 units
Or, the reorder point may be computed as the maximum usage during lead time: 80 units for 22 days	1,760 units

(E) Material RPM of Acceleration Manufacturing Company:

Summary of April Activity:

	Units	Unit Cost	Total Cost
April inventory	40	$20	$ 800
Purchases:			
April 13	50	21	1,050
April 20	80	22	1,760
April 27	30	24	720
Total available for April	200		$4,330

Weighted-Average Method:

Weighted-average cost per unit: $4,330 ÷ 220 units =	$21.65
Multiply by April 30 inventory	60 units
April 30 inventory cost, 60 units	$1,299
Material used in April: 200 − 60 =	140 units
Multiply by weighted-average cost per unit	$21.65
Cost of materials used in April, 140 units	$3,031

FIFO Method

April 27, 30 units at $24	$ 720
April 20, 30 units at $22	660
April 30 inventory cost, 60 units	$1,380
April 1 inventory, 40 units at $20	$ 800
April 13, 50 units at $21	1,050
April 20, 50 units at $22	1,100
Cost of materials used in April, 140 units	$2,950

LIFO Method:

April 1 inventory, 40 units at $20	$ 800
April 13, 20 units at $21	420
April 30 inventory cost, 60 units	$1,220
April 27, 30 units at $24	$ 720
April 20, 80 units at $22	1,760
April 13, 30 units at $21	630
Cost of materials used in April, 140 units	$3,110

Recapitulation:

	FIFO	LIFO	Weighted Average
Cost of April 30 inventory	$1,380	$1,220	$1,299
Cost of materials used in April	2,950	3,110	3,031
Total	$4,330	$4,330	$4,330

CHAPTER 15

(A) 1b, 2c, 3a, 4a, 5c, 6a, 7c, 8c, 9b, 10a, 11b, 12c, 13c

(B) 1 persistent relationships; 2 an intermediate, a final; 3 the cost-allocation base; 4 variable, fixed; 5 predetermined; 6 cause-and-effect, misleading.

(C) Desert Products Company:

1. *Budgeted* fixed costs should be allocated on the basis of *long-run demand* (total KWH: 300,000 + 200,000 = 500,000):

   Dept. A (300,000/500,000) × $80,000 = $48,000
   Dept. B (200,000/500,000) × $80,000 = $32,000

2. Variable costs should be allocated by using the $.05 *predetermined rate* and *actual KWH used:*

   Dept. A 230,000 × $.05 = $11,500
   Dept. B 190,000 × $.05 = $ 9,500

(Unallocated actual costs for 19_6 may be written off to cost of sales at end of year.)

CHAPTER 16

(A) 1a, 2c, 3a, 4e, 5b, 6c, 7c, 8c, 9a, 10c, 11a, 12a, 13e

(B) 1 contribution, costs controllable by division managers; 2 controllable by division (or segment) managers, controllable by others; 3 greatest, least; 4 homogeneous; 5 direct-labor cost, direct-labor hours.

(C)

General Omnibus Company
Contribution-Approach Income Statement by Segments
($000 omitted)

	Company Total	Alpha Division	Omega Division
Net sales	$900	$500	$400
Less variable manufacturing cost of sales	450	300	150

	Company Total	Alpha Division	Omega Division
Manufacturing contribution margin	$450	$200	$250
Less variable selling and administrative costs	130	60	70
Contribution margin	$320	$140	$180
Less fixed costs controllable by division managers	140	60	80
Contribution controllable by division managers	$180	$ 80	$100
Less fixed costs controllable by others	70	30	40
Contribution by segments	$110	$ 50	$ 60
Less unallocated costs	75		
Income before income taxes	$ 35		

(D)

Easy Escalator Company
Budgeted Reallocation of Factory-Overhead Costs ($000 omitted)

	Service Departments			Production Departments		
	A	B	C	X	Y	Z
Overhead costs before reallocation	300	210	240	160	110	105
Costs reallocated from Dept. A to others	300	30	60	90	45	75
Costs reallocated from Dept. B to others		240	30	90	30	90
Costs reallocated from Dept. C to others			330	110	110	110
Total overhead of production departments				450	295	380
Divide by total direct-labor hours				300	100	190
Predetermined overhead rates for product costing				1.50	2.95	2.00

CHAPTER 17

(A) 1d, 2d, 3a, 4b, 5a, 6c, 7b, 8b, 9a, 10c, 11d, 12c, 13a, 14b, 15a, 16a, 17a, 18a, 19a

(B) 1 joint products; 2 the stage of production at which the different individual products can be identified; 3 the revenue-producing properties or abilities of the separate products; 4 relative-sales-value; 5 costs beyond the split-off point, predicted sales values of the fully processed products; 6 product costing; 7 the costs beyond the split-off point; 8 by-products.

(C) Steer Wheeling Corporation:

1.

	Product REV	Product ROL	Total
Quantities produced and processed	150 yd	300 yd	
Multiply by unit selling prices	$40	$10	
Total sales values when completed	$6,000	$3,000	$9,000
Less further processing costs	1,500	1,500	3,000
Approximate values at split-off	$4,500	$1,500	$6,000
Allocation of $4,000 joint costs:			
To REV: (4,500/6,000) (4,000)	$3,000		
To ROL: (1,500/6,000) (4,000)		$1,000	

2.

	Product REV	Product ROL	Total
Sales (computed above)	$6,000	$3,000	$9,000
Less production costs:			
Joint costs (computed above)	$3,000	$1,000	$4,000
Further processing costs	1,500	1,500	3,000
Total costs	$4,500	$2,500	$7,000
Gross profit on sales	$1,500	$ 500	$2,000

3.

	Product REV	Product ROL
Unit selling prices of completely processed products	$ 40	$ 10
Unit selling prices at split-off	32	4
Increase in unit selling prices from further processing	$ 8	$ 6
Multiply by number of units	150	300
Differential revenue from futher processing	$1,200	$1,800
Less differential costs (costs of further processing)	1,500	1,500

	Product REV	Product ROL
Differences	($300)	$300
Decisions	Sell at Split-off	Process beyond split-off

4. Sales:

Product REV at split-off point: 150 yds. at $32 each		$4,800
Product ROL at end of further processing: 300 yds. at $10 each		3,000
Total sales		$7,800
Less costs:		
Joint costs	$4,000	
Product ROL costs of further processing	1,500	5,500
Gross profit on sales		$2,300

(Note that this gross profit is greater than the $2,000 gross profit based upon the further processing of both products as computed in 2 above.)

5. No, because the total joint costs of $4,000 would not be affected by further-processing decisions. Note that because the joint costs would be the same for each of the following four possible combinations of further-processing decisions, the differences in gross profit would be caused only by the incremental costs and revenues:

	Process Both Products	Process REV Only	Process ROL Only	Process Neither Product
Sales: REV	$6,000	$6,000	$4,800	$4,800
ROL	3,000	1,200	3,000	1,200
Total sales	$9,000	$7,200	$7,800	$6,000
Less Costs:				
Joint costs	$4,000	$4,000	$4,000	$4,000
REV processing costs	1,500	1,500	–	–
ROL processing costs	1,500	–	1,500	–
Total costs	$7,000	$5,500	$5,500	$4,000
Gross profit	$2,000	$1,700	$2,300	$2,000

(D) N. C. Dental Products Company:

Sales		$75,000
Less cost of sales		
Gross production costs	$50,000	
Less net realizable value of by-product produced	2,000	
Net production costs of main product	$48,000	
Less ending inventory of main product (10%)	4,800	
Net cost of sales of main product		43,200
Gross margin on sales		$31,800

CHAPTER 18

(A) 1a, 3c, 3b, 4b, 5a, 6a, 7a, 8b, 9c, 10a, 11c, 12b, 13b

(B) 1 process-costing; 2 equivalent units produced; 3 the finished-goods control account, a departmental work-in-process control account; 4 the weighted-average, the first-in, first-out; 5 the first-in, first-out method; 6 standard costing.

(C) EQ Manufacturing Process:

1. By weighted-average method:

	Material Costs	Conversion Costs
Units completed	600	600
Work in process, end:		
(300) (100%)	300	
(300) (60%)		180
Equivalent units for total work done	900	780

2. By first-in, first-out method:	Material Costs	Conversion Costs
Total work done (above)	900	780
Less old equivalent units for work done on beginning inventory in previous periods:		
(200)(100%)	200	
(200) (70%)		140
Remainder, new equivalent units for current month, November	700	640

(D) WA manufacturing process:

Step 1–Units of Physical Flow

Work in process, beginning	300 (40%)	Units completed	700
Units transferred in	600	Work in process, end	200 (50%)
Units to account for	900	Units accounted for	900

Step 2–Equivalent Units	Transferred-in Costs	Conversion Costs
Units completed	700	700
Work-in-process, end:		
(200) (100%)	200	
(200) (50%)		100
Equivalent units for total work done	900	800

Step 3–Summary of Total Costs to Account for	Transferred-in Costs	Conversion Costs	Total Costs
Work-in-process, beginning	$3,000	$ 2,000	$ 5,000
Current costs	5,100	3,600	8,700
Total costs to account for	$8,100	$ 5,600	$13,700

Step 4–Unit Costs	Transferred-in Costs	Conversion Costs	Total Costs
Total costs to account for (Step 3)	$8,100	$ 5,600	
Divide by equivalent units (Step 2)	900	800	
Unit costs	$ 9.00	$ 7.00	$16.00

Step 5–Total Costs of Work Completed and in Process

Units completed: (700) ($16)		$11,200
Work-in-process, end:		
Transferred-in costs: (200) ($9)	$1,800	
Conversion costs: (200) (50%) ($7)	700	2,500
Total costs accounted for		$13,700

(E) FI manufacturing process:

Step 1–Units of Physical Flow

Work-in-process, beginning	200 (75%)
Units transferred in	600
Units to account for	800
Units completed and transferred out during February	500
Work in process, end	300 (50%)
Units accounted for	800

Step 2–Equivalent Units	Transferred-in Costs	Conversion Costs
Units completed and transferred out during February	500	500
Work in process end:		
Transferred-in costs: (300) (100%)	300	
Conversion costs: (300) (50%)		150
Total work done	800	650
Less old equivalent units for work done on beginning inventory in previous periods:		
Transferred-in costs: (200)(100%)	200	
Conversion costs: (200)(75%)		150
Remainder, new equivalent units for current period, February	600	500

Step 3—Summary of Total Costs to Account for	Transferred-in Costs	Conversion Costs	Total Costs
Work-in-process, beginning	$2,200	$ 1,300	$ 3,500
Current costs	6,000	4,000	10,000
Total costs to account for	$8,200	$ 5,300	$13,500

Step 4—Unit Costs	Transferred-in Costs	Conversion Costs	Total Costs
Current costs only	$6,000	$ 4,000	
Divide by equivalent units (Step 2)	600	500	
Unit Costs	$10.00	$ 8.00	$ 18.00

Step 5—Total Costs of Work Completed and in Process		
Units completed:		
From beginning inventory (Step 3)		$ 3,500
Current costs added:		
Conversion costs: (200) ($8) (100% – 75%)		400
Total from beginning inventory		$ 3,900
Started and completed: (500–200) ($18)		5,400
Total costs transferred out (Average unit cost: $9,300 ÷ 500 = $18.60)		$ 9,300
Work in process, end:		
Transferred-in costs: (300) ($10)	$3,000	
Conversion costs: (300) (50%) ($8)	1,200	4,200
Total costs accounted for		$13,500

CHAPTER 19

(A) 1c, 2d, 3d, 4a, 5a, 6b, 7a, 8b, 9b, 10d, 11a, 12d, 13c, 14c, 15a, 16d, 17a

(B) 1 spoilage, quality, disposal value (or salvage value); 2 costs accumulated to the point of rejection, disposal value of the spoiled goods; 3 measurable but relatively minor; 4 net cost of normal; 5 factory-overhead cost; 6 the disposal value of the spoiled goods; 7 Factory Overhead; 8 work-in-process; 9 Factory Overhead, Work in Process; 10 spoilage random fluctuations, exceeds the top of.

(C) Batch-Parcel Company:

	Debit	Credit
1. Normal spoilage common to all jobs:		
Stores	200	
Factory Overhead	700	
Work in Process		900
2. Normal spoilage due to the the nature of particular jobs:		
Stores	200	
Work in Process		200
3. Abnormal spoilage:		
Stores	200	
Special Loss from Abnormal Spoilage	700	
Work in Process		900
4. Normal defective work common to all jobs:		
Factory Overhead	600	
Stores, Accrued Payroll, Factory Overhead Applied		600
5. Normal defective work due to the nature of particular jobs:		
Work in Process	600	
Stores, Accrued Payroll, Factory Overhead Applied		600
6. Abnormal defective work:		
Special Loss from Abnormal Defective Work	600	
Stores, Accrued Payroll, Factory Overhead Applied		600
7. Normal scrap common to all jobs:		
Stores	150	
Factory Overhead		150
8. Abnormal scrap due to the nature of particular jobs:		
Stores	150	
Work in Process		150

(D) Anti-Gravity Process of Negative-Weight Products, Inc.:

1. Lost from normal spoilage	40 units
Lost from abnormal spoilage	60
Good units transferred out	540
Ending work in process: (3/4) (80)	60
Equivalent units for conversion costs	700 units
2. Conversion costs in beginning inventory	$ 2,000
Add current conversion costs	$ 9,200
Total conversion costs	$11,200
Divide by equivalent units	700
Unit conversion cost	$ 16
3. Lost from normal spoilage	40 units
Multiply by unit conversion cost	$ 16
Total conversion costs of normal spoilage	$ 640
4. Lost from abnormal spoilage	60 units
Multiply by unit conversion cost	$ 16
Total conversion costs of abnormal spoilage	$ 960
5. Good units transferred out	540 units
Multiply by unit conversion cost	$ 16
Conversion costs before adding normal spoilage	$ 8,640
Add conversion costs of normal spoilage	640
Total conversion costs transferred out to next process	$ 9,280
6. Ending work in process	80 units
Multiply by completion fraction	3/4
Equivalent units in ending work in process	60 units
Multiply by unit conversion cost	$ 16
Total conversion costs in ending work-in-process inventory	$ 960
Recapitulation or proof (not required by problem):	
Conversion costs in beginning inventory	$ 2,000
Current conversion costs	9,200
Total conversion costs to account for	$11,200
Conversion costs of abnormal spoilage	$ 960
Conversion costs transferred out to next process	9,280
Conversion costs in ending inventory of work in process	960
Total conversion costs accounted for	$11,200

CHAPTER 20

(A) 1c, 2b, 3b, 4c, 5a, 6b, 7d, 8a, 9c, 10a, 11a, 12a, 13d, 14b, 15a, 16d, 17a, 18b

(B) 1 payroll deductions or withholdings; 2 individual federal income, Social Security (or F.I.C.A., or F.O.A.B.); 3 Accrued Payroll, gross; 4 fringe labor costs; 5 unemployment, F.I.C.A. (or F.O.A.B.); 6 Work in Process Control; 7 F.I.C.A.; 8 higher, calendar.

(C) Scrooge and Cratchit Clerical Supplies:

1. Work-in-process	20,000	
Factory overhead control: 5,000 + (14%) (5,000 + 20,000)	8,500	
Selling expense control: 3,000 + (14%) (3,000)	3,420	
Administrative expense control: 2,000 + (14%) (2,000)	2,280	
Accrued payroll		30,000
Estimated liability for vacation pay: (5%) (30,000)		1,500
Employer's F.I.C.A. taxes payable: (6%) (30,000)		1,800
Federal unemployment taxes payable: (0.5%) (30,000)		150
State unemployment taxes payable: (2.5%) (30,000)		750
2. Accrued payroll	30,000	
Employee's income taxes payable		4,000
Employee's F.I.C.A. taxes payable (6%) (30,000)		1,800
Cash: 30,000 − 4,000 − 1,800		24,200

CHAPTER 21

(A) 1b, 2d, 3d, 4c, 5d, 6b, 7b, 8a, 9a, 10a, 11c, 12b, 13a, 14c, 15b, 16c

(B) 1 internal check, errors, fraud, waste; 2 recordkeeping, physical handling of assets; 3 document control; 4 independent accountants (or public accountants), the physical testing or verification of inventories; 5 shoplifting by customers, embezzling by employees; 6 sales volume, unit values of products; 7 factory, credit.

(C) 1U, 2A, 3U, 4A, 5A, 6U, 7U, 8U

(D) Neeman-Markups Company:

		Retail Prices
Beginning merchandise inventory (physical count)		$ 8,000
Merchandise purchases		77,000
Additional retail price changes:		
Markups		3,000
Markdowns		(6,000)
Total merchandise to account for		$82,000
Less:		
Sales	$72,000	
Allowable inventory shrinkage	2,600	74,600
Ending inventory should be		$ 7,400
Less ending inventory (physical count)		6,500
Inventory shortage		$ 900

CHAPTER 22

(A) 1c, 2a, 3b, 4c, 5a, 6c, 7c, 8b, 9b, 10d, 11d, 12b, 13b, 14a, 15c, 16a, 17c, 18a, 19a, 20b, 21c, 22c, 23c

(B) 1 interdependence among subunits; 2 goal congruence; 3 goods and services, divisions (or subunits) of an organization; 4 goal congruence, incentive, subunit autonomy; 5 competitive, minimal; 6 dysfunctional; 7 buying (or purchasing), selling (or supplier); 8 independent, dysfunctional decision making; 9 cost, external, payables, cost of goods sold, gross profit in inventories.

(C) Abacus Calculator Equipment, Inc.:

1.	(a)	(b)
Variable costs per unit	$ 40	$ 40
Outside market price per unit	43	36
Benefit (detriment) per unit	($3)	$4
Multiply by number of units	5,000	5,000
Total benefit (detriment) to the company	($15,000)	$ 20,000
(The fixed costs are irrelevant.)		

2.	(a)	(b)
Benefit (detriment) as above, before considering alternative use of facilities	($ 15,000)	$ 20,000
Benefit from alternative use	26,000	26,000
Total benefit to the company	$ 11,000	$ 46,000
(The fixed costs are irrelevant.)		

CHAPTER 23

(A) 1a, 2d, 3b, 4a, 5b, 6a, 7a, 8b, 9c, 10c, 11c, 12b, 13b

(B) 1 capital turnover, net-income percentage of sales; 2 the imputed interest on its invested capital; 3 the investment controllable by him; 4 current disposal, total present; 5 replacement cost.

(C) 1. (a) **Sales of Capver Company** $900,000
Divide by invested capital 200,000
Capital turnover .... 4.5 times

(b) Net income .... $ 27,000
Divide by sales 900,000
Net income percentage of sales 3%

(c) Net income .... $ 27,000
Divide by invested capital 200,000
Return on investment 13.5%
(Or: Capital Turnover times Net Income Percentage of Sales: (4.5) (3%) = 13.5%)

2. (a) **Invested capital of Investurn Company** $300,000
Multiply by return on investment 10%
Net income .... $ 30,000

(b) Net income 30,000
Divide by net income percentage of sales 4%
Sales $750,000

(c) Sales $750,000
Divide by invested capital 300,000
Capital turnover .... 2.5 times

3. (a) **Sales of Marsales Company** $600,000
Divide by capital turnover 5
Invested capital $120,000

(b) Net income .... $ 24,000
Divide by sales 600,000
Net income percentage of sales 4%

(c) Net income .... $ 24,000
Divide by invested capital 120,000
Return on investment 20%
(Or: Capital Turnover times Net Income Percentage of Sales: (5) (4%) = 20%)

(D) Key Division of Hard Lock Company:

1. Net income .... $ 99,000
Divide by invested capital 450,000
ROI 22%

2. Net income .... $ 99,000
Less 18% of $450,000 81,000
Residual Income .... $ 18,000

3. (a) No, because the additional project would reduce overall ROI.
(b) Yes, because the additional project would increase Residual Income.

(E) Astute Computer Company:

1. Annual net cash inflows from operations .... $ 38,344
Less annual depreciation: 200,000 ÷ 10 20,000
Operating income .... $ 18,344

(a) ROI on gross cost for each year: 18,344 ÷ 200,000 = 9.2%
(b) ROI on net book value:
For first year: 18, 344 ÷ 200,000 = 9.2%
For sixth year: 18, 344 ÷ 100,000 = 18.3%

2. Note the difference between the 14% time-adjusted rate of return and the 9.2% ROI. Although 14% might exceed the minimum desired ROI, a division manager might tend to reject this project, knowing that his subsequent earnings performance would be evaluated by the traditional accrual accounting method and would show only a 9.2% ROI, using the original investment. This example shows that it would be inconsistent–and might therefore induce dysfunctional decisions–to use DCF models to guide the original investment decision but the traditional accrual accounting models to evaluate the performance resulting from those decisions.

3. Gross cost would be preferred as a basis for comparing divisional performances. The increasing ROI rates on net book value (from 9.2% to 18.3%) show that a possibly deceptive higher ROI might be reflected in later years, despite a level operating income ($18,344 per year), or even a declining operating income.

CHAPTER 24

(A) 1c, 2d, 3b, 4c, 5c, 6c, 7d, 8a, 9c, 10a, 11d

(B) 1 objective function; 2 profit, cost (or loss); 3 states, states of nature; 4 exhaustive, exclusive; 5 specific courses of action, specific events; 6 expected future; 7 uncertainty; 8 events or states of nature, probability; 9 the standard deviation; 10 payoffs, its probability of occurrence; 11 the standard deviation, the expected value.

(C) Kismet Fortune Cookies, Inc.:

1. (.1) (10) + (.4) (5) + (.3) (0) + (.2) (− 10) = 1 + 2 + 0 − 2 = $1.00
2. (.1) (15) + (.4) (10) + (.3) (5) + (.2) (−5) = 1.5 + 4 + 1.5 − 1 = $6.00
3. (.1) (20) + (.4) (15) + (.3) (0) + (.2) (0) = 2 + 6 + 0 + 0 = $8.00
4. (.1) (30) + (.4) (10) + (.3) (0) + (.2) (−15) = 3 + 4 + 0 −3 = $4.00
5. (.1) (30) + (.4) (15) + (.3) (5) + (.2) (0) = 3 + 6 + 1.5 + 0 = $10.50
6. Action 3.
7. Item 5 minus item 3 = $10.50 – $8.00 = $2.50

CHAPTER 25

(A) 1c, 2b, 3a, 4c, 5b, 6a, 7b, 8b, 9c, 10a, 11a, 12b, 13a, 14c, 15c, 16c, 17c, 18a, 19c, 20a, 21b, 22a, 23b

(B) 1 cost functions; 2 dependent, independent; 3 variable, fixed, mixed (or semivariable); 4 scatter diagram, visual-fit; 5 simple regression analysis; 6 the slope of the line, the regression coefficient; 7 the method of least squares; 8 constant variance or homoscedasticity; 9 the relevant range.

(C) Verity Statistical Equipment Company:

1. (a) y; (b) x; (c) $50; (d) $y = 200 + (50)(12) = \$800$; (e) $y = 200 + (50)(0) = \$200$.
2. (a) no; (b) no. See the textbook paragraph, "Fixed-Cost Component."

   Although a cost function estimated for a mixed cost (as in this case) may yield a good approximation to the actual cost function over the relevant range, such a relevant range rarely includes zero activity. Therefore, the *intercept* (200 in this case) would probably be neither the expected cost at zero activity nor a valid estimate of fixed cost, because the actual observations probably did not include the point where activity was zero and the cost function was probably not linear beyond the relevant range.

CHAPTER 26

(A) 1a, 2b, 3c, 4a, 5b, 6a, 7c, 8a, 9a, 10a, 11c, 12c, 13b, 14c, 15c, 16a, 17b, 18c, 19a

(B) 1 sales, variable costs; 2 the sales mix; 3 the budgeted contribution margin; 4 the actual quantity of material used; 5 the adjusted expectations; 6 a random deviation; 7 expected benefits from the investigation, expected costs of the investigation; 8 random deviations, nonrandom deviations; 9 Statistical quality control (or SQC).

(C) Textbook-Based Problem:

1. (a) (120,000 × $1) + (40,000 × $7) = $120,000 + $280,000 = $400,000
   (b) (130,000 × $1) + (38,000 × $7) = $130,000 + $266,000 = $396,000
   (c) $400,000 – $396,000 = $4,000 U

2.

Product A: (130,000 – 120,000) × $1	= $10,000 F
Product B: (38,000 – 40,000) × $7	= $14,000 U
Total volume variance	$ 4,000 U

3.

(a) Product A: (130,000 – 120,000) × $2.50	= $25,000 F
Product B: (38,000 – 40,000) × $2.50	= $ 5,000 U
Total quantity variance	$20,000 F
(b) Product A: (130,000 – 120 000) ($1.00 – $2 50)	= $15,000 U
Product B: (38,000 – 40,000) ($7.00 – $2 50)	= $ 9,000 U
Total sales-mix variance	$24,000 U

4. (a) The detailed volume variance in 2 is more helpful.

   (b) It is easier to understand; it seems more direct and simpler. It does not need to use the $2.50 weighted-average unit contribution margin, which would, of course, be altered by any change in sales mix.

(D) Intricate Electronics Inc.:

1. Price variance: $59,100 – $60,200 = ... $1,100 F
2. Efficiency variance: $60,200 – $58,800 = ... $1,400 U
3. Volume variance: $58,800 – $63,000 = ... $4,200 F
4. Order-adjustment variance: $57,500 – $63,000 = . . . $5,500 F
5. Yield variance: $58,800 – $57,500 = ... $1,300 U

Note that the volume variance is the algebraic sum of the order-adjustment variance and the yield variance: $5,500 F – $1,300 U = $4,200 F. For a more detailed and comprehensive case, see the textbook Exhibit 26-4.

(E) Balancing Process of Candid Scales Company:

1. Decision Table:

	In Control	Out of Control
State of nature		
Probability of state of nature	.95	.05
Payoffs for actions:		
Investigate	C = 2,400	C + M = 12,400
Do not investigate	0	L = 40,000

2. Expected cost of decision to investigate:
   (2,400) (.95) + (12,400) (.05) = 2,280 + 620 = $2,900;
   or (2,400) (1.00) + (10,000) (.05) = 2,400 + 500 = $2,900
3. Expected cost of decision not to investigate:
   0 + (40,000) (.05) = $2,000
4. Out-of-control probability at the point of indifference:
   $$\frac{C}{L-M} = \frac{2,400}{40,000 - 10,000} = \frac{2,400}{30,000} = .08$$

CHAPTER 27

(A) 1a, 2d, 3d, 4a, 5b, 6c, 7a, 8a, 9c, 10c, 11d, 12b, 13c, 14c

(B) 1 linear programming; 2 the objective function; 3 the constraints of scarce resources; 4 technical coefficients; 5 feasible alternatives; 6 equal total-contribution-margin; 7 shadow prices.

(C) Effortless Perfume Company:

1. 200 ÷ 400 = .5 hr
2. 400 ÷ 160 = 2.5 hr
3. $7X + 8Y = TCM$
4. $X + .5Y \leqslant 200$; or $2X + Y \leqslant 400$
5. $X + 2.5Y \leqslant 400$; or $.4X + Y \leqslant 160$
6. $Y \leqslant 150$
7. $X \geqslant 0$ and $Y \geqslant 0$

CHAPTER 28

(A) 1c, 2c, 3a, 4b, 5c, 6c, 7c, 8a, 9a, 10a

(B) 1 cost of sales; 2 normal volume (or standard volume); 3 Work-in-Process, Direct Materials Used; 4 Work-in-Process, Finished Goods; 5 a spending, an efficiency.